LITERATURE

The Ends of Literature

THE LATIN AMERICAN "BOOM" IN THE NEOLIBERAL MARKETPLACE

BRETT LEVINSON

"This book will be recognized as one of the major works in Latin American literary and cultural studies of the last twenty years—an instant classic. It is masterfully concise, highly articulate, well written, and powerful as a theoretical statement. Its main contribution is decisive: it signals the beginning of a new paradigm of contemporary Latin American cultural production."

—Alberto Moreiras, Duke University

The Ends of Literature analyzes the part played by literature within contemporary Latin American thought and politics, above all the politics of neoliberalism. The "why?" of contemporary Latin American literature is the book's over-arching concern. Its wide range includes close readings of the prose of Cortázar, Carpentier, Paz, Valenzuela, Piglia, and Las Casas; of the relationship of the "Boom" movement and its aftermath; of testimonial narrative; and of contemporary Chilean and Chicano film. The work also investigates in detail various theoretical projects as they intersect with and emerge from Latin American scholarship: cultural studies, deconstruction, psychoanalysis, and postcolonial studies.

Latin American literature, both as a vehicle of conservatism and as an agent of subversion, is bound from its inception to the rise of the state. Literature's nature, role, and status are therefore altered when the Latin American nation-state succumbs to the process of neoliberalism: as the "too-strong" state (dictatorship) yields to the "too-weak" state (the market), and as the various practices of civil society and public life are replaced by private or privatized endeavors.

However, neither the "end of literature" nor the "end of the state" can be assumed. The end of literature in Latin America is in fact the call for more literature; it is the call of literature, in particular that of the Boom. The end of the state, likewise, is the demand upon this state. The book, then, analyzes the "ends" in question as at once their purpose, direction, future, and conclusion.

Also key to the study is the notion of transition. Within much recent Latin American political discussion *la transición* refers to the passage from dictatorship to democracy, as well as to the failure of this shift, the failure of post-dictatorship. The author argues that the movement from literary to cultural studies, while issuing from intellectual and aesthetic circles, is an integral component of this same transition.

CULTURAL MEMORY IN THE PRESENT

Brett Levinson is Associate Professor of Comparative Literature at SUNY, Binghampton. He is the author of Secondary Moderns: Mimesis, History, and Revolution in Lezama Lima's "American Expression."

Cover illustration: Piercarlo Carella, *Leggendo il mondo,* pencil on paper, copyright 2001 Piercarlo Carella. Cover design: Sandy Drooker.   0-8047-4346-0

STANFORD UNIVERSITY PRESS

www.sup.org

9 780804 743464

Foundations in Evolutionary Cognitive Neuroscience

Edited by

STEVEN M. PLATEK, PH.D.

Georgia Gwinnett College
Lawrenceville, Georgia, USA

TODD K. SHACKELFORD, PH.D.

Florida Atlantic University
Davie, Florida, USA

CAMBRIDGE
UNIVERSITY PRESS

CAMBRIDGE UNIVERSITY PRESS
Cambridge, New York, Melbourne, Madrid, Cape Town, Singapore, São Paulo, Delhi

Cambridge University Press
The Edinburgh Building, Cambridge CB2 8RU, UK

Published in the United States of America by Cambridge University Press, New York

www.cambridge.org
Information on this title: www.cambridge.org/9780521884211

First published 2009

Printed in the United Kingdom at the University Press, Cambridge

A catalog record for this publication is available from the British Library

ISBN 978-0-521-88421-1 hardback
ISBN 978-0-521-71118-0 paperback

Contents

Contributors

Michael A. Arbib
University of Southern California, Los Angeles, Computer Science Department

Alfredo Ardila
Florida International University, Department of Communication Sciences and Disorders

H. Clark Barrett
University of California, Los Angeles, Center for Behavior, Evolution, and Culture and Center for Culture, Brain, and Development

David C. Geary
University of Missouri, Columbia, Department of Psychological Sciences

Aaron T. Goetz
California State University, Fullerton, Department of Psychology

Benedict C. Jones
University of Aberdeen, School of Psychology

James J. Lee
Harvard University, Department of Psychology

Anthony C. Little
University of Stirling, Department of Psychology

Yoshiro Okubo
Nippon Medical School, Tokyo, Japan, Department of Neuropsychiatry

Steven M. Platek
University of Liverpool, School of Biological Sciences

Todd K. Shackelford
Florida Atlantic University, Department of Psychology

Hidehiko Takahashi
National Institute of Radiological Sciences, Chiba, Japan

1

Introduction to evolutionary psychology: A Darwinian approach to human behavior and cognition

AARON T. GOETZ, TODD K. SHACKELFORD, AND
STEVEN M. PLATEK

Charles Darwin's (1859) theory of evolution by natural selection is among the most important scientific theories and is *the* most important theory in all of the life sciences. Some have even argued that the principles of Darwin's theory can explain the laws of physics and the organization of the universe (e.g., Dennett, 1995). Although Darwin's name is synonymous with evolution (which refers to the modification of traits with descent), philosophers and scholars were thinking about evolution long before Darwin. In fact, one of the first discussions of evolution pre-dates Darwin by two and a half millennia. Anaximander, a Greek philosopher, suggested that "in water the first animal arose covered with spiny skin, and with the lapse of time some crawled onto dry land and breaking off their skins in a short time they survived." Even Darwin's grandfather, Erasmus Darwin, wrote of common ancestry and speciation. What Charles Darwin (1859) provided, however, was a viable working mechanism of evolution: natural selection. Darwinian selection has become the centerpiece of biology, and in the last few decades, many psychologists and anthropologists have recognized the value of employing an evolutionary perspective in their work (for early writings see Barkow, Cosmides, and Tooby, 1992; Chagnon and Irons, 1979; Daly and Wilson, 1983; Symons, 1979). With a focus on evolved psychological mechanisms and their information processing, evolutionary psychology has risen as a compelling and fruitful approach to psychological science. This chapter provides an introduction to evolution by natural selection and its modern application to the study of human behavior and cognition.

Foundations in Evolutionary Cognitive Neuroscience, ed. Steven M. Platek and Todd K. Shackelford.
Published by Cambridge University Press. © Cambridge University Press 2009.

The mechanisms of natural and sexual selection

Evolution by natural selection is the resultant process when (a) individuals of a population vary in their characteristics, (b) much of the variation is heritable, and (c) resources are limited so that individuals reproduce differentially (Darwin, 1859; Mayr, 1982). Individuals can vary morphologically, physiologically, psychologically, behaviorally – no two individuals are exactly the same; even identical twins vary. Due to these variations, some individuals may be better able to survive and reproduce in their current environment than other individuals. If the variations are heritable (i.e., if they have a genetic component), the characteristics can be passed down from parents to offspring. Limited resources (e.g., food, available mates) result in a competition between individuals, and those individuals who have inherited characteristics that allow them to compete more effectively will produce more offspring. Thus, all organisms are subject to evolution by natural selection. As long as the ingredients of natural selection are present – variation, heredity, and competition resulting in differential reproduction – organisms will evolve. An example of natural selection follows.

The peppered moth (*Biston betularia*) is typically white with black spots. This coloration provides an effective camouflage for the moths as they rest on certain Birch trees. There exists variation in the coloration of moths so that some are very white and some very black. In a series of studies, Kettlewell (1955, 1956) documented that when the white trees on which the moths rested became dark from industrial pollution, birds ate more of the white moths because they were now conspicuous on the soot-covered trees. In polluted areas, the population of darker, or melanic, moths replaced the lighter form, but in unpolluted areas, more of the light-colored moths had survived. Kettlewell showed that the environment in which the moths were better camouflaged contributed to better survival and reproduction. Kettlewell's work is a classic demonstration of natural selection in action.

Herbert Spencer's summary of natural selection, "survival of the fittest," has, unfortunately, caused more confusion than clarification (Gaulin and McBurney, 2004). Reproduction is a much larger component of natural selection than is survival. If an individual had characteristics that enabled it to survive for hundreds of years, yet it never reproduced, those characteristics could not be favored by selection because without transmission to offspring, characteristics cannot become more common in a population. Survival, therefore, functions only to enable individuals to reproduce (directly or indirectly). Secondly, Spencer's adage suggests that an individual may evolve to be the "fittest." What determines an individual to be "fit" is its design in relation to competing designs in the current environment. What is fit in one generation may be unfit in another generation. Also, fit is often taken to imply physically fit. Fitness, in an evolutionary context, is an organism's success in producing offspring that survive to reproductive age (Williams, 1966).

Sexual selection is the process that favors an increase in the frequency of alleles associated with reproduction (Darwin, 1871). Darwin distinguished sexual selection from natural selection, but today most evolutionary scientists combine the two concepts under the label natural selection. Sexual selection is composed of intrasexual competition (competition between members of the same sex for sexual access to members of the opposite sex) and intersexual selection (differential mate choice of members of the opposite sex). Under sexual selection, even a trait that is a liability to survival can evolve. When the sexual attractiveness, for example, of a trait outweighs the survival costs to maintain it, the trait may be sexually selected. The epitome of a sexually selected trait is the peacock's tail. Maintaining and maneuvering an unwieldy tail is metabolically costly for peacocks, and it is often the target of predators. The cumbersome tail evolved, however, because it was attractive to peahens. The mass and brightness of the plumage is attractive to peahens because it signals a low parasite load (Hamilton and Zuk, 1982). Peacocks with smaller, lackluster tails have been shown to be more susceptible to parasites and to have a higher parasite load. Thus, the large bright tail feathers are an honest signal of health, and peahens would be reproductively wise to select as mates males with such tails (who sire offspring that share their high quality genes).

In many species, particularly polygynous species where male reproductive variance is high and female reproductive variance is low, sexual selection is responsible for prominent sexual dimorphism. In such species, intrasexual competition between males for sexual access to females is fierce, and a size advantage is adaptive. It is often difficult to establish whether a trait evolved via natural selection or sexual selection, but as mentioned previously, this distinction is not often necessary.

In summary, the core premise of natural selection as a mechanism for evolution is that individual variation exists among traits in a population due to random mutations. Those individuals who have traits that better enable them to survive and reproduce will propagate the genes associated with those traits throughout the population.

After Darwin: the Modern Synthesis and Hamilton's inclusive fitness theory

The details of modern evolutionary theory, or neo-Darwinian theory, are the result of the Modern Synthesis. From the early 1930s to the 1950s, advancements in genetics, systematics, and paleontology aligned Darwin's theory with the facts of genetics (Mayr and Provine, 1980). The Modern Synthesis is so called because it was the integration or synthesizing of Darwinian selection with Mendelian genetics. R. A. Fisher, J. B. S. Haldane, Sewall Wright, Ernst Mayr, and Theodosius Dobzhansky are considered the primary authors of the Modern Synthesis (Mayr and Provine, 1980). With a more precise understanding of inheritance, Darwin's theory of evolution by natural selection took flight as a powerful explanatory model.

Following the Modern Synthesis, evolution by natural selection was extended once more to include inclusive fitness theory (Hamilton, 1964). Hamilton reasoned that selection could operate through classical fitness (i.e., the sum of an individual's own reproductive success) and inclusive fitness, which includes the effects of an individual's actions on the reproductive success of genetic relatives. That is, a trait will be naturally selected if it causes an individual's genes to be passed on, regardless of whether the individual directly produces offspring. This addendum to natural selection produced a "gene's eye" view of selection, and could now explain the evolution of altruistic behavior (i.e., behavior that is beneficial to others but costly for the actor). Genes associated with producing an alarm call when sighting a predator, for example, may spread throughout a population even when it is detrimental to the caller if the alarm call is emitted in the presence of genetic relatives and has an overall benefit to those relatives (e.g., Sherman, 1977). Hamilton's inclusive fitness theory is considered the most important advance in our understanding of natural selection, so much so that the term "inclusive fitness theory" is synonymous with "evolution by natural selection."

The products and byproducts of evolution: adaptations, byproducts, and noise

Although natural selection is not the only mechanism of evolution (e.g., mutation, migration, genetic drift), it is the primary means of modification and the primary creative evolutionary force capable of producing functional organization (Fisher, 1954; Mayr, 1963; Williams, 1966). The creative force of natural selection, acting on random genetic variation, designs three products: adaptations, byproducts of adaptations, and noise.

Adaptations are central to the study of evolution. Through the process of natural selection, small incremental phenotypic changes that enhance an organism's ability to survive and reproduce (relative to competing designs) accumulate to form an adaptation. Adaptations are inherited, they develop reliably, are usually species-typical, and were selected for because they were economic, efficient, and reliable solutions to adaptive problems (Buss, Haselton, Shackelford, Bleske, and Wakefield, 1998; Thornhill, 1997; Tooby and Cosmides, 1990; Williams, 1966). An adaptive problem is an obstacle or impediment that was recurrent during a species' evolutionary history and whose solution affected the survival and reproduction (i.e., genetic propagation) of an organism. Furthermore, adaptive problems aren't necessarily "problems," they are the "regularities of the physical, chemical, developmental, ecological, demographic, social, and informational environments encountered by ancestral populations during the course of a species' or population's evolution" (Tooby and Cosmides, 1992, p. 62). In sum, natural selection designs adaptations that solve adaptive problems associated with survival and reproduction. The heart, the production of sweat, and sexual arousal are all adaptations designed by natural selection. The heart is an anatomical adaptation designed to circulate blood throughout an organism's body. The production of sweat is a physiological adaptation designed to thermoregulate an organism. Sexual arousal is a psychological adaptation designed to motivate sexual behavior.

Not all products of natural selection are adaptations. Byproducts of adaptations are side-effects that may or may not be functional but that were not directly selected. They are called byproducts because they are incidentally tied to adaptations and are therefore "carried along" with them. Identifying byproducts is equally as rigorous a process as identifying adaptations because the hypothesis that a trait is a byproduct requires one to identify the adaptation of which it is a byproduct. The human navel and the whiteness of bone are byproducts of adaptations – they do not contribute in any way to an individual's survival or reproduction. In keeping with our mandate: the human navel is a byproduct of an umbilical cord and the whiteness of bone is a byproduct of the calcium in bones.

The third product of evolution is noise, or random effects. Noise is also functionless and cannot solve adaptive problems. Noise can be produced by random changes or perturbations in the genetic or developmental environment or by chance mutations. Noise, unlike a byproduct, is not linked to the adaptive aspect of a characteristic. The random shape of an individual's navel is an example of noise.

In summary, the evolutionary process produces three products: adaptations, byproducts, and noise. Adaptations are the product of natural selection and are functionally organized features that contribute to a species' reproductive success, however indirectly. Byproducts and noise do not solve adaptive problems and are not subject to natural selection themselves. In the following section, we discuss how the study of psychological adaptations has changed the study of human behavior and cognition.

Evolutionary psychology

Evolutionary psychology (EP) attempts to make sense of current human thought, emotion, and behavior by careful consideration of human evolutionary history. Over our evolutionary history, humans have faced many adaptive problems that needed to be solved to survive and reproduce. Generation after generation, over millions of years, natural selection slowly shaped the human brain, favoring circuitry that was good at solving these adaptive problems of our ancestors. The study of psychological adaptations (or evolved psychological mechanisms) is central to EP.

Because the focus of EP is on describing adaptations, some have charged its practitioners as being hyper-adaptationists. Assuming a priori that a trait may be an adaptation is an experimental heuristic that guides research questions and methodology. Biologists have been conducting their research this way for over 70 years. Moreover, byproducts and noise are typically only identifiable after the adaptations of which they are a byproduct or noise have been discovered and described (Tooby and Cosmides, 1990).

Although modern evolutionary psychological theories are relatively new, all psychological theories are evolutionary in nature (Buss, 1995): "All psychological theories – be they cognitive, social, developmental, personality, or clinical – imply the existence of internal psychological mechanisms" (p. 2). If the internal psychological mechanisms implied in any psychological theory were not the product of the evolutionary process, then they would be, by default, unscientific theories.

Psychological mechanisms as information-processing modules

An evolved psychological mechanism is an information-processing module that was selected throughout a species' evolutionary history because it reliably solved a particular adaptive problem (Tooby and Cosmides, 1992). Evolved psychological mechanisms are understood in terms of their specific input, decision rules, and output (Buss, 1995). Each psychological mechanism evolved to take in a narrow range of information – information specific to a specific adaptive problem. The information (or input) that the organism receives signals the adaptive problem that is being confronted. The input (either internal or external) is then transformed into output (i.e., behavior, physiological activity, or input relayed to another psychological mechanism) via a decision rule – an "if, then" procedure. An example of the input, decision rules, and output of a psychological mechanism is appropriate.

Fruit can either be ripe or unripe. Because ripe fruit is more nutritious (i.e., calorically dense) than immature fruit, humans have developed a preference for ripe fruit. The decision rule regarding the selection of fruit might go something like, "If the fruit tastes sweet, then eat it." Supposing all fruit was maximally saturated with sugar all of the time, then that particular decision rule would not exist. The output associated with this mechanism might be to eat the ripe fruit or disregard the unripe fruit. This example illustrates the fact that psychological mechanisms develop and operate without any conscious awareness or formal learning, and we are blind to their underlying logic. Do you enjoy ripe fruit because it is calorically dense and provides nutrition needed to carry out activities related to survival and reproduction? Or do you simply enjoy sweet fruit?

Tooby and Cosmides (1992) have written that the causal link between evolution and behavior is made through psychological mechanisms. That is, the filter of natural selection operates on psychological mechanisms that produce behavior. Natural selection cannot operate on behavior directly, but instead, on the genes associated with the psychological mechanisms that produce the behavior. Williams (1966) spoke similarly, "The selection of genes is mediated by the phenotype [psychological mechanism], and in order to be favorably selected, a gene must produce phenotypic reproductive success [adaptive behavior]" (p. 25).

Psychological mechanisms and domain specificity

The vast majority of psychological mechanisms are presumed to be domain-specific. That is, the mind is composed of content-dependent machinery (i.e., physiological and psychological mechanisms) that is presumed to have evolved to solve a specific adaptive problem. Psychological mechanisms can also be expressed as cognitive biases that cause people to more readily attend to or make sense of some pieces of information relative to others. This presumption of domain specificity or modularity contrasts with the traditional position that humans are endowed with a general set of learning or reasoning mechanisms that are applied to any problem regardless of specific content (e.g., Atkinson and Wheeler, 2004). A system that is domain-general or content-independent, however, is a system that lacks a-priori knowledge about specific situations or problem-domains (Tooby and Cosmides, 1992). Such a system, when faced with a choice in a chain of decisions, must select from all behavioral possibilities (e.g., wink, jump, remember mother, smile, point finger, scream, etc.). This problem of choosing among an infinite range of possibilities when only a small subset are appropriate has been described by researchers in artificial intelligence, linguistics, and other disciplines (see Tooby and Cosmides, 1992 for a review).

Not only are there theoretical arguments against a content-independent system, myriad evidence for domain-specificity comes from, among other areas, evolutionary psychological theory and research (e.g., Cosmides, 1989;

Cosmides and Tooby, 1994; Flaxman and Sherman, 2000; Pinker and Bloom, 1990), cognitive research (e.g., Hirschfeld and Gelman, 1994), studies of animal learning (e.g., Carey and Gelman, 1991; Garcia, Ervin, and Koelling, 1966), and the clinical neurological literature (e.g., Gazzaniga and Smylie, 1983; Ramachandran, 1995; Sergent, Ohta, and MacDonald, 1992). Practitioners of EP concede that relatively domain-general mechanisms may exist, but the vast majority of mechanisms are presumed to be domain-specific.

Some of the controversy surrounding the modularity of the mind seems to be rooted in the use of the term *domain*. Psychologists have often used the term to refer to particular domains of life, such as the mating domain, kinship domain, and parenting domain. Subsequently, many have assumed that labeling a mechanism as domain-specific restricts the proposed mechanism to a particular domain, and if evidence can be garnered to show that the mechanism functions in more than one domain (e.g., the mating domain and the kinship domain), then it is taken as evidence for the domain generality of the proposed mechanism. This, however, is incorrect. A domain, when referring to a psychological mechanism, is a selection pressure, an adaptive problem (Cosmides and Tooby, 1987). Domain, then, is synonymous with *problem*. That is, a domain-specific mechanism refers to a problem-specific mechanism – a mechanism that evolved to solve a specific adaptive problem. So although evolutionary and cognitive psychologists use the term *domain-specific*, perhaps some confusion could be avoided if the more accurate term *problem-specific* were employed instead. Many psychological mechanisms cut across different domains of life. Face recognition is used in all the social domains of life (e.g., mating and kinship domains). Working memory is used in all domains, as is processing speed. Face recognition, working memory, and processing speed still solve specific problems. Working memory, for example, solves the specific problem of holding information in the mind for a brief period of time. So although working memory is used in all domains, it is problem specific (and therefore domain specific) because it solves a single adaptive problem. It has been suggested that evolutionary and cognitive psychologists might be better off avoiding these contentious labels and simply describing the proposed mechanism and its function (personal communication, D. M. Buss, January 2005).

Evolutionary time lags and the environment of evolutionary adaptedness

Because evolution is an excruciatingly slow process, extant humans and their minds are designed for earlier environments of which they are a product. Our minds were not designed to solve the day-to-day problems of our modern society, but instead, were designed to solve the day-to-day problems of our evolutionary past. Examples of evolutionary time lags abound: our difficulty in learning to fear modern threats, such as guns and cars, and our near effortless learning to fear more ancient threats, such as snakes and spiders (Öhman and Mineka, 2001); children's ease in learning biologically primary mathematic abilities, such as counting and their difficulty in learning biologically secondary mathematic abilities, such as arithmetic (Geary, 1995); women will not concede to intercourse indiscriminately even though modern contraception can eliminate the reproductive costs associated with intercourse; our preference for sugar and fat was once adaptive due to their scarcity, but has now become maladaptive. These few examples illustrate that our modern behavior is best understood when placed in the context of our environment of evolutionary adaptedness.

The environment of evolutionary adaptedness (EEA) is not a place or time in history but a statistical composite of the selection pressures (i.e., the enduring properties, components, and elements) of a species', more specifically the *adaptations* that characterize a species', ancestral past (Tooby and Cosmides, 1990). That is, each adaptation evolved due to a specific set of selection pressures. Each adaptation, in principle, has a unique EEA, but there likely would have been significant overlap in the EEAs of related adaptations. Tooby and Cosmides (1990) and other practitioners of EP, however, use "Pleistocene" to refer to the human EEA because this time period, lasting 1.81 to 0.01 million years ago, was appropriate for virtually all adaptations of *Homo sapiens*.

Although our evolutionary past is not available for direct observation, the discovery and description of adaptations allows us to make inferences about our evolutionary past, and the characterization of adaptations is arguably the single most reliable way of learning about the past (Tooby and Cosmides, 1990). Some adaptations provide unequivocal information about our ancestral past. Our cache of psychological mechanisms associated with navigating the social world tells us that our ancestors were a social species (e.g., Cosmides, 1989; Cummins, 1998; Forgas, Haselton, and von Hippel, 2007; Kurzban *et al.*, 2001; Pinker and Bloom, 1990; Trivers, 1971). A multitude of psychological mechanisms associated with cuckoldry avoidance tell us that female infidelity was a recurrent feature of our evolutionary past (Buss, Larsen, Westen, and Semmelroth, 1992; Buss and Shackelford, 1997; Goetz and Shackelford, 2006a; Platek, 2003; Shackelford, Goetz, McKibbin, and Starratt, 2007).

Some adaptations, however, do not make clear (at least upon first inspection) their link with our ancestral past. There exists, for example, a mechanism present in the middle ear of all humans that is able to reduce sound intensity by as much as 30 decibels in 50 milliseconds. The attenuation reflex, as it is known, acts by contracting muscles that pull the stirrup away from the oval window of the cochlea, preventing strong vibrations from damaging the inner ear. The attenuation reflex meets the characteristics of an adaptation (e.g., economic, efficient, reliable), yet it is not obvious what selection pressures drove the evolution of this adaptation. That is, what specific noises did our ancestors recurrently hear that would create this noise reducing mechanism? That the muscles appear to contract as we are about to speak suggests that our own loud voices might have been the impetus for this adaptation. Moreover, sound attenuation is greater at low frequencies than at high ones (and humans speak at low frequencies), also suggesting that ululating was a recurrent (enough) feature of our evolutionary past. Thus, from discovering and describing adaptations, we can tentatively characterize aspects of our evolutionary environment.

This is not to be taken to indicate, however, that the aim of evolutionary psychology is to make inferences about the past. Evolutionary psychology is not *post hoc* storytelling; its practitioners typically use a deductive approach, moving from theory to data. That is, evolutionary psychologists make predictions derived from hypotheses based on middle-level theories – e.g., Trivers' (1972) parental investment theory – then collect data to test their predictions. For example, Buss *et al.* (1992) tested the hypothesis proposed by Symons (1979) and Daly, Wilson, and Weghorst (1982) that the sexes would differ in their reactions to a romantic partner's sexual and emotional infidelity. Buss and his colleagues did not happen to collect the appropriate data, analyze the results, and develop a *post hoc* explanation for what they observed. Furthermore, claims of adaptations are typically stated as tentative until the proposed adaptation has undergone rigorous hypothesis testing (see Schmitt and Pilcher, 2004). The inductive approach, however, should not be disregarded. Moving from data to theory is a common practice in all scientific enterprises (e.g., cosmology, geology, physics) and is known as "explanation" (Tooby and Cosmides, 1992).

Ultimate and proximate explanations

Some psychologists seem to be hostile to the idea of applying evolutionary theories to human behavior. One cause of this unwarranted hostility is the misconception that evolutionary analyses are incompatible with (or less important than) non-evolutionary (e.g., sociological or cultural) analyses. Such critics fail to recognize that evolutionary and non-evolutionary approaches operate at different levels of analysis (Tinbergen, 1963). Evolutionary scientists are typically interested in causation at the ultimate (or distal) level. An ultimate explanation refers to the evolved function of a trait, behavior, or mechanism. This is in contrast to proximate explanations. Proximate explanations refer to the immediate, non-evolutionary causes of a trait, behavior, or mechanism (e.g., the genetic or cellular causes). In our example of the input, decision rules, and output of a psychological mechanism associated with ripe fruit, one could correctly note that humans prefer ripe fruit because it is perceived to be sweet (proximate cause) and because it provides needed calories to perform duties related to survival and reproduction (ultimate cause). Although the explanations are fundamentally different, they are compatible and equally important (Sherman and Alcock, 1994). But it is also possible and not uncommon to have competing explanations at the same level of analysis (e.g., competing evolutionary psychological hypotheses); such debate is a healthy feature of science.

Evolutionary psychology's relationship with sociobiology

Those less familiar with evolutionary psychology often construe the approach as "sociobiology reborn." Although sociobiology, ethology, behavioral ecology, and evolutionary psychology share evolution as a guiding framework, the programs are conceptually distinct for at least three reasons (see also Buss, 1995; Crawford, 2000). First, evolutionary psychology investigates a broader array of phenomena than sociobiology. Sociobiology is the study of plant and animal social behavior. Evolutionary psychology's research agenda includes the social domain but it also addresses all other domains of life and all areas of psychology (e.g., consciousness, memory, sensation, perception, motivation, etc.). Second, the focus on evolved psychological mechanisms and their information processing is a unique and defining feature of evolutionary psychology. The input, decision rules, and output of psychological mechanisms are central to the analysis. Third, evolutionary psychologists do not measure individuals' direct reproductive output (i.e., number of children) or fitness. Many sociobiologists, in contrast, have advocated measuring an individual's reproductive success to understand the adaptive value of behavior. Evolutionary psychology questions the premise that measuring fitness in a recent or current environment provides information about the evolutionary history or selection pressures that caused the evolution of the psychological mechanisms that motivate the particular behavior. The information needed to measure fitness correctly only becomes known generations later, because there is no guarantee that selection pressures remain stable over time. Practitioners of evolutionary psychology have argued that "humans are adaptation executers, not fitness maximizers" (Tooby and Cosmides, 1990, p. 420). Whether a subdiscipline of or a separate field from sociobiology, evolutionary psychology and sociobiology share evolution as a guiding framework (Alcock, 2001).

Discovering new topics and rethinking old topics

The modern application of evolutionary principles to the study of human psychology and behavior has opened up new lines of research and has shaken up old topics in psychology. In this section, we discuss the recently developed area of human sperm competition (with an emphasis on the evolutionary cognitive neuroscience of human sperm competition) and the rethinking of racism and self-deception in light of evolution.

With the recognition that female infidelity was a recurrent feature of our evolutionary past has come the development of a unique field within human mating: sperm competition. A form of male–male postcopulatory competition, sperm competition occurs when the sperm of two or more males simultaneously occupy the reproductive tract of a female and compete to fertilize her egg (Parker, 1970). Males must compete for mates, but if two or more males have copulated with a female within a sufficiently short period of time, sperm will compete for fertilizations. Psychological, behavioral, physiological, anatomical, and genetic evidence indicates that men have evolved solutions to combat the adaptive problem of sperm competition (Gallup *et al.*, 2003; Goetz and Shackelford, 2006a; Goetz *et al.*, 2005; Kilgallon and Simmons, 2005; Pound, 2002; Shackelford and Goetz, 2007; Shackelford, Goetz, McKibbin, and Starratt, 2007; Shackelford *et al.*, 2002; Smith, 1984; Wyckoff, Wang, and Wu, 2000). Shackelford *et al.* (2002), for example, documented that men who spent a greater proportion of time apart from their partner since the couple's last copulation – therefore, facing a high risk of sperm competition – report that they find their partner more sexually attractive, have more interest in copulating with her, and believe that she is more interested in copulating with him (effects were independent of the total time since last copulation and relationship satisfaction). These perceptual changes may motivate men to copulate as soon as possible with their partner, thereby entering their sperm into competition with any rival sperm that may be present in her reproductive tract.

Although there is accumulating evidence that males engage differential psychological strategies that appear to be designed as a response to female infidelity, the neural correlates of such strategies have only recently been investigated. If, as documented above, men's sexual interest in their partners is related to perceptions of infidelity, then two recent studies suggest a network of brain substrates that, in the context of sperm competition, might be implicated in the neural control of physiological changes. Rilling, Winslow, and Kilts (2004) used positron emission tomography (PET) to measure brain activation when male rhesus macaques were allowed to observe their exclusive female mating partner engaging in copulation with a rival male. In this situation, activation was observed in the right superior temporal sulcus (STS) and amygdala. Rilling *et al.* (2004) suggest that activation of these areas might relate to similar reports of humans experiencing increased vigilance and anxiety under conditions of purported sexual infidelity by their partners. A similar study conducted in humans documented similar activation (right amygdala) in men who were asked to read sentences that depicted their partner engaging in sexual infidelity (Takahashi *et al.*, 2006). Because the amygdala is highly innervated with androgen receptors, increased anxiety and vigilance about partner infidelity could subsequently activate a system designed to respond to possible sperm competition. This hypothesis was partially supported by Rilling *et al.* (2004), who also demonstrated increases in circulating testosterone levels when macaques were challenged with the situation described above.

In fact, this neural response system might be "on line" in men prior to any observation or suspicion of infidelity. Shackelford *et al.* (2002) found that perceptions of mate attractiveness increase as a function of time spent apart from a partner; recent research shows that such perceptions of attraction correlate with increased activity in the amygdala (Winston, O'Doherty, Kilner, Perrett, and Dolan, 2007). Similarly, Winston *et al.* (2007) found increased anterior cingulate cortex (ACC) activation in men during rankings of attractiveness, and these authors relate the differential in ACC by sex activation to differences in arousal stemming from internal monitoring. In other words, a man might employ this substrate as part of a mechanism enabling him to make appropriate arousal valuations under circumstances when he suspects or has directly observed his partner's infidelity. This arousal might then lead to increased execution of sperm competitive behaviors and, possibly, to prudent sperm allocation.

Some data are accumulating that implicate the STS in decisions about social interactions (e.g., Frith and Frith, 1999). Thus, the STS activation reported by Rilling *et al.* (2004) and Winston *et al.* (2007) might reflect the degree to which evaluations about infidelity and trustworthiness are made. Processing associated with social evaluation might also feed into the ACC. Platek, Keenan, and Mohamed (2005) identified a sex difference in activation of the ACC in response to children's, but not adults', faces that share the subject's facial resemblance. Because facial resemblance appears to serve as an indicator of paternity (Platek *et al.*, 2002, 2003, 2004), this finding suggests that the ACC might serve as a broad scale evaluation substrate for fidelity judgments.

Although further research is necessary to understand fully how the neural networks cause sperm competition responses – behaviorally, physiologically, and psychologically – preliminary evidence suggests that the networks will involve several key neurocognitive mechanisms: (1) social evaluation of partners on the basis of presumed propensity towards trustworthiness and fidelity (STS), (2) decisions about attractiveness and relation to internal monitoring, or decisions about belief in suspicions (ACC, STS, medial prefrontal cortex), and (3) automatic response generators (amygdala) that serve to moderate prudent sperm allocation and behaviors to "correct" a suspected or discovered partner infidelity (e.g., semen displacement, forced in-pair copulation, violence, or defection from pair bond). This network, apparently specific to men, may be quickly called into action during all phases of anti-cuckoldry tactics (mate guarding, sperm competition, and parental investment decisions; see Platek and Shackelford, 2006).

An evolutionary approach also has encouraged re-evaluating and rethinking old topics in psychology. Tomes of non-evolutionary psychological research argued that people encode automatically the race of individuals they encounter. Kurzban, Tooby, and Cosmides (2001), however, proposed that human psychology did not evolve specifically to encode race but, instead, that the encoding of race is a byproduct of adaptations for detecting coalitional alliances. By varying cues of coalitional affiliation and race, so that the two did not correspond, Kurzban and his colleagues were able to reduce (and in some cases remove) the extent to which people categorize others according to race. Subsequent research on racial prejudice and discrimination will benefit from this work.

The principles of evolutionary psychology have even managed to solve a philosophical debate. Known as the paradox of self-deception, many philosophers have argued that self-deception – the active misrepresentation of reality to the conscious mind (Trivers, 2000) – cannot occur because it is impossible to be, simultaneously, the deceiver and the deceived. Considering, however, that the mind is comprised of many information-processing mechanisms, some highly interconnected and some connected to just a few other mechanisms, a self-deception mechanism could evolve if the mechanisms responsible for conscious experience were unconnected to the mechanisms responsible for ultimate intentions. Without being consciously aware of particular ultimate intentions or goals, we may be better able to deceive others in order to reach such goals. Self-deception research from an evolutionary psychological perspective is in its infancy, but is growing as we employ new techniques to study this phenomenon (e.g., Keenan, 2005; Stevens, Guise, Kelly, and Keenan, 2005).

Evolutionary psychology's future

Although this modern approach to human behavior and cognition is relatively young – about 25 years old, EP's impact is already permeating all areas of psychology and opening up lines of research missed entirely by previous psychologists. EP's merit and future are also demonstrated in the fact that the number of publications using an evolutionary psychological approach is growing exponentially (Durrant and Ellis, 2003).

Moreover, evolutionary psychology's influence on cognitive neuroscience is on the rise. Using quantitative methods, Webster (2007) has documented a strong positive trend in the "evolutionizing" of neuroscience. The observed growth of evolutionary cognitive neuroscience is consistent across several neuroscience journals. Webster notes that "evolution's penetration into evolutionary cognitive neuroscience has increased at a rate that is roughly equivalent to its penetration into personality and social psychology over the last two decades; however, its penetration into neuroscience in general appears to have happened at an even faster rate" (p. 529). It's clear from Webster's analyses, and this volume in particular, that cognitive neuroscientists are recognizing the utility of an evolutionary perspective.

Another promising direction of future work is signaled by the emergence of evolutionary development psychology. The subdiscipline of evolutionary developmental psychology considers how natural selection might have influenced human psychology and behavior at all stages of development (e.g., Bjorklund and Pellegrini, 2002; Hernández Blasi and Bjorklund, 2003). Hypothesizing functions for humans' extended development, children's cognitive immaturity, and children's play behavior, for example, evolutionary developmental psychology asserts that development is as much an influential factor on psychology and behavior as evolution (Bjorklund and Pellegrini, 2000; Smith, 2005).

A future task of evolutionary psychology will be to describe the phylogenetic origins of mental traits. Phylogenetics – an area in biology dealing with identifying and understanding the evolutionary relationships between species and traits – is not well represented in the evolutionary psychological literature, but some have discussed the emergence of some adaptations (e.g., Bering and Shackelford, 2004; Marcus, 2006; Wynn, 2002). Incorporating phylogenetic studies into evolutionary psychology may help to clarify a proposed mechanism's relative domain-specificity or generality.

As new psychologists are impartially introduced to EP, as "traditional" (i.e., anti-evolutionary) psychologists retire, as EP's empirical output grows, as findings from genetics corroborate findings from EP (e.g., Cherkas *et al.*, 2004), as the neural substrates underlying hypothesized psychological mechanisms are identified (e.g., Platek, Keenan, and Mohamed, 2005 and this volume) and as cross-disciplinary frameworks of evidence are utilized (Schmitt and Pilcher, 2004), EP will emerge as *the* metatheory for psychological science.

Conclusion

In this chapter we introduced evolutionary theory and its modern impact on psychological science. We discussed how, with a focus on evolved psychological mechanisms and their information processing, evolutionary psychology has risen as a compelling and fruitful approach to the study of human behavior and cognition.

Because the design of the mind owes its functional organization to a natural, evolutionary process, an evolutionarily psychological approach is a logical framework on which to base all psychological theories. Evolutionary psychological theories specify what problems our cognitive mechanisms were designed to solve, thereby providing important information about what their design features are likely to be. In other words: "Is it not reasonable to anticipate that our understanding of the human mind would be aided greatly by knowing the purpose for which it was designed?" (Williams, 1966, p. 16).

It is possible to do research in psychology with little or no knowledge of evolution. Many psychologists do. But without an evolutionary perspective, psychology becomes a disparate set of fields. Evolutionary explanations pervade all fields in psychology and provide a unifying metatheoretical framework within which all of psychology can be organized.

Note

Portions of this manuscript were reproduced from Goetz and Shackelford (2006b).

References

Alcock, J. (2001). *The Triumph of Sociobiology*. New York: Oxford University Press.

Atkinson, A. P. and Wheeler, M. (2004). The grain of domains: the evolutionary-psychological case against domain-general cognition. *Mind and Language*, **19**, 147–176.

Barkow, J. H., Cosmides, L., and Tooby, J. (1992). *The Adapted Mind: Evolutionary Psychology and the Generation of Culture*. New York: Oxford University Press.

Bering, J. M. and Shackelford, T. K. (2004). The causal role of consciousness: A conceptual addendum to human evolutionary psychology. *Review of General Psychology*, **8**, 227–248.

Bjorklund, D. F. and Pellegrini, A. D. (2000). Child development and evolutionary psychology. *Child Development*, **71**, 1687–1798.

Bjorklund, D. F. and Pellegrini, A. D. (2002). *The Origins of Human Nature*. Washington, DC: APA Press.

Buss, D. M. (1995). Evolutionary psychology: A new paradigm for psychological science. *Psychological Inquiry*, **6**, 1–20.

Buss, D. M., Haselton, M. G., Shackelford, T. K., Bleske, A. L., and Wakefield, J. C. (1998). Adaptations, exaptations, and spandrels. *American Psychologist*, **53**, 533–548.

Buss D. M., Larsen R., Westen D., and Semmelroth J. (1992). Sex differences in jealousy: Evolution, physiology, and psychology. *Psychological Science*, **3**, 251–255.

Buss, D. M. and Shackelford, T. K. (1997). From vigilance to violence: Mate retention tactics in married couples. *Journal of Personality and Social Psychology*, **72**, 346–361.

Carey, S. and Gelman, R. (1991). *The Epigenesis of Mind: Essays on Biology and Cognition.* Hillsdale, NJ: Erlbaum.

Chagnon, N. A. and Irons, W. (1979). *Evolutionary Biology and Human Social Behavior: An Anthropological Perspective.* North Scituate, MA: Duxbury Press.

Cherkas, L. F., Oelsner, E. C., Mak, Y. T., Valdes, A., and Spector, T. (2004). Genetic influences on female infidelity and number of sexual partners in humans: A linkage and association study of the role of the Vasopressin Receptor Gene (*AVPR1A*). *Twin Research*, **7**, 649–658.

Cosmides, L. (1989). The logic of social exchange: Has natural selection shaped how humans reason? Studies with the Wason selection task. *Cognition*, **31**, 187–276.

Cosmides, L. and Tooby, J. (1987). From evolution to behavior: Evolutionary psychology as the missing link. In J. Dupre (Ed.), *The Latest on the Best: Essays on Evolution and Optimality* (pp. 277–306). Cambridge, MA: MIT Press.

Cosmides, L. and Tooby. J. (1994). Origins of domain specificity: The evolution of functional organization. In L. A. Hirschfeld and S. A. Gelman (Eds.) *Mapping the Mind: Domain Specificity in Cognition and Culture* (pp. 85–116). New York: Cambridge University Press.

Crawford, C. (2000). Evolutionary psychology: Counting babies or studying information processing mechanisms. *Annals of the New York Academy of Sciences*, **907**, 21–38.

Cummins, D. D. (1998). Social norms and other minds: The evolutionary roots of higher cognition. In D. D. Cummins and C. Allen (Eds.), *The Evolution of Mind* (pp. 30–50). New York: Oxford University Press.

Daly, M. and Wilson, M. (1983). *Sex, Evolution, and Behavior (2nd edn.).* Boston: Willard Grant.

Daly, M., Wilson, M., and Weghorst, S. J. (1982). Male sexual jealousy. *Ethology and Sociobiology*, **3**, 11–27.

Darwin, C. (1859). *On the Origin of Species.* London: John Murray.

Darwin, C. (1871). *The Descent of Man and Selection in Relation to Sex.* London: John Murray.

Dennett, D. (1995). *Darwin's Dangerous Idea: Evolution and the Meanings of Life.* London: Penguin

Durrant, R. and Ellis, B. J. (2003). Evolutionary psychology: Core assumptions and methodology. In M. Gallagher and R. J. Nelson (Eds.), *Comprehensive Handbook of Psychology, Vol. 3: Biological Psychology* (pp. 1–33). New York: John Wiley & Sons, Inc.

Fisher, R. A. (1954). Retrospect of the criticisms of the theory of natural selection (pp. 84–98). In J. S. Huxley, A. C. Hardy, and E. B. Ford (Eds.) *Evolution as a Process.* London: Allen and Unwin.

Flaxman, S. M. and Sherman, P. (2000). Morning sickness: A mechanism for protecting mother and embryo. *The Quarterly Review of Biology*, **75**, 113–148.

Forgas, J. P., Haselton, M. G., and von Hippel, W. (2007). *Evolution and the Social Mind: Evolutionary Psychology and Social Cognition.* New York: Psychology Press.

Frith, C. D. and Frith, U. (1999). Interacting minds – a biological basis. *Science*, **286**, 1692–1695.

Futuyma, D. J. (1986). *Evolutionary Biology (2nd edn.).* Sunderland, MA: Sinauer Assoc.

Gallup, G. G., Burch, R. L., Zappieri, M. L., Parvez, R. A., Stockwell, M. L., and Davis, J. A. (2003). The human penis as a semen displacement device. *Evolution and Human Behavior*, **24**, 277–289.

Garcia, J., Ervin, F. R., and Koelling, R. A. (1966). Learning with prolonged delay of reinforcement. *Psychonomic Science*, **5**, 121–122.

Gaulin, S. J. C. and McBurney, D. H. (2004). *Evolutionary Psychology (2nd edn.)*. Upper Saddle River, NJ: Pearson Education.

Gazzaniga, M. S. and Smylie, C. S. (1983). Facial recognition and brain asymmetries: Clues to underlying mechanisms. *Annals of Neurology*, **13**, 536–540.

Geary, D. C. (1995). Reflections of evolution and culture in children's cognition: Implications for mathematical development and instruction. *American Psychologist*, **50**, 24–37.

Goetz, A. T. and Shackelford, T. K. (2006a). Sexual coercion and forced in-pair copulation as sperm competition tactics in humans. *Human Nature*, **17**, 265–282.

Goetz, A. T. and Shackelford, T. K. (2006b). Modern application of evolutionary theory to psychology: Key concepts and clarifications. *American Journal of Psychology*, **119**, 256–584.

Goetz, A. T., Shackelford, T. K., Weekes-Shackelford, V. A., Euler, H. A., Hoier, S., Schmitt, D. P, and LaMunyon, C. W. (2005). Mate retention, semen displacement, and human sperm competition: Tactics to prevent and correct female infidelity. *Personality and Individual Differences*, **38**, 749–763.

Hamilton, W. D. (1964). The genetical evolution of social behaviour. *Journal of Theoretical Biology*, **7**, 1–52.

Hamilton, W. D. and Zuk, M. (1982). Heritable true fitness and bright birds: A role for parasites? *Science*, **218**, 384–387.

Hernández Blasi, C. and Bjorklund, D. F. (2003). Evolutionary developmental psychology: A new tool for better understanding human ontogeny. *Human Development*, **46**, 259–281.

Hirschfeld, L. A. and Gelman, S. A. (1994). *Mapping the Mind: Domain Specificity in Cognition and Culture*. New York: Cambridge University Press.

Keenan, J. P. (2005). *The Selfish Brain*. Paper presented at the 17th Annual Meeting of the Human Behavior and Evolution Society. Austin, TX.

Kettlewell, H. B. D. (1955). Selection experiments on industrial melanism in the Lepidoptera. *Heredity*, **9**, 323–342.

Kettlewell, H. B. D. (1956). Further selection experiments on industrial melanism in the Lepidoptera. *Heredity*, **10**, 287–301.

Kilgallon, S. J. and Simmons, L. W. (2005). Image content influences men's semen quality. *Biology Letters*, **1**, 253–255.

Kurzban, R., Tooby, J., and Cosmides, L. (2001). Can race be erased? Coalitional computation and social categorization. *Proceedings of the National Academy of Sciences*, **98**, 15387–15392.

Marcus, G. F. (2006). Cognitive architecture and descent with modification. *Cognition*, **101**, 443–465.

Mayr, E. (1963). *Animal Species and Their Evolution*. Cambridge: Harvard University Press.

Mayr, E. (1982). *The Growth of Biological Thought: Diversity, Evolution, and Inheritance*. Cambridge: Harvard University Press.

Mayr, E. and Provine, W. B. (1980). *The Evolutionary Synthesis: Perspectives on the Unification of Biology*. Cambridge: Harvard University Press.

Öhman, A. and Mineka, S. (2001). Fears, phobias, and preparedness: Toward an evolved module of fear and fear learning. *Psychological Review*, **108**, 483–522.

Parker, G. A. (1970). Sperm competition and its evolutionary consequences in the insects. *Biological Reviews*, **45**, 525–567.

Pinker, S. and Bloom, P. (1990). Natural language and natural selection. *Behavioral and Brain Sciences*, **13**, 707–727.

Platek, S. M. (2003). An evolutionary model of the effects of human paternal resemblance on paternal investment. *Evolution and Cognition*, **9**, 189–197.

Platek, S. M., Burch, R. L., Panyavin, I. S., Wasserman, B. H., and Gallup, G. G., Jr. (2002). Reactions to children's faces: Resemblance matters more for males than females. *Evolution and Human Behavior*, **23**, 159–166.

Platek, S. M., Critton, S. R., Burch, R. L., Frederick, D. A., Myers, T. E., and Gallup Jr., G. G. (2003). How much resemblance is enough? Sex difference in reactions to resemblance, but not the ability to detect resemblance. *Evolution and Human Behavior*, **24**, 81–87.

Platek, S. M., Keenan, J. P., & Mohamed, F. B. (2005). Neural correlates of facial resemblance. *NeuroImage*, **25**, 1336–1344.

Platek, S. M., Raines, D. M., Gallup Jr., G. G., Mohamed, F. B., Thomson, J. W., Myers, T. E., Panyavin, I. S., Levin, S. L., Davis, J. A., Fonteyn, L. C. M., and Arigo, D. R. (2004). Reactions to children's faces: Males are still more affected by resemblance than females are, and so are their brains. *Evolution and Human Behavior*, **25**, 394–405.

Platek, S. M., and Shackelford, T. K. (Eds.). (2006). *Female Infidelity and Paternal Uncertainty*. New York: Cambridge University Press.

Pound, N. (2002). Male interest in visual cues of sperm competition risk. *Evolution and Human Behavior*, **23**, 443–466.

Ramachandran, V. S. (1995). Anosognosia in parietal lobe syndrome. *Consciousness Cognition*, **4**, 22–51.

Rilling, J. K., Winslow, J. T., and Kilts C. D. (2004). The neural correlates of mate competition in dominant male rhesus macaques. *Biological Psychiatry*, **56**, 364–375.

Schmitt, D. P. and Pilcher, J. J. (2004). Evaluating evidence of psychological adaptation: How do we know one when we see one? *Psychological Science*, **15**, 643–649.

Sergent, J., Ohta, S., and MacDonald, B. (1992). Functional neuroanatomy of face and object processing. *Brain*, **115**, 15–36.

Shackelford, T. K. and Goetz, A. T. (2007). Adaptation to sperm competition in humans. *Current Directions in Psychological Science*, **16**, 47–50.

Shackelford, T. K., Goetz, A. T., McKibbin, W. F., and Starratt, V. G. (2007). Absence makes the adaptations grow fonder: Proportion of time apart from partner, male sexual psychology, and sperm competition in humans (*Homo sapiens*). *Journal of Comparative Psychology*, **121**, 214–220.

Shackelford, T. K., LeBlanc, G. J., Weekes-Shackelford, V. A., Bleske-Rechek, A. L., Euler, H. A., and Hoier, S. (2002). Psychological adaptation to human sperm competition. *Evolution and Human Behavior*, **23**, 123–138.

Sherman, P. W. (1977). Nepotism and the evolution of alarm calls. *Science*, **197**, 1246–1253.

Sherman, P. W. and Alcock, J. (1994). The utility of the proximate-ultimate dichotomy in ethology. *Ethology*, **96**, 58–62.

Silverman, I. (2003). Confessions of a closet sociobiologist: Personal perspectives on the Darwinian movement in psychology. *Evolutionary Psychology*, **1**, 1–9.

Smith, R. L. (1984). Human sperm competition. In R. L. Smith (Ed.), *Sperm Competition and the Evolution of Animal Mating Systems* (pp. 601–660). New York: Academic Press.

Smith, P. K. (2005). Play: Types and functions in human development. In B. J. Ellis and D. F. Bjorklund (Eds.), *Origins of the Social Mind* (pp. 271–291). New York: Guilford.

Stevens, S., Guise, K., Kelly, K., and Keenan, J. P. (2005). *Self-deception and the brain: Using transcranial magnetic stimulation (TMS) to investigate the evolutionary origins of deception.* Poster presented at the 17th Annual Meeting of the Human Behavior and Evolution Society. Austin, TX.

Symons, D. (1979). *The Evolution of Human Sexuality*. New York: Oxford University Press.

Symons, D. (1992). On the use and misuse of Darwinism in the study of behavior. In J. H. Barkow, L. Cosmides, and J. Tooby (Eds.), *The Adapted Mind: Evolutionary Psychology and the Generation of Culture* (pp. 137–159). New York: Oxford University Press.

Takahashi, H., Matsuura, M., Yahata, N., Koeda, M., Suhara, T., and Okubo, Y. (2006). Men and women show distinct brain activation during imagery of sexual and emotional infidelity. *NeuroImage*, **32**, 1299–1307.

Thornhill, R. (1997). The concept of an evolved adaptation. In G. R. Bock and G. Cardew (Eds.), *Characterizing Human Psychological Adaptations* (pp. 4–22). West Sussex, England: John Wiley & Sons, Ltd.

Tinbergen, N. (1963). On aims and methods of ethology. *Zeitschrift für Tierpsychologie*, **20**, 410–433.

Tooby, J. and Cosmides, L. (1990). The past explains the present: Emotional adaptations and the structure of ancestral environments. *Ethology and Sociobiology*, **11**, 375–424.

Tooby, J. and Cosmides, L. (1992). The psychological foundations of culture. In J. H. Barkow, L. Cosmides, and J. Tooby (Eds.), *The Adapted Mind: Evolutionary Psychology and the Generation of Culture* (pp. 19–136). Oxford: Oxford University Press.

Trivers, R. L. (1971). The evolution of reciprocal altruism. *Quarterly Review of Biology*, **76**, 35–57.

Trivers, R. L. (1972). Parental investment and sexual selection. In B. Campbell (Ed.), *Sexual Selection and the Descent of Man: 1871–1971* (pp. 136–179). Chicago: Aldine.

Trivers, R. (2000). The elements of a scientific theory of self-deception. *Annals of the New York Academy of Sciences*, **907**, 114–131.

Webster, G. D. (2007). Evolutionary theory in cognitive neuroscience: A 20-year quantitative review of publication trends. *Evolutionary Psychology*, **5**, 520–530.

Williams, G. C. (1966). *Adaptation and Natural Selection*. Princeton, NJ: Princeton University Press.

Winston, J. S., O'Doherty, J., Kilner, J. M., Perrett, D. I., and Dolan, R. J. (2007). Brain systems for assessing facial attractiveness. *Neuropsychologica*, **45**, 195–206.

Wyckoff, G. J., Wang, W. and Wu, C. (2000). Rapid evolution of male reproductive genes in the descent of man. *Nature*, **403**, 304–308.

Wynn, T. (2002). Archaeology and cognitive evolution. *Behavioral and Brain Sciences*, **25**, 389–402.

2

The evolution of general fluid intelligence

DAVID C. GEARY

The evolution of general fluid intelligence

In the decades following Darwin's (1859) publication of *On the Origin of Species*, there was a flurry of proposals and theories regarding human evolution (Darwin, 1871; Huxley, 1863; Wallace, 1864), including the evolution of human intelligence. The proposals of these early evolutionists were very similar to theories of cognitive and intellectual evolution offered by this generation's theorists (Alexander, 1989; Ash and Gallup, 2007; Dunbar, 1998; Flinn, Geary, and Ward, 2005; Geary, 2005; Kanazawa, 2004, 2007; Kaplan, Hill, Lancaster, and Hurtado, 2000; Miller, 2000; Mithen, 1996, 2007). Many of the themes and contrasting views that emerged during the middle decades of the nineteenth century are echoed by theorists in the first decade of the twenty-first century. The central theme that cuts across generations and theories is that the core of intelligence is the ability to anticipate and predict variation and novelty and to devise strategies to cope with this novelty. The core issue that divides theorists is the source of novelty; specifically, whether the primary source of this variation is due to climatic change, the vagaries and nuances of hunting other species, or from the dynamics of competition within and between human groups. Darwin (1871, pp. 158–160) suggested that each of these contributed to the evolution of human intelligence:

> He [humans] has great power of adapting his habits to new conditions of life. He invents weapons, tools and various stratagems, by which he procures food and defends himself. When he migrates into a colder climate he uses clothes, builds sheds, and makes fires; and, by the aid of fire, cooks food otherwise indigestible. He aids his fellow-men in many ways, and anticipates future events ... from the remotest times successful tribes have supplanted other tribes.

Foundations in Evolutionary Cognitive Neuroscience, ed. Steven M. Platek and Todd K. Shackelford.
Published by Cambridge University Press. © Cambridge University Press 2009.

It is likely that some combination of selection pressures – climatic, ecological (e.g., hunting), and social – influenced the evolution of the human brain and mind and the evolution of what is now called general fluid intelligence, as defined below. The key question concerns the selection pressure that was central to the evolution of these competencies, following the emergence of the genus *Homo* and especially the emergence of *H. sapiens*. In the first two sections, I provide respective reviews of the empirical research on hominid brain evolution and psychometric and cognitive neuroscientific research on fluid intelligence. These reviews provide the background needed to appreciate the changes that have occurred in brain and mind during human evolution and to understand the component competencies that define fluid intelligence. In the final section, I place these findings in the context of models of climatic, ecological, and social selection pressures and within an integrative model of human brain, cognitive, and psychological evolution.

Brain evolution

Brain volume and organization

One common method for estimating the brain volume of extinct homi-nids is to reconstruct the fossilized cranium and then make a plaster cast of the cranium (Holloway, Broadfield, and Yuan, 2004). In some cases, these endocasts provide an impression of the architecture of the outer surface of the neocortex and thus allow inferences to be drawn about gross evolutionary change in the structure of this part of the brain (Falk, 1983; Holloway and de la Coste-Lareymondie, 1982; Tobias, 1987). These and related methods have been used to estimate the brain volume of the various species of *Homo* and species of the predecessor genus, *Australopithecus*. The mean estimates for these species are shown in the top portion of Figure 2.1 and are based on multiple sources for all species (Falk *et al.*, 2000; Holloway, 1973a, 1973b; McHenry, 1994; Tobias, 1987; Wood and Collard, 1999), with the exception of *A. garhi* which is estimated from a single source (Asfaw, White, Lovejoy, Latimer, Simpson, and Suwa, 1999). The middle section of the figure presents estimated times of existence of these species; these estimates are subject to change with the discovery of additional hominid fossils (e.g. Spoor, Leakey, Gathogo, Brown, Antón, McDougall, Kiarie, Manthi, and Leakey, 2007).

The evolutionary pattern is clear. The australopithecines (*A. afarensis*, *A. africanus*, and *A. garhi*) show a significantly but modestly larger brain volume than chimpanzees (*Pan troglodytes*) and thus presumably a larger brain volume than the ancestor common to australopithecines, chimpanzees, and humans

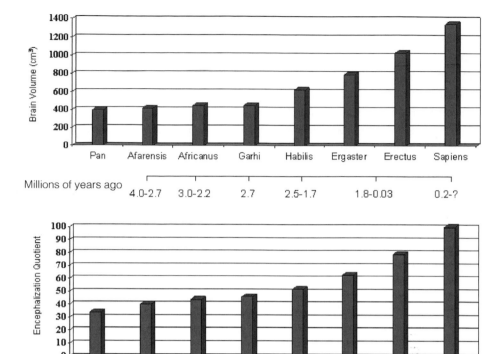

Figure 2.1. The top portion presents the estimated brain volume for chimpanzees (*Pan troglodytes*) and key species of australopithecines (*A. afarensis*, *A. africanus*, *A. garhi*) and Homo (*H. habilis*, *H. ergaster*, *H. erectus*, *H. sapiens*). The middle portion presents estimated time of existence of these species; *H. ergaster* and *H. erectus* are presented together because they may be earlier and later forms of the same species. The bottom portion presents estimated encephalization quotients (EQ) for these species as a percentage of the EQ of modern humans (*H. sapiens*).

(McHenry, 1994; Tobias, 1987). Whether the brain morphology of australopithecines was more similar to that of chimpanzees and other great apes or to humans is debated (e.g., Falk, 1983; Holloway and Kimbel, 1986). Either way, one pattern that is not found in great apes but is consistently found in australopithecines and other hominids, including humans, is a difference in the shape of the posterior portions of the left hemisphere and anterior portions of the right hemisphere. The visual area of the left hemisphere – for instance, area 18 in Figure 2.2 – is smaller than expected based on body and brain size and the left parietal area and right frontal area (area 10, Figure 2.2) are larger than expected (Holloway and de la Coste-Lareymondie, 1982). Expansion of the right frontal area is potentially important, because this area appears to be important for self-awareness, awareness of one's behavior in social contexts, and the ability to

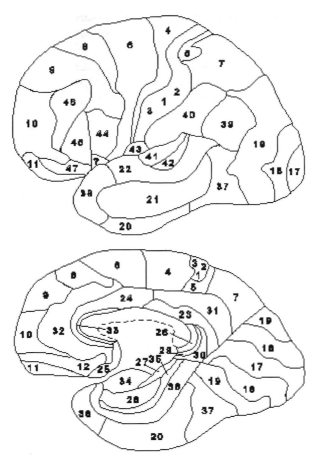

Figure 2.2. Cartoon maps of Brodmann's (1909) areas of the human neocortex. The top section is a lateral (outer) view of the cortex, whereas the bottom section is a medial (center, between the two hemispheres) view. Many of these areas can be subdivided into specialized subregions that may process different forms of information. Generally, areas 1, 2, 3, 5, 31, 39, 40, and 43 are part of the parietal cortex and support a variety of functions including sense of body position, attention, and spatial competencies; areas 17, 18, and 19 are part of the occipital cortex and support simple and complex visual perception; areas 22, 41, 42, and subregions of areas 40 and 38 are part of the temporal cortex and support simple and complex auditory and speech perception; areas 20, 21, 26–28, 34–37, and 52 are also part of the temporal lobe, but support a variety of complex visual competencies; areas 4, 6, and 8 are involved in complex motor movements and are part of the frontal cortex; area 44 and subregions of area 45 are involved in speech generation and are part of the frontal cortex; areas 9, 10, 11, 25, 46, 47, and subregions of 45 are part of the prefrontal cortex and support behavioral control, executive functions, and many complex social competencies; areas 23, 24, 30, (parts of 31), 32, and 33 are part of the cingulate and support attentional and emotional functions. Illustration by Mark Dubin.

anticipate future events (Levine, 1999; Platek *et al.*, 2006; Platek, Keenan, Gallup, and Mohamed, 2004; Tulving, 2002).

Further increases in brain volume and added changes in the morphology are evident in *H. habilis* (Falk, 1983; Tobias, 1987), including modest expansion of the frontal and parietal lobes and extensive remodeling – specifically, evidence for more folding and thus more surface area of the frontal lobes relative to *A. africanus*. One area of the frontal lobe implicated in human speech and gesture, specifically, Broca's area (area 44, Figure 2.2), appears to have expanded with the emergence of *H. habilis* and had an architecture similar to that of modern humans. The increase in the size of the parietal cortex (e.g., area 40) is potentially important as well (Holloway, 1996), because it is coincident with increasingly sophisticated tool use with and after the emergence of *H. habilis*, and because areas of the parietal cortex are engaged during tool use in modern humans (Johnson-Frey, 2003), and contribute to the attentional control components of fluid intelligence (discussed below). Further increases in brain volume and morphology are evident with the emergence of *H. erectus* and continue in modern humans (McHenry, 1994; Ruff, Trinkaus, and Holliday, 1997; Wood and Collard, 1999).

The threefold increase in brain volume comparing *A. afarensis* to modern humans belies another important pattern, that is, relative stasis for long periods of time. The modest increase in brain volume from *A. afarensis* to *A. garhi* evolved over the course of 1.5 million years; there was relatively little change in brain volume from about 4 million years ago (MYA) until the emergence of *H. habilis* about 2.5 MYA (McHenry, 1994; Wood and Collard, 1999). Another period of relative stasis occurred from about 1.8 MYA until about 500 000 years ago (Ruff *et al.*, 1997), followed by substantial increases in brain volume over the past several hundred thousand years and continuing until about 20 000 years ago (Holloway, 1996; Ruff *et al.*, 1997).

Encephalization quotient

Although evolutionary change in absolute brain volume is important, it can also be misleading. The absolute size of the brain increases with increases in overall body size, and thus confounds cross-species comparisons (Harvey and Clutton-Brock, 1985). For instance, the weight of an adult male *A. africanus* is estimated to have been 30% less than that of a modern adult human male. It is therefore possible that some proportion of the difference in absolute brain volume comparing these two species is due to differences in overall body size and not to selection pressures for increased brain size (McHenry, 1994). The encephalization quotient (EQ) is an often-used measure to control for the relation between brain and body size; EQ indexes brain size relative to that of a mammal of the same body weight (Jerison, 1973; for discussion see Holloway, 1996). Domestic cats have an EQ of about 1.0, that is, their brain size relative to their body size is average for mammals.

The EQ of primates and that of other highly social species is typically greater than 1.0. McHenry (1994) estimated the EQ of chimpanzees to be 2.0. For modern humans, EQ values range from less than 5.0 (Aiello and Wheeler, 1995) to more than 7.0 (Jerison, 1973; Tobias, 1987), with estimates commonly ranging between 5.0 and 6.0 (McHenry, 1994; Ruff et al., 1997). As shown in the bottom portion of Figure 2.1, EQ has increased dramatically over the past 4 million years of hominid evolution. The estimates are expressed in terms of a percentage of that of modern humans and thus although the EQ of chimpanzees is twice that of the typical mammal, it is estimated to be only 34% of that of modern humans. The EQ of australopithecines is greater than that of chimpanzees but less than 50% that of modern humans, whereas the EQ of H. habilis was slightly more than 50% of modern humans. Large increases in EQ are evident with the emergence of H. ergaster and H. erectus, with values at the high end close to 80% that of modern humans. Following the emergence of H. ergaster, there was a period of little change in EQ for about 1.2 million years, followed by a modest 12% increase from 500 000 to 400 000 years ago, and then very rapid increases until about 20 000 years ago.

The EQ of modern humans appears to have peaked about 20 000 years ago and declined 3% to 4% since then (Holloway, 1996; Ruff et al., 1997). The gradual decline in EQ values suggests that the selection pressures that resulted in the rapid increase in EQ beginning about 500 000 years ago have been relaxed during the last 10 000 to 20 000 years. During this timeframe, agriculture, economic specialization, city-states, and other changes were becoming increasingly central features of human subsistence activities and social organization (Brace, 1995; Clutton-Brock, 1992; Hole, 1992). These changes appear to have resulted in a relaxation of the selection pressures that drove the rapid increase in EQ from 500 000 years ago to about 20 000 years ago. Evolutionary declines in EQ are in fact common when day-to-day living becomes easier. For instance, domesticated *canids* (i.e., dogs) and *felines* (i.e., cats) have EQ values about 20% lower than that of their feral cousins (Burghardt, 2005).

Selection pressures and brain evolution

The three principal classes of selection pressure and hominid brain evolution are climatic, ecological, and social. In the following sections, I overview and update reviews of these pressures presented in earlier work (i.e., Geary, 2005).

Climatic. Climatic and geological changes are common and can result in change in temperature, rainfall, and other ecological conditions that in turn can influence the mix of vegetation, woodland, and other factors that can have dramatic evolutionary effects on multiple species (e.g., deMenocal, 2001; Vrba, Denton, Partridge, and Burckle, 1995). One of the more influential models of climatic change and evolution is Vrba's the turnover-pulse hypothesis (e.g., 1974, 1995). The gist is that large-scale climatic changes, such as those associated with global cooling, can result in large-scale changes in habitat (e.g., change in the distribution of food sources) and physical ecology (e.g., ambient temperature). The result is pulses of speciation and extinction events. The hypothesis is that new species evolve as habitat change results in geographic isolation – due, for instance, to deforestation and resulting pockets of woodlands within savanna – of populations of the same species, and subsequent adaptations of these populations to local conditions. Extinction follows for those species that are unable to adapt to these changes.

Vrba (1995) argued that significant glaciation between 2.8 and 2.5 MYA resulted in decreased temperature and rainfall in Africa and a corresponding turnover pulse of many species of large fauna, including hominids. Evolutionary responses to decreasing temperature often include increases in physical size to enable greater retention of body heat and a prolonged period of physical development to enable growth of a larger body. Vrba proposed that these physical adaptations resulted in an accompanying change in brain volume and EQ: "The conclusion is inescapable that hominine encephalization in the latest Pliocene started a new trend, of higher evolutionary rates than before" (Vrba, 1995, p. 406). The specific mechanisms driving or at least maintaining the increase in hominid EQ are not detailed, but the implication is that EQ changes were not the direct result of ecological or social pressures but rather an incidental effect of broader physical adaptations.

Vrba's (1974) hypothesis has been vigorously debated (e.g., Kimbel, 1995; Potts, 1998; Turner and Wood, 1993; White, 1995). Consistent with the hypothesis and related climatic models (Potts, 1998), there is evidence that global cooling may have contributed to the expansion of the African savanna during the time when multiple species of australopithecine emerged (Kimbel, 1995). Ash and Gallup (2007) analyzed the relation between estimates of global temperature and variability in global temperature since the emergence of *H. habilis* and brain volume and EQ estimates from *Homo* cranial fossils from *H. habilis* to early modern humans. Among other findings, brain volume was strongly correlated with a measure of temperature variability ($rho = 0.73$). Temperatures are cooler and typically more variable as latitude moves north or south of the equator, and brain volume was significantly ($rho = 0.48$) correlated with distance from the equator.

At the same time, there are other results that weaken the climate hypothesis. If increases in brain volume and EQ of *Homo* were associated with climatic change and variability, then similar increases in other African hominids and primates that lived in the same regions and during the same timeframe should be found. Falk *et al.* (2000) tested this hypothesis by comparing the brain volumes of *H. habilis* and *H. erectus* to the brain volumes of three sister species of African hominids (*Paranthropus robustus*, *P. boisei*, *P. aethiopicus*) from roughly 2.0 to 1.5 MYA. With the possible exception of *P. boisei* (Elton, Bishop, and Wood, 2001), the brain volumes of these species did not change substantively during this timeframe. Elton *et al.* examined change in the brain volume of a species of now extinct baboon (*Theropithecus*) that appears to have lived in the same localities as *H. habilis* and *H. erectus*. Again, there was no change in the brain volume of this species of baboon during the timeframe when there were significant increases in brain volume and EQ in *Homo*.

Evidence for Vrba's (1974) turnover pulse hypothesis and related climate models (e.g., Potts, 1998) is mixed. The emergence of various species of australopithecine 3.0 to 2.0 MYA, including the emergence of the line that eventually led to modern humans, may have been driven, at least in part, by climatic and ecological changes in Africa during this epoch. Since that time, climate change and variation may have contributed to changes in brain volume and EQ in *Homo*, but does not appear sufficient in and of itself. If it were, then other primates and hominids exposed to the same climate conditions would have shown the same pattern of brain evolution as *Homo*, but they do not.

Ecological. In traditional societies today and in preindustrial Western nations, parasites, food shortages, and occasional predator attacks were significant sources of human mortality and morbidity (Hed, 1987; Hill and Hurtado, 1996; Morrison, Kirshner, and Molho, 1977). These were almost certainly components of natural selection during human evolution but, as with climatic pressures, they do not appear to be sufficient explanations of the increases in hominid brain volume and EQ. If they were, then many species would have evidenced the same increases in brain volume and EQ because parasites, predators, and food shortages are common selection pressures across species. Ecological models of hominid brain evolution have instead focused on improvements in the ability of hominids to extract biological resources from the ecology and through this reduce premature mortality. The latter results in population increases and eventually geographic expansions. The basic idea is supported by a common pattern across nonhuman species: species with complex foraging or predatory demands have a larger brain volume and higher EQ values than related species with less complex foraging or predatory demands (Barton, 1996; Barton and Dean, 1993; Kaplan & Robson, 2002).

The argument is taken one step further with the proposal that hominids evolved into super predators (Martin, 1967; Wrangham *et al.*, 1999). Humans in traditional societies are indeed highly efficient at extracting life-supporting resources from the ecology through hunting and foraging (Kaplan *et al.*, 2000; Hill *et al.* 2001). If this ability to extract and process (e.g., through cooking) biological resources from the ecology was the driving force in hominid brain evolution, then there should be evidence of social, behavioral, and other adaptations that allowed evolving hominids to forage and hunt in increasingly sophisticated ways.

Analyses of tooth size, shape, and wear patterns of australopithecines suggest a substantive shift in diet in comparison to their predecessors (e.g., Jolly, 1970; Teaford and Ungar, 2000). There is preliminary evidence that *A. garhi* constructed stone tools, including tools used to cut and process meat (Semaw *et al.*, 2003). These features of tooth morphology and behavioral adaptation suggest that australopithecines were able to eat a wider range of foods than their predecessors and thus were able to exploit a wider range of ecologies. Wrangham *et al.* (1999) presented evidence consistent with the position that *H. erectus* used fire for cooking, which enables the use of a wider range of plant and animal species as foods, as noted by Darwin (1871). Foley and others have demonstrated that tools related to hunting and foraging (e.g., digging sticks) have become increasingly sophisticated since the appearance of *A. afarensis* (de Heinzelin *et al.*, 1999; Foley and Lahr, 1997). *H. habilis* appears to have used simple stone tools, with increases in the complexity of these tools and their wide geographic distribution coinciding with the emergence and migration patterns of *H. erectus*. These advances continued with the appearance of early modern humans (Clark *et al.*, 2003), although the most complex stone tools are found in archeological sites dating less than 50 000 years ago (Foley and Lahr, 1997). The pattern of tool "evolution" and the likely function of these tools, including hunting and foraging, is consistent with ecological models of human brain evolution (e.g., Kaplan *et al.*, 2000).

Evidence that these changes resulted in the evolution of a super-predator comes from patterns of human migration and subsequent mass extinctions of other species. Wallace noted as much in 1911 (p. 264) – "the rapidity of the extinction of so many large Mammalia is actually due to man's agency." Five decades later, Martin (1967, 1973) presented systematic evidence that indeed mass extinctions of some megafauna (prey species weighing 40 kg or more) were evident in Africa about 50 000 years ago, and later mass extinctions occurred in Australia, Asia, America, and New Zealand after the migration of humans into these regions. Martin (1973) and Alroy (2001) presented evidence suggesting the mass extinction of megafauna in North America occurred about 12 000 years ago, that is, roughly 1000 to several thousand years after the arrival of humans. These mass extinctions have not been correlated with climatic or other ecological changes (e.g., glaciers; Miller *et al.*, 1999), although the extinction of some species is related to climate and ecological changes and not to human activity. Guthrie (2003, 2006) presents evidence that the Alaskan horse (*Equus ferus*) was extinct before the arrival of humans and that populations of mammoths (*Mammuthus primigenius*) were declining; humans may have contributed to the final demise of the mammoth, however. In any case, declines in populations of species of large fish and mammals have been directly linked to human hunting and fishing from the time humans were hunter-gathers to the modern day (e.g., Hsieh *et al.*, 2006; Myers and Worm, 2003; Pandolfi *et al.*, 2003).

Further evidence for a co-evolving relation between EQ and hunting and other dietary changes comes from the metabolic requirements of the human brain (Armstrong, 1990). Specifically, there is evidence that the evolutionary increase in brain volume was associated with a corresponding decrease in the mass of the metabolically expensive gastrointestinal tract (Aiello and Wheeler, 1995), although this evidence is not conclusive (Aiello, Bates, and Joffe, 2001). Reduction in the size of the gastrointestinal tract requires change from a low quality (e.g., plants) to a high quality (e.g., fruits, meat) diet. The above noted shift in the australopithecine diet is thus consistent with the corresponding change in EQ, as is the rapid increase in EQ associated with the increasingly effective hunting competencies of *H. erectus* and *H. sapiens*. It is not that reduction in the gastrointestinal tract directly caused the evolutionary expansion of brain volume and EQ but rather it released a significant constraint and thus resulted in an opportunity for evolutionary change.

Social pressures. The foregoing pattern of gradual improvement in the hunting and foraging abilities of hominids, especially after the emergence of *Homo*, is consistent with Alexander's (1989) model of *ecological dominance*. Once achieved, an evolutionary Rubicon was crossed:

> the ecological dominance of evolving humans diminished the effects of "extrinsic" forces of natural selection such that within-species competition became the principal "hostile force of nature" guiding the long-term evolution of behavioral capacities, traits, and tendencies (Alexander, 1989, p. 458).

Ecological dominance would manifest as the ability to efficiently extract biological resources – as exemplified by the pattern of overkill of megafauna – from the ecology and the ability to manipulate the ecology in ways that reduce mortality risks and support subsequent population expansions (Hill *et al.*, 2001; Kaplan *et al.*, 2000). Pressures for ecological manipulation, as in building of shelters, use of fire, clothing, and so forth, would in theory be stronger in harsh and variable climates. These climates would be more common as latitude moves north or south of the equator (Ash and Gallup, 2007). There are also fewer parasites in these colder environments (Low, 1990), which should result in fewer demands on the metabolically expensive immune system. As with dietary change and gut evolution, reduction in metabolic demands of the immune system may have released a significant constraint on brain evolution. The release of this metabolic constraint would provide an opportunity for further evolutionary change in brain volume and EQ, but only if other conditions favored this evolution. These conditions are hypothesized to include social competition.

The lower mortality that would follow from ecological dominance would have necessarily resulted in population increases. These increases would support migration to new regions, as happened with *H. erectus*, but also carries the risk of expansion beyond the carrying capacity of the ecology. As the population increases, the available resources diminish per capita and thus social competition for these diminishing resources will necessarily increase in intensity. As detailed by Malthus (1798) and confirmed in subsequent studies (e.g., Hed, 1987; Morrison *et al.*, 1977; United Nations, 1985), the end result is often a population crash that disproportionately affects individuals who are economically poor and of lower social status. The inverse relation between social status, resource control and mortality risk creates a never ending cycle whereby Darwin's and Wallace's (1858, p. 54) conceptualization of natural selection as a "struggle for existence," becomes in addition a *struggle with other human beings for control* of the resources that support life and allow one to reproduce (Geary, 1998, 2005). In this situation, the stage is set for a form of runaway selection, whereby the more cognitively, socially, and behaviorally sophisticated individuals are able to out-maneuver and manipulate other individuals in order to gain control of resources in the local ecology, and to gain control of the behavior of other people (West-Eberhard, 1983). To the extent that access to these resources covaries with survival and reproductive outcomes – and it does in many contexts (Betzig, 1986; Hed, 1987; Malthus, 1798; United Nations, 1985) – the associated sociocognitive competencies, and supporting brain systems, will necessarily evolve.

My point is that an ecological-dominance–social-competition model (see Alexander, 1989; Flinn *et al.*, 2005; Geary, 2005; see also Gavrilets and Vose, 2006) accommodates most of the core features of the climatic and ecological theories of human brain evolution. The model is also in keeping with other evolutionary models that focus primarily on the importance of social competition during human evolution (e.g., Dunbar, 1998; Humphrey, 1976). I should note that social competition is nested between and within groups. The maintenance of ecological dominance in human populations requires extensive cooperation and a division of labor among members of the in-group, typically kin. These groups also cooperate in ways that allow them to better compete with other groups for control of ecologically rich land and control of social and political dynamics between groups. Across species and for human populations, larger group size typically results in competitive advantage (Horowitz, 2001; Wrangham, 1999), and thus pressures for mechanisms that support in-group cooperation.

Empirical studies of fluid intelligence

Across the various theories of the evolution of the human brain and intelligence, there has been surprisingly little attention paid to the definition and measurement of the core concept of "intelligence." The gist is similar across these theories and includes planning, foresight, scenario building, and so forth, but reference to the more than 100 years of psychological studies of intelligence is rarely, if ever found. In an earlier work (Geary, 2005) I attempted to integrate theories of human brain and cognitive evolution with findings from psychological studies of intelligence. The core ideas are that the evolved "intelligence" referred to in these evolutionary theories is the general fluid intelligence identified by psychometric psychologists, and that these theories, fluid intelligence, and many other aspects of human cognition (e.g., in-group, out-group attributional biases) can be integrated within a broader theoretical framework. I summarize this framework in a later section. In the following sections, I provide a brief review of empirical studies of general intelligence.

Psychometric research

Quantitative studies of individual differences in intelligence began with Spearman (1904). In this study, elementary- and high-school students as well as adults were administered sensory and perceptual tasks and were rated by teachers and peers on their in-school intelligence and out-of-school common sense. Scores on exams in classics, French, English, and mathematics were also available for the high-school students. Correlational analyses revealed that above average performance on one task was associated with above average performance on all other tasks, on exam scores, and for ratings of intelligence and common sense. On the basis of these findings, Spearman (1904, p. 285) concluded "that all branches of intellectual activity have in common one fundamental function (or group of functions)." Spearman termed the fundamental function or group of functions general intelligence or g.

Six decades later, Cattell and Horn (Cattell, 1963; Horn, 1968; Horn and Cattell, 1966) proposed that the single general ability proposed by Spearman should be subdivided into two distinct abilities. The first is called *crystallized intelligence* (Gc) and is manifested as the result of experience, schooling, and acculturation and is referenced by over-learned skills and knowledge, such as vocabulary. The second ability is called *fluid intelligence* (Gf), and represents a biologically based ability to acquire skills and knowledge. As Cattell (1963, p. 3) stated: "Fluid general ability ... shows more in tests requiring adaptation to new situations, where crystallized skills are of no particular advantage." This empirically based conclusion is critical to the current analysis, because it links Gf with theoretical models of the evolution of the human brain and mind; specifically, that this evolution was driven by selection pressures that required humans and our ancestors to cope with variation and novelty in their day-to-day lives. In other words, the ability to anticipate and cope with novelty and change – adaptation to new situations – that are central to models of human brain and cognitive evolution is reliably assessed by tests of Gf.

Cognitive research

In the decades following Cattell and Horn's (Cattell, 1963; Horn, 1968; Horn and Cattell, 1966) discovery, hundreds of studies aimed at identifying the cognitive components of g and especially Gf have and continue to be conducted (see Jensen, 1998). These efforts led to the identification of speed of information processing and working memory as core components of Gf. In the following reviews, I refer to measures that likely assessed a combination of Gf and Gc as tests of g, and measures that largely tap fluid abilities as Gf.

Speed of processing. Three important findings have emerged from studies of the relation between speed of processing simple pieces of information, such as speed of retrieving a word name from long-term memory, and performance on measures of g (Hunt, 1978; Jensen, 1998). The first is that faster speed of cognitive processing is related to higher scores on measures of g (Jensen, 1982; Jensen and Munro, 1979), although strength of the relation is moderate ($rs \sim 0.3$ to 0.4). The second finding is that variability in speed of processing is also related to scores on measures of g ($rs \sim 0.4$; Jensen, 1992). The variability measure assesses consistency in speed of executing the same process multiple times; individuals who are consistently fast in executing these processes have the higher scores on measures of g (Deary, 2000; Jensen, 1998; Neubauer, 1997). Finally, the speed with which individuals can identify very briefly (e.g., 50 ms) presented information (e.g., whether '>' is pointed left or right) is moderately correlated with g (Deary and Stough, 1996).

The gist of this research is that performance on psychometric tests of g and especially Gf is related to the speed and accuracy with which information is identified, and then processed by sensory and perceptual systems. For

individuals who score highly on measures of Gf, the processing of this information occurs more rapidly than for other individuals. For all individuals, the
information is first implicitly (i.e., below conscious awareness) represented in
short-term memory. For the information to become available to conscious
awareness and thus amenable to explicit problem solving, it must become
represented in working memory.

Working memory. The processing of the majority of information gathered by
our sensory and perceptual systems and represented in short-term memory
occurs automatically, and implicitly. Much of the time, any required mental or
behavioral response also occurs automatically, that is, without the need to
engage attentional and working memory resources (Gigerenzer, Todd, and
ABC Research Group, 1999). As Gigerenzer and his colleagues have demonstrated, these automatic responses are the result of evolved heuristics – fast
and efficient behavioral or cognitive responses that require minimal, explicit
cognitive resources – or heuristics learned during the life span. However, when
information cannot be automatically processed by evolved systems or through
access to learned information stored in long-term memory, the result is an
automatic shift in attention to this information (Botvinick *et al.* 2001).
Situations that trigger attentional shifts are, by this definition, novel or rapidly
changing and thus are not easily coped with through evolved or learned
strategies.

The focusing of attention results in an explicit representation of this information in working memory, and simultaneous inhibition of irrelevant
information (Cowan, 1995; Engle, Conway, Tuholski, and Shisler, 1995). Once
represented in working memory and available to conscious awareness, the
information is amenable to explicit, controlled problem solving, that is, the
information can be mentally operated on to adjust pre-existing heuristics or
generate new ones to cope with the novel or changing situation. The attentional
system that controls the explicit manipulation of information during problem
solving is called the central executive, and the modalities in which the information is represented are called slave systems. The latter include auditory, visual,
spatial, or episodic representations of information (Baddeley, 1986, 2000); episodic memory binds information from multiple systems and is important for
recall of memories of personal experiences (Tulving, 2002).

If working memory is a core component of Gf, then individual differences in
performance on measures of Gf should be strongly associated with individual
differences in working memory capacity and this is indeed the case (e.g.,
Carpenter, Just, and Shell, 1990; Conway *et al.*, 2002; Engle, Tuholski, Laughlin,
and Conway, 1999; Kyllonen and Christal, 1990; Mackintosh and Bennett, 2003).
The strength of the relation between performance on working memory tasks

and scores on measures of Gf range from moderate ($rs \sim 0.5$; Ackerman, Beier, and Boyle, 2005; Mackintosh and Bennett, 2003) to very high ($rs > 0.8$; Conway *et al.*, 2002). On the basis of these patterns, Horn (1988) and other scientists (Carpenter *et al.*, 1990; Stanovich, 1999) have argued that measures of strategic problem solving and abstract reasoning define Gf, and the primary cognitive system underlying problem solving, reasoning, and thus Gf is attention-driven working memory. The relation between speed of processing and working memory is debated (Ackerman, Beier, and Boyle, 2005; Fry and Hale, 1996, 2000), but a potential solution is presented below (see also Geary, 2005).

Summary. Intelligent individuals identify, process, and bind together bits of social and ecological information more easily and quickly than do other people. Their perceptual systems process this information such that the information is activated quickly and accurately in short-term memory. If evolved or learned heuristics are available for responding to the situation, then intelligent people will be able to execute these responses more quickly and consistently (across situations requiring the same response) than other people. If evolved or learned heuristics are not available, there is an automatic shifting of attention to the novel or rapidly changing information represented in short-term memory. Once attention is focused, intelligent people are able to represent more information in working memory than are other people and have an enhanced ability to consciously manipulate this information. The manipulation is guided and constrained by reasoning and inference making mechanisms (Embretson, 1995; Stanovich, 1999).

Neuroscience research

I have proposed that this attention-driven ability to explicitly represent and systematically and logically manipulate information in working memory are core features of an evolved human ability to adapt to social and ecological variation and novelty within the life span (Geary, 2005). In other words, the focus of evolutionary theorists on the importance of the human ability to anticipate and adapt to novelty and change converges with decades of empirical findings on the component skills that underlie human intelligence and especially Gf. If this proposal is correct, then the evolutionary emergence of Gf should track the above described evolutionary changes in brain size and EQ. Unfortunately, a direct test of this hypothesis is not possible, due to the absence of Gf data in the palaeontological record and the extinction of, and thus the inability to assess on measures of Gf, other species of *Homo*. It is possible to indirectly test this hypothesis by examining the relation between brain size and organization and performance on measures of Gf in contemporary humans. This is because the evolution Gf and changes in brain size and organization would presumably have been dependent on the same individual differences found in modern populations.

Brain size. Neuroimaging methodologies now allow for a relatively easy assessment of gross brain volume and volume of specific brain regions. The studies that have examined individual differences in gross brain volume and performance on measures of g has revealed the bigger the better, but the relation is modest ($r \sim 0.3$ to 0.4); Deary, 2000; McDaniel, 2005; Rushton and Ankney, 1996). In one of the more comprehensive of these studies, Wickett, Vernon, and Lee (2000) examined the relations between total brain volume and performance on measures of Gf, Gc, short-term memory, and speed of processing. Larger brain volumes were associated with higher Gf scores ($r = 0.49$), a larger short-term memory capacity ($r = 0.45$), and faster speed of processing ($rs \sim 0.4$), but were unrelated to Gc scores ($r = 0.06$). Raz *et al.* (1993) examined the relation between performance on measures of Gf and Gc and total brain volume, and volume of the dorsolateral prefrontal cortex (areas 9 and 46, Figure 2.2) – associated with attentional control and explicit representation of information in working memory – portions of the parietal cortex (e.g., areas 39 and 40) – associated with visuospatial ability, attentional control, and tool use – the hippocampus – associated with consolidation of short-term memories into long-term memories – and several other brain regions. Higher Gf scores were associated with larger total brain volume ($r = 0.43$), a larger dorsolateral prefrontal cortex ($r = 0.51$), and more white matter (i.e., neuronal axons) in the prefrontal cortex ($r = 0.41$), but were unrelated to size of the other brain regions. Performance on the Gc measure was not related to size of any of these brain regions or to total brain volume.

Regional activation. Multiple studies have now examined the brain regions that become activated or deactivated while individuals solve items on measures of Gf or other reasoning tasks (Duncan *et al.* 2000; Gray, Chabris, and Braver, 2003; Haier *et al.*, 1988; Kalbfleisch, Van Meter, and Zeffiro, 2006; Prabhakaran *et al.*, 1997). Most of the studies reveal a pattern of activation and deactivation in several brain regions, much of which is likely due to task-specific (e.g., verbal vs. spatial) content of the reasoning measures (e.g., Stephan *et al.*, 2003). The results from studies that have employed the most sensitive imaging technologies are consistent with the brain volume studies; performance on measures of Gf are supported, in part, by the same system of brain regions that support the central executive components of working memory, that is, attentional and inhibitory control. These areas include the dorsolateral prefrontal cortex, anterior cingulate cortex (area 24, Figure 2.2), and regions of the parietal cortex (Duncan *et al.*, 2000), although size and white matter organization in other brain regions may also contribute to individual differences in Gf (for a recent review see Jung and Haier, 2007).

The engagement of areas of the anterior cingulate cortex is important. This is because this brain region is activated when goal achievement requires dealing with some degree of novelty, conflict, or making a difficult decision (Miller and Cohen, 2001; Ranganath and Rainer, 2003) – these are situations in which a goal cannot be readily achieved by means of heuristics. Areas of the anterior cingulate cortex are thus the potential mechanism that results in the automatic attentional shift to novel, conflicted, or changing information represented in short-term memory and a corresponding activation of the dorsolateral and other prefrontal areas (Botvinick et al., 2001). These areas in turn enable the attentional focus and explicit, controlled problem solving needed to cope with novel situations, resolve conflicts, and make decisions that involve cost-benefit trade-offs (Kerns et al., 2004; Miller and Cohen, 2001). Botvinick and colleagues' proposal that novelty and conflict result in automatic attentional shifts and activation of executive functions is important, as it addresses the *homunculus* question. The central executive does not activate itself, but rather is automatically activated when heuristic-based processes are not sufficient for dealing with current information patterns or tasks.

Integration

Brain imaging studies on the whole support the hypothesis that the same brain regions that underlie working memory and explicit controlled problem solving are engaged when people solve items on measures of Gf (Duncan et al., 2000; Gray et al., 2003; Kane and Engle, 2002). High scores on measures of Gf are associated with activation of the dorsolateral prefrontal cortex and several other brain regions associated with attentional control, including the anterior cingulate cortex and regions of the parietal cortex (Jung and Haier, 2007). These same regions also appear to support the ability to inhibit irrelevant information from intruding into working memory and conscious awareness (Esposito et al., 1999) and inhibit the execution of evolved or learned heuristics (Geary, 2005). Awareness of information represented in working memory and the ability to mentally manipulate this information may result from a synchronization of the prefrontal brain regions that subserve the central executive and the brain regions that process the specific forms of information (e.g., voice, face, object; Damasio, 1989; Dehaene and Naccache, 2001; Posner, 1994).

An attention-driven synchronization of the activity of dorsolateral prefrontal cortex and the brain regions that support explicit working memory representations of external information or internal mental simulations would be facilitated by faster speed of processing and rich interconnections among these brain regions. The latter are associated with larger brain size and especially a greater volume of white matter (i.e., axons): the corresponding prediction that Gf will be positively correlated with the quantity of white matter connections between the prefrontal cortex and posterior cortical regions is testable with use of diffusion tensor imaging. Functionally, speed of processing may be important for the synchronization process, because faster speed of processing would enable more accurate adjustments in synchronization per feedback cycle. With repeated synchronized activity, the result appears to be the formation of a neural network that automatically links the processing of these information patterns (Sporns, Tononi, and Edelman, 2000). In other words, speed of processing and an attention-driven working memory system are not competing explanations of Gf (Ackerman *et al.*, 2005; Engle, 2002; Kane and Engle, 2002), but rather may be coevolved and complementary mechanisms (Geary, 2005).

Integrated model: the motivation to control

The theoretical model that places general fluid intelligence in the context of human brain and cognitive evolution can be organized around a "motivation to control." This does not mean that individuals necessarily have a conscious, explicit, and Machiavellian motivation to control other individuals. Rather, the "motivation to control" is a framework for conceptualizing the function of evolved traits and for integrating seemingly different traits. A clarification and example is provided by the evolution of the size and shape of the beaks of various species of Galápagos finch (Grant, 1999); several examples are shown in Figure 2.3. All 14 species of finch arose during the past 3 million years from a single ancestral species that originated from the South American mainland (Sato *et al.*, 1999). The across-species differences in beak size and shape are the evolutionary result of specialization in different types of foods – the evolved function of the beak is to facilitate access to and control of different types of food (e.g., insects vs. seeds encased in shells). These birds have no conscious motivation to control, but they have evolved such that their behavior and physical traits (beaks in this example) are focused on obtaining control of resources that have covaried with survival prospects during the species' evolutionary history. I apply this framework to various aspects of human functioning in the first section, and then focus on cognition, including fluid intelligence, in the second.

General theory

The basic proposal is that the brain and mind of all species evolved to process the forms of information (e.g., facial expressions, movement patterns of predators) that covaried with survival and reproductive prospects during the

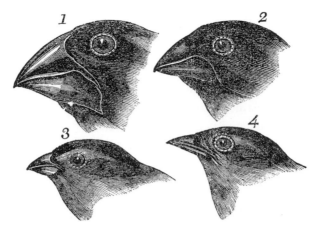

Figure 2.3 Four species of finch from the Galápagos islands; 1. Large ground finch (*Geospiza magnirostris*); 2. Medium ground finch (*G. fortis*); 3. Small tree finch (*Camarhynchus parvulus*); 4. Warble finch (*Certhidea olivacea*) from *Journal of Researches into the Natural History and Geology of the Countries Visited During the Voyage of H.M.S. Beagle Round the World, Under the Command of Capt. Fitz Roy, R. N. (2nd edition)*, by C. Darwin, 1845, London: John Murray, p. 379.

species' evolutionary history. These systems operate implicitly and bias the organism to behavior in ways that result in attempts to gain control of these outcomes, such as capturing prey or avoiding being captured by a predator (Gigerenzer *et al.*, 1999; Simon, 1956). The gist of the framework is consistent with the well replicated finding that peoples' subjective wellbeing and physical health are associated with having some level of control over relationships, events, and resources that are of significance in their life (Fiske, 1993; Heckhausen and Schulz, 1995; Marmot, 2004; Shapiro, Schwartz, and Astin, 1996). As noted earlier, in conditions with higher risk of premature mortality than is found in modern societies, achieving control of social relationships (e.g., as related to social status) and biological (e.g., food) and physical (e.g., safe shelter, water) resources often meant the difference between living and dying, especially during population crashes.

The control-related behavioral focus is represented by the apex and adjoining section of Figure 2.4. The bottom of the figure represents the folk modules that result in implicit and automatic, bottom-up processing of social (e.g., facial expressions), biological (e.g., features of hunted species), and physical (e.g., objects potentially useable as tools) information patterns that have tended to be the same across generations and within lifetimes, and have covaried with survival or reproductive prospects during human evolution. A taxonomy and description of the corresponding modular brain and cognitive systems in the

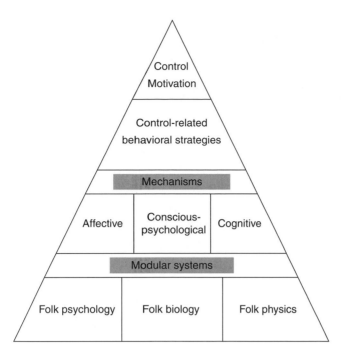

Figure 2.4 The apex and following section represent the focus of behavior on achieving control of the social, biological, and physical resources that have tended to covary with survival and reproductive outcomes during human evolution. The midsection shows the supporting affective, conscious-psychological (e.g., self awareness), and cognitive (e.g., working memory) mechanisms that support the motivation to control and operate on the modular systems shown at the base.

respective domains of folk psychology, folk biology, and folk physics is provided elsewhere (Geary, 2005; Geary and Huffman, 2002). If the evolution of the human brain and fluid intelligence was driven by the need to deal with rapid change in climatic, ecological, or social conditions, then cognitive systems that function to represent and manipulate dynamic change in information patterns should be identifiable. These systems are represented by the center section of Figure 2.4, and are the key to understanding the evolution of general fluid intelligence. I focus on the specifics of this center section of the figure in the sections that follow.

Conscious-psychological. The core of the conscious-psychological mechanism is the human ability to form a conscious, explicit mental representation of situations that are centered on the self and one's relationship with other people or one's access to biological and physical resources. The representations often involve a form of mental time travel, that is, mental simulations of past, present, or potential future states and can be cast as visual images, in language, or as episodic memories (Suddendorf and Corballis, 1997; Tulving, 2002). A key component is the ability to create a mental representation of a desired or fantasized state and to compare this to a mental representation of one's current situation. This might involve, for instance, fantasizing about developing a relationship with a potential romantic partner and ways to bring about this outcome. These are self-centered conscious-psychological representations of present and potential future states that are of personal significance and are the content on which more conscious and effortful reasoning and problem-solving processes are applied (Evans, 2002; Stanovich and West, 2000).

Explicit attributions about the self, other people, or group dynamics can also be components of these representations. The well-studied attributional biases about members of the in-group (favorable) and members of an out-group (unfavorable) provide an example; these biases are predicted to have resulted from an evolutionary history of coalitional competition in humans. These biases are particularly salient during times of intergroup competition and hostilities in the laboratory (Stephan, 1985) and real world (Horowitz, 2001). The latter are often centered around ethnic conflicts and are invariably over resource control. Negative attributions about the character and intentions of the out-group often include rumors of an intended out-group attack or conspiracy to, for instance, poison the in-group's food supply. These types of rumors justify, facilitate, and very often precede often deadly violence. A common result is the self-serving elimination of economic or social competitors. The attributional biases not only justify this self-serving violence, they protect individuals from the affective consequences, such as guilt, that could result if the violence were directed against members of the in-group.

Brain imaging studies suggest that areas 32 and 9 (Figure 2.2) of the prefrontal cortex are particularly active when people mentally simulate the behavior of other people or simulate future social or other scenarios (Gallagher and Frith, 2003). These systems appear to reconstitute the activity of the brain regions that were engaged during personal experiences or activate more abstracted representations of common features of these experiences (Damasio, 1989). These regions are highly integrated (physically and functionally) with the prefrontal regions described in the next section (Miller and Cohen, 2001).

Cognitive. The cognitive mechanisms include working memory, attentional control, and the ability to inhibit automatic processing of folk-related or learned behavioral responses or cognitive biases (e.g., attributional biases; Baddeley, 2000; Bjorklund and Harnishfeger, 1995; Cowan, 1995; Wheeler and Fiske, 2002). The mechanisms also include the ability to systematically problem solve and to reason about patterns represented in working memory (Newell and Simon, 1972). These cognitive and problem-solving processes are the mechanisms that allow individuals to represent and manipulate information processed by the folk modules. In terms of the motivation to control, the most important evolutionary function concerns the relation between these cognitive and problem-solving mechanisms and the generation and manipulation of conscious-psychological representations. Working memory and attentional and inhibitory control are the content-free mechanisms that enable the integration of a current conscious-psychological state with memory representations of related past experiences, and the generation of mental models or simulations of potential future states (Alexander, 1989; Johnson-Laird, 1983).

Attentional and executive control is dependent on several regions of the prefrontal cortex, such as the dorsolateral regions (Kane and Engle, 2002). Other regions of the prefrontal cortex, such as the ventromedial areas (e.g., area 11, Figure 2.2) of both hemispheres and the right frontal pole (area 10) support social cognition, including a sense of self (Tulving, 2002); as noted, endocast patterns suggest substantial expansion of the latter region (Holloway and de la Coste-Lareymondie, 1982). The brain regions that support self aware-ness are intimately tied to episodic memories and the ability to mentally time travel (Suddendorf and Corballis, 1997; Wheeler, Stuss, and Tulving, 1997). The latter is the ability to project the self back in time to recreate a personal experience, and to project the self forward in time to create simulations of situations that might arise in the future. Individuals who do not have a sense of self and who cannot mentally time travel, due to brain injury, have a very difficult time dealing with complex, dynamic situations that vary from the routine. These situations are typically social in nature, and are consistent with the hypothesis that social dynamics were an important pressure driving the evolved human ability to anticipate and cope with novelty and change.

The prefrontal cortex and working memory systems thus enable individuals to form conscious representations of a variety of social and ecological situations and to explicitly change the form of these representations. When these representations are infused with a sense of self and the ability to mentally time travel, the result is a mental capacity that may be uniquely human. Self awareness and other functions associated with the prefrontal cortex and executive control can be integrated with the motivation to control; specifically, the motivation to control is facilitated by the ability to mentally simulate potential future social scenarios or changes in ecological conditions, and then to rehearse potential responses to these situations. One way to deal with unpredictable situations is to mentally generate potential variations of these conditions and then rehearse behavioral strategies for controlling outcomes associated with each of these variants. The brain and cognitive systems that have evolved to support this function are the central executive component of working memory (i.e., attentional and inhibitory control), and a variety of regions of prefrontal cortex, among others (see Geary, 2005).

Affective. Following Damasio (2003), affective mechanisms include emotions, that is, observable behaviors (e.g., facial expressions or social withdrawal), and feelings, that is, conscious representations of an emotional state or other conditions that can potentially influence the individual's wellbeing. Affective mechanisms influence behavioral strategies. Emotions result in observable feedback to others and feelings provide unobservable feedback to the individual (Campos, Campos, and Barrett, 1989). The latter is a useful indicator of the effectiveness of control-related behavioral strategies and an indicator of the potential benefits of a simulated behavior. Positive feelings provide reinforcement when strategies are resulting in the achievement of significant goals, or at least a reduction in the difference between the current and desired state, and negative feelings provide punishment and promote disengagement when behaviors are not resulting in this end (Gray, 1987). The supporting brain systems, such as the amygdala (not shown in Figure 2.2), are predicted to function in part to amplify attention to evolutionarily significant forms of information and produce emotions, feelings, and corresponding behavioral biases that are likely to automatically reproduce outcomes that have covaried with survival or reproduction during hominid evolution (Damasio, 2003).

General fluid intelligence

My proposal is that research on Gf has identified the core cognitive processes and brain systems that support the use of self-centered mental simulations represented at the center of Figure 2.4. From this perspective, Gf evolved as a result of the benefits associated with the ability to anticipate dynamic and variable circumstances and to mentally construct and rehearse potential behavioral responses to these circumstances (Geary, 2005). The ability to use these mental simulations is dependent on the core components of Gf, that is, working memory and attentional control and, as Cattell (1963) proposed, function to deal with variation and novelty in social and ecological conditions. In other words, the more than 100 years of empirical research on general intelligence has isolated those features of self-centered mental models – the conscious-psychological and cognitive components of the motivation to control (Figure 2.4) – that are not strongly influenced by content and that enable explicit representations of symbolic information in working memory and an attention-dependent ability to manipulate this information in the service of strategic problem solving.

One important difference comparing research on Gf and my model involves self awareness; this is a core feature of self-aware mental models but not an aspect of Gf. The reason for the discrepancy lies in the initial development of intelligence tests, that is, to predict school performance, not social functioning or awareness of the self; see Geary (2007b, 2007c) for extension of the model presented herein to learning in school. Although not a focus of the current chapter, note that from the evolutionary perspective described here, Gc is predicted to be composed of two general classes of knowledge. The first includes information learned during an individual's lifetime, as proposed by Cattell (1963). The second includes inherent modular competencies and folk knowledge.

Conclusion

Since the emergence of *A. afarensis* roughly 4 MYA, the hominid brain has tripled in absolute size and in terms of EQ. Much of this change occurred following the emergence of the genus *Homo* and the most substantial increases occurred over the past several hundred thousand years. The selection pressures that drove this comparatively rapid change in the human brain are vigorously debated and include climatic variation (Ash and Gallup, 2007; Kanazawa 2004; Vrba, 1995), the complexities of hunting and foraging in natural ecologies (Kaplan *et al.*, 2000), and social dynamics (Alexander, 1989; Dunbar, 1998; Humphrey, 1976). There is evidence consistent with each of these proposals and it may be that each class of pressure contributed to the evolution of the human brain over the past 4 million years. The most interesting issue concerns the particularly rapid and substantial increases in brain volume and EQ following the emergence of *H. erectus* and continuing through to modern humans. Alexander's model of ecological dominance provides a framework for integrating various forms of selection pressure and for making inferences about when the various pressures may have been most critical in driving human brain and cognitive evolution. On the basis of this model, my colleagues and I have argued that the complexity and dynamics of social competition and cooperation within and between groups is likely to have been the most potent selection pressure for human brain and cognitive evolution since the emergence of *H. erectus* (Flinn *et al.*, 2005; Geary, 2005; Bailey and Georg, 2009).

The combination of selection pressures and especially those related to social competition can be integrated with psychological research using the "motivation to control" framework. Although I have not elaborated here, the folk physical modules at the base of Figure 2.4 and described elsewhere are consistent with the evolution of modularized brain and cognitive systems that enable humans to conceptualize, construct, and use very complicated tools (Geary, 2005; see also Povinelli, 2000). These competencies are consistent with Kaplan *et al.*'s (2000) focus on the relation between the complexities of hunting in natural ecologies and human brain evolution. The modular competencies are also consistent with Alexander's (1989) ecological dominance model. As noted, the model also predicts the evolution of modularized folk psychological or social-cognitive competencies that are uniquely human; these would include language and theory of mind, among others (Geary, 2005).

Much of human behavior and cognition and perhaps all of that of most other species can be accommodated by the fast, implicit functioning of such modularized systems. Of course, different species are predicted to have evolved different constellations of modules, but most of these will be encompassed within the same domains; specifically, for processing and responding to conspecifics (folk psychology), other species (folk biology), and the physical environment (folk physics). The motivation-to-control model includes modules in these domains as well as mechanisms that enable organisms to anticipate and cope with variation, novelty, and change within their life span. The critical differences comparing humans to other species appears to be in the ability of generate representations of the self in working memory – self awareness – and to mentally time travel (Suddendorf and Corballis, 1997; Tulving, 2002). The combination enables the generation of self-centered mental models, that is, a conscious-psychological (explicit) representation of past, present, or potential future situations that are of personal relevance.

Although climatic and ecological conditions can create variation and novelty and thus may have contributed to the evolution of mental time travel and the ability to form self-aware mental simulations of potential future states, the most dynamic and variable conditions faced by most humans are those that arise from the competing interests of other people. My proposal is that the evolved function of these mental models is to generate a self-centered simulation of the "perfect" world, one in which other people behave in ways consistent with one's best interest, and biological and physical resources are under one's control. The function of mental simulations is to create and rehearse strategies that can be used to reduce the difference between this perfect world and current conditions. The cognitive systems that evolved to support the use of these self-centered mental models are known as working memory and attentional control, that is, the core cognitive components of general fluid intelligence.

References

Ackerman, P. L., Beier, M. E., and Boyle, M. O. (2002). Individual differences in working memory within a nomological network of cognitive and perceptual speed abilities. *Journal of Experimental Psychology: General*, **131**, 567–589.

Ackerman, P. L., Beier, M. E., and Boyle, M. O. (2005). Working memory and intelligence: The same or different constructs? *Psychological Bulletin*, **131**, 30–60.

Aiello, L. C., Bates, N., and Joffe, T. (2001). In defense of the expensive tissue hypothesis. In D. Falk and K. R. Gibson (Eds.), *Evolutionary Anatomy of the Primate Cerebral Cortex* (pp. 57–78). Cambridge, UK: Cambridge University Press.

Aiello, L. C. and Wheeler, P. (1995). The expensive-tissue hypothesis: The brain and digestive system in human and primate evolution. *Current Anthropology*, **36**, 199–221.

Alexander, R. D. (1989). Evolution of the human psyche. In P. Mellars and C. Stringer (Eds.), *The Human Revolution: Behavioural and Biological Perspectives on the Origins of Modern Humans* (pp. 455–513). Princeton, NJ: Princeton University Press.

Alroy, J. (2001). A multispecies overkill simulation of the end-Pleistocene megafaunal mass extinction. *Science*, **292**, 1893–1896.

Armstrong, E. (1990). Brains, bodies and metabolism. *Brain, Behavior and Evolution*, **36**, 166–176.

Asfaw, B., White, T., Lovejoy, O., Latimer, B., Simpson, S., and Suwa, G. (1999). Australopithecus garhi: A new species of early hominid from Ethiopia. *Science*, **284**, 629–635.

Ash, J. and Gallup, G. G. Jr. (2007). Paleoclimatic variation and brain expansion during human evolution. *Human Nature*, **18**, 109–124.

Baddeley, A. D. (1986). *Working Memory*. Oxford: Oxford University Press.

Baddeley, A. (2000). The episodic buffer: A new component of working memory? *Trends in Cognitive Sciences*, **4**, 417–423.

Bailey, D. H. and Georg, D. C. (2009). Hominid brain evolution: testing climatic, ecological, and social competition models. *Human Nature*, **20**.

Barton, R. A. (1996). Neocortex size and behavioural ecology in primates. *Proceedings of the Royal Society of London B*, **263**, 173–177.

Barton, R. A. and Dean, P. (1993). Comparative evidence indicating neural specialization for predatory behaviour in mammals. *Proceedings of the Royal Society of London B*, **254**, 63–68.

Betzig, L. L. (1986). *Despotism and Differential Reproduction: A Darwinian View of History*. New York: Aldine Publishing Company.

Bjorklund, D. F. and Harnishfeger, K. K. (1995). The evolution of inhibition mechanisms and their role in human cognition and behavior. In F. N. Dempster and C. J. Brainerd (Eds.), *New Perspectives on Interference and Inhibition in Cognition* (pp. 141–173). New York: Academic Press.

Botvinick, M. M., Braver, T. S., Barch, D. M., Carter, C. S., and Cohen, J. D. (2001). Conflict monitoring and cognitive control. *Psychological Review*, **108**, 624–652.

Brace, C. L. (1995). Biocultural interaction and the mechanism of mosaic evolution in the emergence of "modern" morphology. *American Anthropologist*, **97**, 711–721.

Brodmann, K. (1909). *Vergleichende Lokalisationslehre der Grosshirnrinde in ihren Prinzipien dargestellt auf Grund des Zellenbaues*. [Comparative Localization of the Cerebral Cortex Based on Cell Composition.] Leipzig: Barth.

Burghardt, G. M. (2005). *The Genesis of Animal Play: Testing the Limits*. Cambridge, MA: Bradford/MIT Press.

Campos, J. J., Campos, R. G., and Barrett, K. C. (1989). Emergent themes in the study of emotional development and emotion regulation. *Developmental Psychology*, **25**, 394–402.

Carpenter, P. A., Just, M. A., and Shell, P. (1990). What one intelligence test measures: A theoretical account of processing in the Raven Progressive Matrices Test. *Psychological Review*, **97**, 404–431.

Cattell, R. B. (1963). Theory of fluid and crystallized intelligence: A critical experiment. *Journal of Educational Psychology*, **54**, 1–22.

Clark, J. D., Beyene, Y., WoldeGabriel, G., Hart, W. K., Renne, P. R., Gilbert, H., Defleur, A., Suwa, G., Katoh, S., Ludwig, K. R., Boisserie, J.-R., Asfaw, B., and White, T. D. (2003). Stratigraphic, chronological and behavioral contexts of Pleistocene *Homo sapiens* from Middle Awash, Ethiopia. *Nature*, **423**, 747–752.

Clutton-Brock, J. (1992). Domestication of animals. In S. Jones, R. Martin, and D. Pilbeam (Eds.), *The Cambridge Encyclopedia of Human Evolution* (pp. 380–385). New York: Cambridge University Press.

Conway, A. R. A., Cowan, N., Bunting, M. F., Therriault, D. J., and Minkoff, S. R. B. (2002). A latent variable analysis of working memory capacity, short-term memory capacity, processing speed, and general fluid intelligence. *Intelligence*, **30**, 163–183.

Cowan, N. (1995). *Attention and Memory: An Integrated Framework*. New York: Oxford University Press.

Damasio, A. R. (1989). Time-locked multiregional retroactivation: A systems-level proposal for the neural substrates of recall and recognition. *Cognition*, **33**, 25–62.

Damasio, A. (2003). *Looking for Spinoza: Joy, Sorrow, and the Feeling Brain*. Orlando, FL: Harcourt, Inc.

Darwin, C. R. (1845). *Journal of Researches into the Natural History and Geology of the Countries Visited During the Voyage of H. M. S. Beagle Round the World, Under the Command of Capt. Fitz Roy, R.N.* (2nd Edn.). London: John Murray.

Darwin, C. (1859). *The Origin of Species by Means of Natural Selection*. London: John Murray.

Darwin, C. (1871). *The Descent of Man, and Selection in Relation to Sex*. London: John Murray.

Darwin, C. and Wallace, A. (1858). On the tendency of species to form varieties, and on the perpetuation of varieties and species by natural means of selection. *Journal of the Linnean Society of London, Zoology*, **3**, 45–62.

Deary, I. J. (2000). *Looking Down on Human Intelligence: From Psychophysics to the Brain*. Oxford, UK: Oxford University Press.

Deary, I. J. and Stough, C. (1996). Intelligence and inspection time: Achievements, prospects, and problems. *American Psychologist*, **51**, 599–608.

Dehaene, S. and Naccache, L. (2001). Towards a cognitive neuroscience of consciousness: Basic evidence and a workspace framework. *Cognition*, **79**, 1–37.

de Heinzelin, J., Clark, J. D., White, T., Hart, W., Renne, P., WoldeGabriel, G., Beyene, Y., and Vrba, E. (1999). Environment and behavior of 2.5-million-year-old Bouri hominids. *Science*, **284**, 625–629.

deMenocal, P. B. (2001). Cultural responses to climatic change during the late Holocene. *Science*, **292**, 667–673.

Dunbar, R. I. M. (1998). The social brain hypothesis. *Evolutionary Anthropology*, **6**, 178–190.

Duncan, J., Rüdiger, J. S., Kolodny, J., Bor, D., Herzog, H., Ahmed, A., Newell, F. H., and Emslie, H. (2000). A neural basis for general intelligence. *Science*, **289**, 457–460.

Elton, S., Bishop, L. C., and Wood, B. (2001). Comparative context of Plio-Pleistocene hominin brain evolution. *Journal of Human Evolution*, **41**, 1–27.

Embretson, S. E. (1995). The role of working memory capacity and general control processes in intelligence. *Intelligence*, **20**, 169–189.

Engle, R. W. (2002). Working memory capacity as executive attention. *Current Directions in Psychological Science*, **11**, 19–23.

Engle, R. W., Conway, A. R. A., Tuholski, S. W., and Shisler, R. J. (1995). A resource account of inhibition. *Psychological Science*, **6**, 122–125.

Engle, R. W., Tuholski, S. W., Laughlin, J. E., and Conway, A. R. A. (1999). Working memory, short-term memory, and general fluid intelligence: A latent-variable approach. *Journal of Experimental Psychology: General*, **128**, 309–331.

Esposito, G., Kirkby, B. S., van Horn, J. D., Ellmore, T. M. and Berman, K. F. (1999). Context-dependent, neural system-specific neurophysiological concomitants of ageing: Mapping PET correlates during cognitive activation. *Brain*, **122**, 963–979.

Evans, J. St. B. T. (2002). Logic and human reasoning: An assessment of the deduction paradigm. *Psychological Bulletin*, **128**, 978–996.

Falk, D. (1983, September 9). Cerebral cortices by East African early hominids. *Science*, **221**, 1072–1074.

Falk, D., Redmond, J. C. Jr., Guyer, J., Conroy, G. C., Recheis, W., Weber, G. W., and Seidler, H. (2000). Early hominid brain evolution: A new look at old endocasts. *Journal of Human Evolution*, **38**, 695–717.

Fiske, S. T. (1993). Controlling other people: The impact of power on stereotyping. *American Psychologist*, **48**, 621–628.

Flinn, M. V., Geary, D. C., and Ward, C. V. (2005). Ecological dominance, social competition, and coalitionary arms races: Why humans evolved extraordinary intelligence. *Evolution and Human Behavior*, **26**, 10–46.

Foley, R. A. (1999). Hominid behavioral evolution: Missing links in comparative primate socioecology. In P. C. Lee (Ed.), *Comparative Primate Socioecology* (pp. 363–386). Cambridge, UK: Cambridge University Press.

Foley, R. and Lahr, M. M. (1997). Mode 3 technologies and the evolution of modern humans. *Cambridge Archaeology Journal*, **7**, 3–36.

Fry, A. F. and Hale, S. (1996). Processing speed, working memory, and fluid intelligence: Evidence for a developmental cascade. *Psychological Science*, **7**, 237–241.

Fry, A. F. and Hale, S. (2000). Relationships among processing speed, working memory, and fluid intelligence in children. *Biological Psychology*, **54**, 1–34.

Gallagher, H. L. and Frith, C. D. (2003). Functional imaging of 'theory of mind'. *Trends in Cognitive Sciences*, **7**, 77–83.

Gavrilets, S. and Vose, A. (2006). The dynamics of Machiavellian intelligence. *Proceedings of the National Academy of Sciences USA*, **103**, 16823–16828.

Geary, D. C. (1998). *Male, Female: The Evolution of Human Sex Differences*. Washington, DC: American Psychological Association.

Geary, D. C. (2005). *The Origin of Mind: Evolution of Brain, Cognition, and General Intelligence.* Washington, DC: American Psychological Association.

Geary, D. C. (2007a). An integrative model of human brain, cognitive, and behavioral evolution. *Acta Psychological Sinica*, **39**, 383–397.

Geary, D. C. (2007b). Educating the evolved mind: Conceptual foundations for an evolutionary educational psychology. In J. S. Carlson and J. R. Levin (Eds.), *Educating the Evolved Mind* (pp. 1–99, Vol. 2, *Psychological Perspectives on Contemporary Educational Issues*). Greenwich, CT: Information Age.

Geary, D. C. (2007c). An evolutionary perspective on learning disability in mathematics. *Developmental Neuropsychology*, **32**, 471–519.

Geary, D. C. and Huffman, K. J. (2002). Brain and cognitive evolution: Forms of modularity and functions of mind. *Psychological Bulletin*, **128**, 667–698.

Gigerenzer, G., Todd, P. M., and ABC Research Group (Eds.) (1999). *Simple Heuristics that Make us Smart.* New York: Oxford University Press.

Grant, P. R. (1999). *Ecology and Evolution of Darwin's Finches.* Princeton, NJ: Princeton University Press.

Gray, J. A. (1987). Perspectives on anxiety and impulsivity: A commentary. *Journal of Research in Personality*, **21**, 493–509.

Gray, J. R., Chabris, C. F., and Braver, T. S. (2003). Neural mechanisms of general fluid intelligence. *Nature Neuroscience*, **6**, 316–322.

Guthrie, R. D. (2003). Rapid body size decline in Alaskan Pleistocene horses before extinction. *Nature*, **426**, 169–171.

Guthrie, R. D. (2006). New carbon dates link climatic change with human colonization and Pleistocene extinctions. *Nature*, **441**, 207–209.

Haier, R. J., Siegel, B. V. Jr., Nuechterlein, K. H., Hazlett, E., Wu, J. C., Paek, J., Browning, H. L., and Buchsbaum, M. S. (1988). Cortical glucose metabolic rate correlates of abstract reasoning and attention studied using positron emission tomography. *Intelligence*, **12**, 199–217.

Harvey, P. H. and Clutton-Brock, T. H. (1985). Life history variation in primates. *Evolution*, **39**, 559–581.

Heckhausen, J. and Schulz, R. (1995). A life-span theory of control. *Psychological Review*, **102**, 284–304.

Hed, H. M. E. (1987). Trends in opportunity for natural selection in the Swedish population during the period 1650–1980. *Human Biology*, **59**, 785–797.

Hill, K., Boesch, C., Goodall, J., Pusey, A., Williams, J., and Wrangham, R. (2001). Mortality rates among wild chimpanzees. *Journal of Human Evolution*, **40**, 437–450.

Hill, K. and Hurtado, A. M. (1996). *Ache Life History: The Ecology and Demography of a Foraging People.* New York: Aldine de Gruyter.

Hole, F. (1992). Origins of agriculture. In S. Jones, R. Martin, and D. Pilbeam (Eds.), *The Cambridge Encyclopedia of Human Evolution* (pp. 373–379). New York: Cambridge University Press.

Holloway, R. L. (1973a). New endocranial values for the East African early hominids. *Nature*, **243**, 97–99.

Holloway, R. L. (1973b). Endocranial volumes of early African hominids, and the role of the brain in human mosaic evolution. *Journal of Human Evolution*, **2**, 449–459.

Holloway, R. (1996). Evolution of the human brain. In A. Lock and C. R. Peters (Eds.), *Handbook of Human Symbolic Evolution* (pp. 74–116). New York: Oxford University Press.

Holloway, R. L., Broadfield, D. C., and Yuan, M. S. (2004). *The Human Fossil Record, Volume Three: Brain Endocasts – The Paleoneurological Record*. Hoboken, NJ: John Wiley & Sons.

Holloway, R. L. and de la Coste-Lareymondie, M. C. (1982). Brain endocast asymmetry in pongids and hominids: Some preliminary findings on the paleontology of cerebral dominance. *American Journal of Physical Anthropology*, **58**, 101–110.

Holloway, R. L. and Kimbel, W. H. (1986, May 29). Endocast morphology of Hadar hominid AL 162-28. *Nature*, **321**, 536–537.

Horn, J. L. (1968). Organization of abilities and the development of intelligence. *Psychological Review*, **75**, 242–259.

Horn, J. L. (1988). Thinking about human abilities. In J. R. Nesselroade and R. B. Cattell (Eds.), *Handbook of Multivariate Experimental Psychology* (2nd Edn, pp. 645–685). New York: Plenum.

Horn, J. L. and Cattell, R. B. (1966). Refinement and test of the theory of fluid and crystallized general intelligence. *Journal of Educational Psychology*, **57**, 253–270.

Horowitz, D. L. (2001). *The Deadly Ethnic Riot*. Berkeley, CA: University of California Press.

Hsieh, C.-H., Reiss, C. S., Hunter, J. R., Beddington, J. R., May, R. M., and Sugihara, G. (2006). Fishing elevates variability in the abundance of exploited species. *Nature*, **443**, 859–862.

Humphrey, N. K. (1976). The social function of intellect. In P. P. G. Bateson and R. A. Hinde (Eds.), *Growing Points in Ethology* (pp. 303–317). New York: Cambridge University Press.

Hunt, E. (1978). Mechanics of verbal ability. *Psychological Review*, **85**, 109–130.

Huxley, T. H. (1863). *Evidence as to Man's Place in Nature*. New York: Appleton and Company.

Jensen, A. R. (1982). Reaction time and psychometric g. In H. J. Eysenck (Ed.), *A Model for Intelligence* (pp. 93–132). New York: Springer-Verlag.

Jensen, A. R. (1992). The importance of intraindividual variation in reaction time. *Intelligence*, **13**, 869–881.

Jensen, A. R. (1998) *The g Factor: The Science of Mental Ability*. Westport, CT: Praeger.

Jensen, A. R. and Munro, E. (1979). Reaction time, movement time, and intelligence. *Intelligence*, **3**, 121–126.

Jerison, H. J. (1973). *Evolution of the Brain and Intelligence*. New York: Academic Press.

Johnson-Frey, S. H. (2003). What's so special about human tool use? *Neuron*, **39**, 201–204.

Johnson-Laird, P. N. (1983). *Mental Models*. Cambridge, England: Cambridge University Press.

Jolly, C. J. (1970). The seed eaters: A new model of hominid differentiation based on a baboon analogy. *Man*, **5**, 5–26.

Jung, R. E. and Haier, R. J. (2007). The parieto-frontal integration theory (P-FIT) of intelligence: Converging neuroimaging evidence. *Behavioral and Brain Sciences*, **30**, 135–187.

Kalbfleisch, M. L., Van Meter, J. W., and Zeffiro, T. A. (2006). The influences of task difficulty and response correctness on neural systems supporting fluid reasoning. *Cognitive Neurodynamics*, **1**, 71–84.

Kanazawa, S. (2004). General intelligence as a domain-specific adaptation. *Psychological Review*, **111**, 512–523.

Kanazawa, S. (2007). The g-culture coevolution. In S. Gangestad and J. Simpson (Eds.), *The Evolution of Mind: Fundamental Questions and Controversies* (pp. 313–318). New York: Guilford Publications.

Kane, M. J. and Engle, R. W. (2002). The role of prefrontal cortex in working-memory capacity, executive attention, and general fluid intelligence: An individual-differences perspective. *Psychonomic Bulletin and Review*, **9**, 637–671.

Kaplan, H. S. and Robson, A. J. (2002). The emergence of humans: The coevolution of intelligence and longevity with intergenerational transfers. *Proceedings of the National Academy of Sciences USA*, **99**, 10221–10226.

Kaplan, H., Hill, K., Lancaster, J., and Hurtado, A. M. (2000). A theory of human life history evolution: Diet, intelligence, and longevity. *Evolutionary Anthropology*, **9**, 156–185.

Kerns, J. G., Cohen, J. D., MacDonald, A. W.III, Cho, R. Y., Stenger, V. A., and Carter, C. S. (2004, February 13). Anterior cingulate conflict monitoring and adjustments in control. *Science*, **303**, 1023–1026.

Kimbel, W. H. (1995). Hominid speciation and Pliocene climatic change. In E. S. Vrba, G. H. Denton, T. C. Partridge, and L. H. Burckle (Eds.), *Paleoclimate and Evolution, with Emphasis on Human Origins* (pp. 425–437). New Haven, CT: Yale University Press.

Kyllonen, P. C. and Christal, R. E. (1990). Reasoning ability is (little more than) working-memory capacity?! *Intelligence*, **14**, 389–433.

Levine, B. (1999). Self-regulation and autonoetic consciousness. In E. Tulving (Ed.), *Memory, Consciousness, and the Brain: The Tallinn conference* (pp. 200–214). Philadelphia, PA: Psychology Press.

Low, B. S. (1990). Marriage systems and pathogen stress in human societies. *American Zoologist*, **30**, 325–339.

Mackintosh, N. J. and Bennett, E. S. (2003). The fractionation of working memory maps onto different components of intelligence. *Intelligence*, **31**, 519–531.

Malthus, T. R. (1798). *An Essay on the Principle of Population as it Affects the Future Improvement of Society with Remarks on the Speculations of Mr. Godwin, M. Condorcet, and Other Writers*. London: Printed for J. Johnson, in St. Paul's church-yard.

Marmot, M. (2004). *The Status Syndrome: How Social Standing Affects our Health and Longevity*. New York: Henry Holt and Company, LLC.

Martin, P. S. (1967). Prehistoric overkill. In P. S. Martin and H. E. Wright, Jr. (Eds.), *Pleistocene Extinctions: The Search for a Cause* (pp. 75–120). New Haven, CT: Yale University Press.

Martin, P. S. (1973, March 9). The discovery of America: The first Americans may have swept the Western Hemisphere and decimated its fauna in 1000 years. *Science*, **179**, 969–974.

McDaniel, M. A. (2005). Big-brained people are smarter: A meta-analysis of the relationship between in vivo brain volume and intelligence. *Intelligence*, **33**, 337–346.

McHenry, H. M. (1994). Tempo and mode in human evolution. *Proceedings of the National Academy of Sciences USA*, **91**, 6780–6786.

Miller, E. K. and Cohen, J. D. (2001). An integration of theory of prefrontal cortex function. *Annual Review of Neuroscience*, **24**, 167–202.

Miller, G. F. (2000). *The Mating Mind: How Sexual Choice Shaped the Evolution of Human Nature*. New York: Doubleday.

Miller, G. H., Magee, J. W., Johnson, B. J., Fogel, M. L., Spooner, N. A., McCulloch, M. T., and Ayliffe, L. K. (1999, January 8). Pleistocene extinction of Genyornis newtoni: Human impact on Australian megafauna. *Science*, **283**, 205–208.

Mithen, S. (1996). *The Prehistory of the Mind: The Cognitive Origins of Art and Science*. New York: Thames and Hudson, Inc.

Mithen, S. (2007). General intellectual ability. In S. Gangestad and J. Simpson (Eds.), *The Evolution of Mind: Fundamental Questions and Controversies* (pp. 319–324). New York: Guilford Publications.

Morrison, A. S., Kirshner, J., and Molho, A. (1977). Life cycle events in 15th century Florence: Records of the *Monte Delle Doti*. *American Journal of Epidemiology*, **106**, 487–492.

Myers, R. A. and Worm, B. (2003, May 15). Rapid worldwide depletion of predatory fish communities. *Nature*, **423**, 280–283.

Neubauer, A. C. (1997). The mental speed approach to the assessment of intelligence. In J. Kingma and W. Tomic (Eds.), *Advances in Cognition and Education: Reflections on the Concept of Intelligence* (pp. 149–173). Greenwich, CT: JAI Press.

Newell, A. and Simon, H. A. (1972). *Human Problem Solving*. Englewood Cliffs, NJ: Prentice-Hall.

Pandolfi, J. M., Bradbury, R. H., Sala, E., Hughes, T. P., Bjorndal, K. A., Cooke, R. G., McArdle, D., McClenachan, L., Newman, M. J. H., Paredes, G., Warner, R. R., and Jackson, J. B. C. (2003). Global trajectories of the long-term decline of coral reef ecosystems. *Science*, **301**, 955–958.

Platek, S. M., Keenan, J. P., Gallup, G. G. Jr., and Mohamed, F. B. (2004). Where am I? The neurological correlates of self and other. *Cognitive Brain Research*, **19**, 114–122.

Platek, S. M., Loughead, J. W., Gur, R. C., Busch, S., Ruparel, K., Phend, N., Panyavin, I. S., and Langleben, D. D. (2006). Neural substrates for functionally discriminating self-face from personally familiar faces. *Human Brain Mapping*, **27**, 91–98.

Posner, M. I. (1994). Attention: The mechanisms of consciousness. *Proceedings of the National Academy of Sciences USA*, **91**, 7398–7403.

Potts, R. (1998). Variability selection in hominid evolution. *Evolutionary Anthropology*, **7**, 81–96.

Povinelli, D. J. (2000). *Folk Physics for Apes: The Chimpanzees Theory of How the World Works.* New York: Oxford University Press.

Prabhakaran, V., Smith, J. A. L., Desmond, J. E., Glover, G. H., and Gabrieli, J. D. E. (1997). Neural substrates of fluid reasoning: An fMRI study of neocortical activation during performance of the Raven's progressive matrices test. *Cognitive Psychology*, **33**, 43–63.

Ranganath, C. and Rainer, G. (2003). Neural mechanisms for detecting and remembering novel events. *Nature Reviews: Neuroscience*, **4**, 193–202.

Raz, N., Torres, I. J., Spencer, W. D., Millman, D., Baertschi, J. C., and Sarpel, G. (1993). Neuroanatomical correlates of age-sensitive and age-invariant cognitive abilities: An in vivo MRI investigation. *Intelligence*, **17**, 407–422.

Ruff, C. B., Trinkaus, E., and Holliday, T. W. (1997, May 8). Body mass and encephalization in *Pleistocene Homo*. *Nature*, **387**, 173–176.

Rushton, J. P. and Ankney, C. D. (1996). Brain size and cognitive ability: Correlations with age, sex, social class, and race. *Psychonomic Bulletin & Review*, **3**, 21–36.

Sato, A., O'Huigin, C., Figueroa, F., Grant, P. R., Grant, B. R., Tichy, H., and Klein, J. (1999). Phylogeny of Darwin's finches as revealed by mtDNA sequences. *Proceedings of the National Academy of Sciences USA*, **96**, 5101–5106.

Semaw, S., Rogers, M. J., Quade, J., Renne, P. R., Butler, R. F., Dominquez-Rodrigo, M., Stout, D., Hart, W. S., Pickering, T., and Simpson, S. W. (2003). 2.6-million-year-old stone tools and associated bones from OGS-6 and OGS-7, Gona, Afar, Ethiopia. *Journal of Human Evolution*, **45**, 169–177.

Shapiro, D. H., Jr., Schwartz, C. E., and Astin, J. A. (1996). Controlling ourselves, controlling our world: Psychology's role in understanding positive and negative consequences of seeking and gaining control. *American Psychologist*, **51**, 1213–1230.

Simon, H. A. (1956). Rational choice and the structure of the environment. *Psychological Review*, **63**, 129–138.

Spearman, C. (1904). General intelligence, objectively determined and measured. *American Journal of Psychology*, **15**, 201–293.

Spoor, F., Leakey, M. G., Gathogo, P. N., Brown, F. H., Antón, S. C., McDougall, I., Kiarie, C., Manthi, F. K., and Leakey, L. N. (2007, August 9). Implications of new early *Homo* fossils from Ileret, east lake of Turkana, Kenya. *Nature*, **448**, 688–691.

Sporns, O., Tononi, G., and Edelman, G. M. (2000). Connectivity and complexity: The relationship between neuroanatomy and brain dynamics. *Neural Networks*, **13**, 909–922.

Stanovich, K. E. (1999). *Who is Rational? Studies of Individual Differences in Reasoning.* Mahwah, NJ: Erlbaum.

Stanovich, K. E. and West, R. F. (2000). Individual differences in reasoning: Implications for the rationality debate? *Behavioral and Brain Sciences*, **23**, 645–726.

Stephan, K. E., Marshall, J. C., Friston, K. J., Rowe, J. B., Ritzl, A., Zilles, K., and Fink, G. R. (2003, July 18). Lateralized cognitive processes and lateralized task control in the human brain. *Science*, **301**, 384–386.

Stephan, W. G. (1985). Intergroup relations. In G. Lindzey and E. Aronson (Eds.), *Handbook of Social Psychology: Volume II: Special Fields and Applications* (pp. 599–658). New York: Random House.

Suddendorf, T. and Corballis, M. C. (1997). Mental time travel and the evolution of the human mind. *Genetic, Social, and General Psychology Monographs*, **123**, 133–167.

Teaford, M. F. and Ungar, P. S. (2000). Diet and the evolution of the earliest human ancestors. *Proceedings of the National Academy of Sciences USA*, **97**, 13506–13511.

Tobias, P. V. (1987). The brain of *Homo habilis*: A new level of organization in cerebral evolution. *Journal of Human Evolution*, **16**, 741–761.

Tulving, E. (2002). Episodic memory: From mind to brain. *Annual Review of Psychology*, **53**, 1–25.

Turner, A. and Wood, B. (1993). Comparative palaeontological context for the evolution of the early hominid masticatory system. *Journal of Human Evolution*, **24**, 301–318.

United Nations (1985). *Socio-economic Differentials in Child Mortality in Developing Countries*. New York: Author.

Vrba, E. S. (1974). Chronological and ecological implications of the fossil Bovidae at the Sterkfontein Australopithecine site. *Nature*, **250**, 19–23.

Vrba, E. S. (1995). The fossil record of African antelopes (Mammalia, Bovidae) in relation to human evolution and paleoclimate. In E. S. Vrba, G. H. Denton, T. C. Partridge, and L. H. Burckle (Eds.), *Paleoclimate and Evolution, with Emphasis on Human Origins* (pp. 385–424). New Haven, CT: Yale University Press.

Vrba, E. S., Denton, G. H., Partridge, T. C., and Burckle, L. H. (Eds.) (1995). *Paleoclimate and Evolution, with Emphasis on Human Origins*. New Haven, CT: Yale University Press.

Wallace, A. R. (1864). The origin of human races and the antiquity of man deduced from the theory of "natural selection". *Journal of the Anthropological Society*, **2**, clviii–clxxxvii.

Wallace, A. R. (1911). *The World of Life: A Manifestation of Creative Power, Direction Mind and Ultimate Purpose*. New York: Moffat, Yard and Company.

West-Eberhard, M. J. (1983). Sexual selection, social competition, and speciation. *Quarterly Review of Biology*, **58**, 222–234.

Wheeler, M. A., Stuss, D. T., and Tulving, E. (1997). Toward a theory of episodic memory: The frontal lobes and autonoetic consciousness. *Psychological Bulletin*, **121**, 331–354.

Wheeler, M. E. and Fiske, S. T. (2002). Controlling racial prejudice and stereotyping: Changing social cognitive goals affects human amygdala and stereotype activation. *Psychological Bulletin*, **121**, 331–354.

White, T. D. (1995). African omnivores: Global climatic change and Plio-Pleistocene hominids and suids. In E. S. Vrba, G. H. Denton, T. C. Partridge, and L. H. Burckle (Eds.), *Paleoclimate and Evolution, with Emphasis on Human Origins* (pp. 369–384). New Haven, CT: Yale University Press.

Wickett, J. C., Vernon, P. A., and Lee, D. H. (2000). Relationships between factors of intelligence and brain volume. *Personality and Individual Differences*, **29**, 1095–1122.

Wood, B. and Collard, M. (1999). The human genus. *Science*, **284**, 65–71.

Wrangham, R. W. (1999). Evolution of coalitionary killing. *Yearbook of Physical Anthropology*, **42**, 1–30.

Wrangham, R. W., Holland Jones, J., Laden, G., Pilbeam, D., and Conklin-Brittain, N. (1999). The raw and stolen: Cooking and the ecology of human origins. *Current Anthropology*, **40**, 567–594.

3

The role of a general cognitive factor in the evolution of human intelligence

JAMES J. LEE

Introduction

The evolution of human intelligence is one of the outstanding problems in the sciences of life and mind. It is a problem that so struck Alfred Russel Wallace, the codiscoverer of natural selection, that he categorically ruled out evolutionary hypotheses and invoked divine infusion as the source of higher cognition in humans. This turn by Wallace has become a paradigmatic illustration of the difficulty and fascination that attends the scientific investigation into the genesis of our extraordinary cognitive powers (Gould, 1980).

Although in many ways as daunted as their great predecessor, few psychologists and human evolutionists today endorse Wallace's solution. In the modern context the problem appears to pose two aspects with an as-yet uncertain degree of interdependence. The first aspect addresses the species-universal architecture of human cognition and its antecedents in more basal systems (Pinker, 1997). The second aspect is concerned with quantitative differences among individuals along dimensions of cognitive abilities and changes in the distributions of the traits represented by these dimensions over the course of evolutionary time. This second aspect, however, has been less well explored by evolutionary psychologists and other workers concerned with the stated outstanding problem. The aim of this chapter with respect to this underdevelopment is twofold: (1) to propose possible resolutions to problematic issues that may to some extent be responsible for this relative neglect, and (2) to discuss future prospects for the integration of differential psychology into human evolutionary studies.

We begin with some background to the *domain-specific modularity* as an overarching principle of evolutionary psychology. This is important because the

Foundations in Evolutionary Cognitive Neuroscience, ed. Steven M. Platek and Todd K. Shackelford.
Published by Cambridge University Press. © Cambridge University Press 2009.

principle is often perceived to be incompatible with an important role in human evolution for a *general factor* of cognitive abilities. By "general" we mean that the latent trait represented by the factor is a source of variance common to a wide array of conceptually distinguishable abilities. Such a factor, often abbreviated as *g*, plays a central role in the taxonomies and theories of many differential psychologists (Humphreys, 1994; Brand, 1996; Jensen, 1998; Carroll, 2003). Given the abundant evidence for the importance of the abilities measured by *g*-loaded IQ tests in diverse spheres of human activity (Brand, 1987; Herrnstein and Murray, 1994; Murray, 1998; Gottfredson and Deary, 2004), any incompatibility between the ecological significance of *g* and the modularity principle would present an awkward difficulty. However, as will be argued subsequently, such an incompatibility does not necessarily follow from any conceptual or empirical considerations bearing on these two types of theoretical constructs. We then critically discuss an argument sometimes made in the literature as to why a highly heritable trait such as *g* should be of little interest to human evolutionists. It turns out that the relationship between the high heritability of a quantitative trait and its evolutionary history is not fully constrained a priori but rather remains open to empirical investigation. Finally, we give a cursory review of some recent and prospective empirical work of particular relevance to the study of a general cognitive factor in an evolutionary context.

The relationship between domain-specific modules and broad dimensions of individual differences

The notion of modularity employed in evolutionary psychology may owe its roots to a now-famous book review by Chomsky (1959). In this review Chomsky convincingly argued that Skinner's (1957) minimal principles of domain-general associative learning cannot support the rapid acquisition of language that we observe in children. The natural alternative left by the inadequacies of a purely environmentalist account is that children are endowed with a "language acquisition device" dedicated to the tuning of mental structures to the particularities of the languages spoken around them. As an innate module devoted to a particular function, the language faculty was arguably the first of its kind to be proposed in the modern era of psychology. The notion of such a faculty as a special biological adaptation of our species has since been integrated into a rich and fruitful research program (Pinker, 1994).

The concept of modularity has permeated into psychology far beyond the confines of language. In his influential book *The Modularity of Mind*, Fodor

(1983) developed an abstract concept of modularity that is potentially applicable to any aspect of cognition. One distinguishing feature of Fodor's account is what he calls *informational encapsulation*. As an example of this principle, Fodor points to the persistence of visual illusions such as the Müller–Lyer effect despite the subject's knowledge that the perceived disparity in line length is in fact only perceived and not actual. This invariant illusoriness suggests to Fodor that the lower levels of visual processing giving rise to the illusion are sealed off from the part of the mind where the subject's knowledge of the world resides. Because of this visual circuit's autonomy from other parts of cognition, it meets an important criterion for a mental module. Cognitive scientists have continued to debate the extent to which modules must be encapsulated in order to qualify as such, but there is widespread agreement that the respective outputs of distinct mental organs enjoy some degree of autonomy from whatever else the subject perceives of this kind more or less exhaust Fodor's list of plausible candidates for modularity. Memory, attention, reasoning, and the other central processes of cognition that receive the outputs of these low-level circuits are thought by Fodor not to possess the attributes of narrowness and independence that characterize true modules.

Some evolutionary psychologists have rejected Fodor's separation of domain-general central functions from modularized perceptual processors and proposed that a strongly modular architecture underlies even highly complex thought processes and behaviors. The most well-known proponents of this school are the evolutionary psychologists John Tooby and Leda Cosmides. In their own words, "[e]volutionary psychologists expect a mind packed with domain-specific, content-rich programs specialized for solving ancestral problems" (Tooby and Cosmides, 2005, p. 42). Perhaps the starkest contrast between these evolutionary psychologists and their predecessors lies in the emphasis on *content*. Whereas Fodor mostly limits his account to cognitive processes that operate over a given modality without regard to the semantic nature of the input, Tooby and Cosmides carve up the mind into specialized systems each devoted to a highly particular substantive domain. One of their chief arguments in favor of this partition is an appeal to the limited applicability of truly domain-general inference rules. For example, content-free logic bars the inference *Q implies P* from the premise *P implies Q*, as the permission of this inference would lead to invalid conclusions in many applications. A case in point is the derivation of the erroneous statement "If you are taller than most women, then you are a man" from the legitimate premise "If you are a man, then you are taller than most women." But suppose that a particular logic is triggered only in the context of social exchange, where P and Q take on a restricted set of representations that include BENEFIT, ENTITLEMENT, OBLIGATION, and the like. If the inference Q *implies* P is derivable from the premise P *implies* Q in this logic, then the valid conclusion "If you satisfy the requirement, then you are entitled to take the benefit" is available from the given statement "If you take the benefit, then you must satisfy the requirement." The advantage of domain-specific inference systems of this kind is that their adaptation to the peculiarities of their domain structures allows the generation of many valid deductions that are unavailable to a domain-general reasoning mechanism, which is restricted to the limited set of inference rules that hold across all interactions between the organism and its environment. Tooby and Cosmides argue that the latter constraint weighs against the viability of domain-general processes in high-level cognition.

Much recent thought addressing the difficulty in conceptualizing the nature of the trait undergoing evolution has been inspired by the synthetic work of Tooby and Cosmides. It follows naturally from their writings that "intelligence" is in fact a label for a constellation of distinct capacities with separable mechanistic and evolutionary bases, each designed by natural selection in response to a particular adaptive problem faced recurrently in the history of the species. Such a view must inevitably interact in some interesting way with any thesis emphasizing the importance of g in human evolution, and a few commentators have offered the opinion that the interaction is in fact a nullification. Thus, we find statements in the literature from evolutionary psychologists to the effect that "general purpose notions such as the g factor for intelligence are doomed to fail in the face of computational complexity" (Raab and Gigerenzer, 2004, p. 196).

Our own exploration of the interaction between g and functional specialization begins with a somewhat idealized examination of the lay conception of intelligence that is being implicitly criticized by evolutionary psychologists such as Raab and Gigerenzer. This is because the construct of g can plausibly be described as a formalization of a concept in folk psychology that has become firmly entrenched in natural language. This formalization is well supported by data that might conceivably have contradicted it, which shows that its place in prescientific intuition is not wholly unfounded. Over the course of this exposition, we will attempt to show that a general factor of human cognitive abilities conceptually survives the concept of modularity whose historical development has been outlined above.

The word *intelligence* seems to embrace a quantitative dimension along which individuals can be ranked (Bartholomew, 2004). Some people are judged to be "more intelligent" or "smarter" than others. Indeed, to the extent that dictionaries are records of common usage, the *Shorter Oxford Dictionary* affirms that intelligence is "understanding as a quality admitting of degree." This quantitative conception of intelligence is of ancient provenance. Characters in the earliest exemplars of poetry, drama, and fiction are variously described as clever or stupid, quick or slow, sharp or dull. What is the basis of these informal rankings? In the *Iliad* and the *Odyssey*, Homer calls his hero Odysseus "the great tactician," "the master mariner," "the shrewd captain," and so on. But we would not need these epithets to realize that Odysseus is distinguished from the other heroes in a particular way. We would be able to infer this from a sample of his behavior. When Odysseus and Diomedes make their nocturnal foray into the Trojan camp, Odysseus has the foresight to drag the bodies of the Trojans slain by Diomedes out of their escape path; he realizes that their stolen horses are unaccustomed to battle and may shy away from blood. The ruse of the gift horse that seals the doom of the Trojans is famously of Odysseus' devising. Perhaps the most amusing of Odysseus' ploys is a trick that "only an intellectually challenged giant would fall for" (Mackintosh, 1998, p. 3). When the Cyclops Polyphemus asks for his name, Odysseus replies, "Nobody." Later, when the other Cyclopes ask the blinded Polyphemus who is responsible for his distress, Polyphemus answers, "Nobody." The Cyclopes retort that if nobody is bothering him, then he must need not their help, and so they leave him unaided.

These are examples of Odysseus's response to a "problem" that justifiably counts as a "correct answer." It is the novelty and diversity of these occasions that defeats any attempt to explain this regularity in terms of distinct bits of skill and knowledge more or less accidentally acquired. An unobserved attribute of Odysseus is instead invoked, an attribute whose stability over time accounts for the consistency of his behavioral emissions. Crucially, because the domain of problems that tend to elicit the correct response from an exceptional individual such as Odysseus is so wide, it is to first order a single attribute that is invoked as differentiating all individuals. In other words, the space of cognitive performances contains a clear dominant dimension that serves us well in the data reduction that we intuitively employ in the characterization of our fellows. Other dimensions also have their place in natural language, as one might comprehensibly say, "I am not at all mathematical" or "She is more spatial than I am." However, as telling as these occasional expansions of dimensionality may be, the implicit uni-dimensional image in the language that scientists, lawyers, writers, intellectual specialists more generally, and laypeople use to distinguish their outstanding individuals (*smartest, most intelligent, most brilliant*) retains its striking vividness and utility.

This bit of dim and untutored multivariate reasoning can explain why no fourth-grader fails to understand the question, "Who is the smartest in your class?" It may have also motivated the psychologist Charles Spearman when he published his first results regarding factor analysis and *g*. Spearman's (1904) original data in support of his views may be rejected as inadequate by most psychologists today. The essence of his methods and conclusions, however, have turned out to be remarkably robust. The term *factor analysis* describes a family of methods for constructing or testing models where measured variables are hypothesized to be indicators of unobserved quantitative variables called *factors* (McDonald, 1985). Suppose that the measured variables are mental ability tests of individually homogenous content. There are an infinite number of mental measurements that might conceivably be devised, but it is assumed that they measure only a finite number of important factors. The tests measure a subset of these factors and may vary in the sensitivity with which a given factor is measured. If the scores on a test could be regressed on the unobserved factor scores, the resulting regression coefficients would represent the sensitivity of each test as a measure of the respective factors. The regression coefficients in this model have come to be known as *factor loadings*. Our factor analysis aims to uncover or confirm what factors are measured by this set of ability tests and the degree to which each test is "loaded" with each factor. The pattern of factor loadings that is recovered from the data then implies a covariance matrix for the tests. For example, if two tests are both strong measures of a particular factor, then their covariance should be correspondingly large. The adequacy of the model can be tested by examining the difference between the sample and model-implied covariance matrices. If the data fit the model well, then the elements of the residual matrix are interpretable as chance perturbations around zero. It is more or less this methodology that was employed by Spearman to demonstrate the empirical discovery for which he is most famous: the consistency of mental test data with the existence of *g*, a single dominant dimension in human cognitive abilities.

We illustrate this finding with a subset of the data collected for Project TALENT, an exemplarily massive longitudinal study including the administration of numerous ability tests to a representative sample of 400 000 American high school students (Flanagan *et al.*, 1962). Table 3.1 presents the correlation matrix for seven of the Project TALENT tests. The small number of observed variables in this example in no way affects the typicality of the result.

Table 3.1 *Correlation matrix of selected aptitude tests administered in Project TALENT*

	(1)	(2)	(3)	(4)	(5)	(6)
(1) Vocabulary	–					
(2) Reading Comprehension	7117	–				
(3) Introductory Mathematics	5827	5320	–			
(4) Arithmetic Reasoning	5744	4962	6825	–		
(5) Abstract Reasoning	5018	4463	5239	5359	–	
(6) Mechanical Reasoning	5308	4414	4901	5192	5762	–
(7) 3D Visualization	4438	3793	4205	4203	5389	5885

Vocabulary: knowledge of word meanings
Reading Comprehension: understanding of written text covering a broad range of topics
Introductory Mathematics: all forms of mathematics taught through ninth grade
Arithmetic Reasoning: problems requiring arithmetic for their solution
Abstract Reasoning: induction of logical relationships in figural patterns
Mechanical Reasoning: deductions based on primitive mechanisms such as gears, pulleys, and
    springs, and knowledge of common physical forces such as gravity
3D Visualization: identification of 2D figures after they have been folded into 3D figures
Note. These data from large sub-samples of male seniors, adjusted to ensure consistency among
the correlations, are taken from Shaycoft (1967). Decimals are omitted.

Notice that in these data every element of the correlation matrix is positive and often substantially so. This so-called *positive manifold* is one of the best-replicated findings in all of psychology (Carroll, 1993). Note also the diversity of abilities encompassed by the positive manifold; the tests cover domains of verbal, numerical, and spatial content and call for both novel reasoning and recall of previously acquired knowledge. "[These are] human cognitive abilities that, in cognitive science terms, would be viewed as distinct modules, with their own operating characteristics and research agendas" (Deary, 2000, pp. 14, 16).

We see that the prominence of the positive manifold mandates a sophisticated view of what is meant by "distinct." But for now we might wonder whether this prominence is consistent with a single factor accounting for individual differences in this test battery. Are the correlations among the tests compatible with each test being a better or worse indicator of one and only one latent ability dimension? Such a single-factor model conforms to Spearman's original theory. It turns out that a fit of these data to a single-factor model is extremely poor, as even the best-fitting parameters produce unacceptably large residual correlations between tests of noticeably similar content.

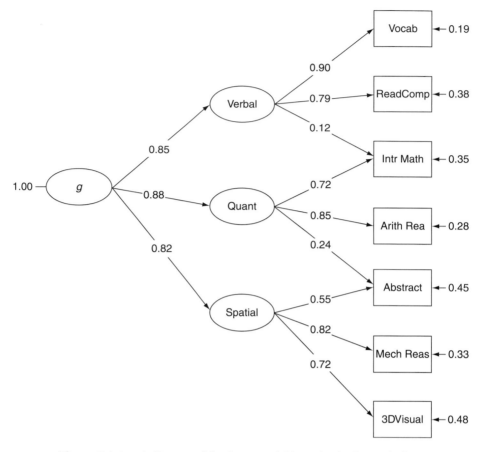

Figure 3.1 A path diagram of the factor model hypothesized to underlie the data in Table 3.1. All factor loadings are standardized. The standardized root mean square residual of 0.0098 indicates an excellent fit. An observed variable that is an indicator of two or more latent factors is said to be *factorially complex*. For example, some of the variance in Abstract Reasoning is attributable to the higher-order *g* factor and to both of the residualized non-*g* sources (not depicted) contributing to the quantitative and spatial factors. Although an exploratory analysis supports a path from the verbal factor to Introductory Mathematics, this path can be deleted with negligible deterioration of fit.

We must invoke *group factors* that affect performance on only a subset of the tests in the battery. This is a theoretically and practically important result: the mental ability tests that have thus far been devised, with meaningful relationships with important external biological and behavioral variables, conform to a measurement model including a general factor common to all

Table 3.2 *Orthogonalized factor pattern of selected aptitude tests administered in Project TALENT*

	g	Verbal	Quantitative	Spatial
Vocabulary	0.77	0.47	–	–
Reading Comprehension	0.67	0.42	–	–
Introductory Mathematics	0.74	0.06	0.34	–
Arithmetic Reasoning	0.75	–	0.40	–
Abstract Reasoning	0.66	–	0.11	0.31
Mechanical Reasoning	0.67	–	–	0.47
3D Visualization	0.63	–	–	0.41

of them and several group factors each influencing a subset of somewhat homogenous content.

We now present a model accommodating both general and group factors. These data fit a three-factor model extremely well, and the strong correlations among these factors support a hierarchical model in which the covariation among the group factors follows from their common indication in turn of a higher-order general factor corresponding to Spearman's g. Figure 3.1 presents the results of a confirmatory analysis in which this explicit structure has been specified. Note how strongly the verbal, quantitative, and spatial factors load on the higher-order general factor. It is possible to represent this factor model in a manner that orthogonalizes the latent sources of variance, permitting a direct inspection of their relative importance and whether the general factor is truly dominant. Table 3.2 presents the orthogonalized factor loadings of the Project TALENT ability tests. Note that g accounts for more of the variance in any given test than do the group factors that the test measures in addition to g. In light of this finding, it is in retrospect unsurprising that an implicit concept of unidimensionality has come to underlie the informal understanding of ability differences that is both inherited from previous generations and recapitulated in each one. Although many of the broad and narrow group factors are also indispensable in substantive understanding and practical relevance (Lubinski, 2004), the g factor is indeed the dominant dimension across the full range of individual differences in human cognitive abilities.

At least one feature of Table 3.2 is worthy of extended further comment. The fact that Vocabulary is the test with the highest g loading is not an idiosyncratic feature of this particular test battery but rather a quite typical result (Sternberg, 1987; Jensen, 2001). This may seem like a point in favor of those skeptics who believe that mental ability tests measure primarily the degree of passive exposure to the amenities of a privileged upbringing (Richardson, 1999). Such a strong inference, however, would rely on a distortion of how people actually learn the meanings of words. The acquisition of the knowledge that a *sound* stands for a particular *concept* is an extraordinarily elaborate process that requires, at a minimum, the capacity to represent the concept and then to infer the sound-concept mapping from the fleeting and ambiguous data presented by the contexts in which the word is used. According to the first requirement, the capacity to form a rich and abstractive understanding of the world is a prerequisite to the acquisition of an indefinitely expanding repertoire of concepts – chunks of world knowledge – labeled by sounds.

Bloom (2000) spells out in detail how children might manage the second requirement of assigning a word to its correct referent. According to our best current understanding, this is an eminently rational process that does not in the least resemble the associative learning of arbitrary stimulus pairs. The dependence of word learning on a deeper substrate of cognition is supported by studies in which Vocabulary has been the subscale of the Wechsler IQ battery showing the most susceptibility to the deleterious effects of inbreeding depression and the greatest resemblance between parents and their adopted-away offspring (Schull and Neel, 1965; Capron and Duyme, 1996). In light of the evidence for the high heritability of g (Luo, Petrill, and Thompson, 1994; Alarcón *et al.*, 1999; Rijsdijk, Vernon, and Boomsma, 2002; Wainwright *et al.*, 2004; Johnson *et al.*, 2007), the strong g loadings of vocabulary tests become not an embarrassment to the construct validity of g but rather a point of convergence between genetic and phenotypic evidence.

The nature of the relationship between the domain generality of individual differences and the modularity paradigm of evolutionary psychology has been our motivation behind this foray into psychometric principles and data, and we should not allow our insight into the intellectual content and demands of word learning to obscure the intrinsic interest that the high g loading of Vocabulary holds for our inquiry. Some students of word learning hold that a dedicated module applies domain-specific constraints and biases to this process (Markman, 1992). Now recall that Tooby and Cosmides have set forth, as an argument in favor of modularity, the gains offered by a divide-and-conquer approach when a learner is faced with substantive domains that are susceptible to varying sets of inference rules. Markman's proposal is in line with this reasoning. However, in the Project TALENT data, Vocabulary shows a large loading on g that is nearly equal to the g loading of Arithmetic Reasoning, a test of precisely the amodular and content-free inference rules of logic and mathematics that should not be expected in the front lines of cognition. The contrast between Vocabulary and Abstract Reasoning is even starker, as the latter is intended to rely as little as possible on any processes other than the content-poor operations inherent in the analysis of figural patterns that have no counterpart in the ecology of the examinees. Such tests are often claimed to be especially good indicators of g. Yet their g loadings are typically comparable to those of vocabulary tests and are often exceeded.

Words have been a recurring feature of the human environment for as long as our lineage has been able to speak. Some form of the conceptual apparatus underlying the semantics of language, a "language of thought" so to speak, is no doubt even older. Researchers have proposed a variety of mechanisms, some devoted in particular to word learning, by which humans are able to label the bits of world knowledge assembled by the conceptual apparatus with the acoustic tags that have been chosen by their linguistic communities. Yet, however these mechanisms accomplish this formidable task, individual differences in their overall efficiency are largely along the same dimension that underlies performance on tests that have been deliberately stripped of content from any recurring substantive domain of human experience. This extremely abstract quality is one feature of g contributing to its status as one of the most mysterious constructs in the behavioral sciences. By "abstract," to be clear, we refer to the pervasive influence of g without any regard for the functional boundaries of the mind set down by otherwise coherent bodies of investigation. We have seen that one reaction to this puzzling superposition has been a denial of the importance of the positive manifold. Other authors have not gone to this empirically untenable extreme, but nevertheless have felt a need to propose resolutions to a perceived conflict between the construct of g and the modular organization of cognition (Miller, 2000; Kanazawa, 2004; Geary, 2005).

A module devoted to computations in the domain of social exchanges is the favorite didactic example of Tooby and Cosmides, and we employ it as well in the development of our own proposed resolution. The existence of the module posited by Tooby and Cosmides is supported by many persuasive items of evidence, including a much higher pass rate when a reasoning problem is presented in the context of a social contract rather than in a logically equivalent symbolic format and the selective impairment of reasoning with respect to social exchanges in one case of brain damage (Cosmides, 1989; Stone et al., 2002). An interesting feature of these evidentiary items is that we can conduct thought experiments where each item is gathered from a *single* subject. A lone within-subject bivariate observation may be enough to find worsened performance in a content-deprived task relative to its logical equivalent in the domain of social contracts, and any expansion of the sample serves not a theoretical purpose but only the practical one of averaging out random perturbations. Similarly, we can imagine a specific decline in reasoning with respect to social exchanges as the sequel of brain damage deliberately inflicted on a single individual in an unethical within-subject experiment. These examples show that the architecture of cognition, including any functional subdivisions, might in principle be inferable from observations of a single individual. Note, however, that our exposition of g as a construct has repeatedly emphasized its necessary outgrowth from observations of variation in a *population*. For instance, the exceptionality of Odysseus would be imperceptible if not for the familiarity of Homer and his audience with a wide range of individual differences in the population. Likewise, a Martian differential psychologist would require two specimens at a minimum to establish the plausibility of a single dimension contributing to the variability in responses across an array of high-level cognitive tasks.

We have identified a methodological difference between the cognitive scientists whose aim is to discover "how the mind works" and those differential psychologists whose goals have been to identify important dimensions of variation. Whereas the former might content themselves with a sample of $N = 1$, the latter must seek $N \geq 2$. If this methodological difference is in correspondence with a substantive one, then the subject matters of these two disciplines might be distinguishable. Jensen (2000) has made the case for a substantive divide most forcefully, and his essential point can be made through the analogy of the mind to a manmade computer. Suppose that another Martian scientist, interested in both the nature of the algorithms devised by an alien intelligence and the causes of differences in performance among their machines, arrives on Earth and procures a large sample of computers. Suppose also that for whatever reason he has no access to the code implementing the programs installed on these computers. By observing the behavior of a single computer carefully, however, the Martian develops hypotheses regarding the algorithms underlying the computer's capabilities. For example, by taking note of run time as a function of input size and incorporating whatever constraints are available from other sources of evidence, he might rule out certain algorithms whose efficiencies are incompatible with his observations. The ultimate success of this endeavor would be to write code that perfectly reproduces the behavior of a computer with respect to input-output relations and whatever can be inferred about intermediate processes and data structures. Note that this is very roughly the job description of the cognitive scientist. The subset of cognitive scientists who are also evolutionary psychologists often employ selective forces plausibly at work in human prehistory to generate hypotheses regarding the algorithms that constitute the mind.

Now suppose that the Martian goes on to record differences in task performance among the various computers. This differential setting reveals certain phenomena that were not evident in the analysis of a single computer, namely the strong positive correlations among the proficiencies with which the computers perform the various tasks of which they are capable. For example, one computer takes all night to process a particularly cumbersome batch of data, and it turns out to suffer in addition from choppy animation of video files. At this point the Martian might be tempted to speculate that all of the diverse tasks performed by the computers are in fact manifestations of a single general-purpose program, thus attributing the positive manifold in his data to qualitative variation in this program's design. Just as the algorithms designed by programming students of different skill levels to compute the binomial expansion may vary by an order of magnitude in efficiency, the different versions of the hypothesized general-purpose program may vary in overall performance because of irregularities in abstract structural features. Of course, it is very likely that such a speculation would be incorrect. The true explanation of the positive manifold probably lies in the fact the different tasks must all be executed on hardware with finite CPU clock speed and RAM capacity. As these processing limitations necessarily affect all of the programs in common, they cause variation in the efficiencies of these programs to be correlated in the sample of computers. On this hypothesis the sample may represent an archeological record of progressive achievements on the part of the silicon industry. Regardless, in locating the causes of the positive manifold in the properties of hardware rather than algorithm design, the hypothesis appeals to a level of explanation that does not necessarily intersect with the mechanistic innards of the programs that execute whatever intelligent behavior any given computer can support.

We are in a similar position to that of our fabled Martian scientist. The ability factors hypothesized by differential psychologists do not necessarily correspond to functional subdivisions of the mind, although they may turn out to do so. The important group factors of verbal and spatial ability are certainly natural candidates, and this accounts for part of their theoretical appeal. But the logical point that the locus of the g factor may lie in an entirely different level of the reductionist hierarchy than the internal structure of cognition shows that there is no necessary contradiction between domain-specific modular processes and the domination of individual differences by a large general factor. This point clearly emerges in the following comment on the apparent preserved correlation between verbal and spatial abilities in women with Turner's syndrome, despite the dissociability of these abilities implied by the specific impairment of the latter:

> Correlations between phenotypically different mental tests may arise, not because of any causal connection among the mental elements required for their correct solutions or because of the physical sharing of neural tissue, but because each test in part requires the same "qualities" of brain for successful performance. For example, the efficiency of neural conduction or the extent of neural arborization may be correlated in different parts of the brain because of a similar epigenetic matrix, not because of concurrent functional overlap. (Willerman and Bailey, 1987, p. 943).

For this reason the dismissive comments of Raab and Gigerenzer are wholly unwarranted, and the speculations of other researchers attempting to contain both phenomena within the same level of explanation may be superfluous. See Borsboom and Dolan (2006) for criticism of Kanazawa (2004) that takes more or less this line. In order to retain the advantages of both types of constructs in explaining available data, it may be best to proceed with a heuristic suggestion that has been made by Jensen:

> [T]here is another reason why researchers in cognitive neuroscience have generally paid so little attention to the g factor: the failure to recognize the important distinction between the essential design features of the brain … which show distinct modules and specific localization of functions for various distinct cognitive functions, on the one hand, and individual differences in the speed and efficiency with which these functions operate … on the other. But I would argue that both of these facets are proper subject matter for brain research. I suggest as a heuristic hypothesis that the design features of the brain – its neural structures and functions – that are necessary for the many distinct processes that enter into information-processing, or intelligence … are essentially the same for all biologically normal *Homo sapiens*, i.e., those free of chromosomal and major gene anomalies or brain damage.
>
> Correlated individual differences in the functioning of these various information processes are a result of other quantitative biochemical and physiological conditions in the brain, most of them highly heritable, that are separate from the brain's essential design features, or "hard-wiring," but are, as it were, superimposed on all of them in common, and affect the overall speed and efficiency of their functioning. (Chabris *et al.*, 1998, pp. 20–21)

Interestingly, in response to this comment by Jensen, the AI pioneer John McCarthy (2004) points out that "the situation in AI today is the reverse" of

Jensen's proposal of design universality and quantitative differences as a first approximation for humans. What Jensen speculates are "quantitative biochemical and physiological conditions," McCarthy places in correspondence with "speed, short term memory, and the ability to form accurate and retrievable long term memories." The situation is reversed because manmade computers "have plenty of speed and memory" and their limitations arise instead from the sophistication of the "intellectual mechanisms that program designers understand well enough to put in programs." The apparently greater ease with which quantitative hardware capacities can be advanced relative to "intellectual mechanisms" demonstrates little definitively but is suggestive for reasons that are discussed in the conclusion of this chapter.

In passing, we note that correct responses in both the abstract and social versions of the Wason task are predicted by scores on the g-loaded SAT (Stanovich and West, 2000). While the experimental manipulation produces a change in the mean response, the g factor may contribute to individual differences in both conditions. This nicely illustrates the compatibility of narrow domain-specific modules with broad dimensions of individual differences and the need for both types of constructs.

The genetics and evolution of g

That "intelligence" has progressively increased in the primate lineage leading to *Homo sapiens* is uncontroversial, despite the conceptual difficulties discussed in the previous section regarding the nature of the trait that has evolved. Moreover, it is certainly the case that narrow cognitive modules do evolve to support rapid solutions to recurring problems in the ecology of a given species. Perhaps an even more striking example in humans than social reasoning is face recognition (Kanwisher, 2000). Patients suffering from hereditary *prosopagnosia* cannot recognize conspecifics by their facial features but are still able to distinguish the two sexes, assess physical attractiveness, and recognize emotional expressions (Kennerknecht *et al.*, 2006). Evidence from pedigrees indicates that the hereditary form of the disorder may be caused by a single dominant allele. Such a narrow deficit resulting from the knockout of a single gene in a critical pathway is striking because it suggests a hypermodular capacity shaped by natural selection to process a highly particular and ecologically relevant class of inputs. The conjecture that selection has sculpted such a capacity for the swift recognition of individuals by facial features seems very natural given what we know about human ecology. Humans must calibrate relations toward numerous conspecifics of varying relatedness and social standing (Hamilton, 1964; Trivers, 1971) and the fashioning of a dedicated module for recognition by facial features seems a plausible means toward the adaptive end of being able to make quick and effortless discriminations.

On the other hand, with players of only this kind, the stage of human cognition seems somewhat barren. Some of the capacities that seem most representative of advanced and distinctively human intellectual accomplishment, including language comprehension and quantitative reasoning, are supported by highly specialized modules that have either evolved or been adapted for these purposes (Pinker, 1994; Dehaene, 1997). But this statement is unsatisfying because it neglects the fact that these accomplishments are most conspicuously manifested in individuals with a high standing on the g factor. If the distribution of g were shifted substantially to the left, the doubtlessly profound consequences would include the diminishment of literature, philosophy, science, and mathematics. To what do we owe the abundance of these fruits? The question as to why natural selection has favored a distinct behavioral phenotype can be a difficult one. For now we augment existing theories within evolutionary psychology by suggesting the mere fact of movement along a g-like dimension in human cognitive evolution. The genotypic distribution of any trait is of course not time-invariant. To the extent that some g-like construct can be extended beyond *Homo sapiens* to its precursors and sister lineages, it may be that selection-induced rightward shifts in the genotypic distribution of g have contributed substantially to the ascent of the great apes and ultimately our own species.

The dramatic expansion of brain size and the accelerating advance of cultural innovation over the course of human evolution seem to present a *prima facie* case that such a rightward shift has indeed occurred (Klein and Edgar, 2002). At this point, however, we run into an apparent paradox posed by the high heritability of g. See Table 3.3 for a summary of the evidence on this point from recent studies where g-loaded IQ tests have been administered to adults or late adolescents. Recall that the *narrow-sense heritability* of trait Y, denoted by $h^2 = \sigma_A^2/\sigma_Y^2$, is equivalent under certain conditions to the total variance in Y accounted for by the linear regression of trait value on the number of enhancing alleles in the genotype (Lynch and Walsh, 1998). The numerator of this fraction is called the *additive genetic variance*. The data in Table 3.3 are consistent with a narrow-sense heritability of 0.50 or greater, which stands out as a high value when compared to estimated heritabilities of various traits in a wide variety of organisms (Mousseau and Roff, 1987). The source of the aforementioned paradox is the widespread assumption, often said to follow from Fisher's Fundamental Theorem of Natural Selection, that the genetic variation underlying traits exposed to selection is inevitably consumed (Roff, 1997). From this assumption it follows that a trait that has been important in the ecology and evolution of a species should *not* show a high heritability.

Table 3.3 *Familial correlations for IQ*

Relationship	Correlation	SE	Reference
Adoptive relatives			
Adoptive father–adopted child	0.08	0.06	Loehlin *et al.* (1997)
Adoptive father–adopted child	0.11	0.08	Plomin *et al.* (1997)
Adoptive mother–adopted child	−0.02	0.06	Loehlin *et al.* (1997)
Adoptive mother–adopted child	−0.05	0.08	Plomin *et al.* (1997)
Unrelated adoptive siblings	−0.02	0.12	Loehlin *et al.* (1997)
Unrelated adoptive siblings	0.07	0.09	Petrill *et al.* (2004)
Parent-offspring			
Biological father–reared child	0.20	0.10	Loehlin *et al.* (1997)
Biological father–reared child	0.33	0.08	Plomin *et al.* (1997)
Biological mother–reared child	0.21	0.10	Loehlin *et al.* (1997)
Biological mother–reared child	0.28	0.08	Plomin *et al.* (1997)
Biological father–adopted-away child	0.33	0.16	Plomin *et al.* (1997)
Biological mother–adopted-away child	0.33	0.06	Loehlin *et al.* (1997)
Biological mother–adopted-away child	0.39	0.07	Plomin *et al.* (1997)
Ordinary full sibs and dizygotic twins			
Full sibs reared together	0.33	0.18	Loehlin *et al.* (1997)
Full sibs reared together	0.22	0.10	Petrill *et al.* (2004)
Dizygotic twins reared together	0.46	0.07	McGue *et al.* (1993)
Dizygotic twins reared together	0.22	0.11	Pedersen *et al.* (1992)
Dizygotic twins reared together	0.30	0.09	Rijskijk *et al.* (2002)
Dizygotic twins reared apart	0.32	0.10	Pedersen *et al.* (1992)
Monozygotic twins			
Monozygotic twins reared together	0.80	0.05	Pedersen *et al.* (1992)
Monozygotic twins reared together	0.85	0.03	Rijskijk *et al.* (2002)
Monozygotic twins reared apart	0.75	0.07	Bouchard *et al.* (1990)
Monozygotic twins reared apart	0.78	0.06	Pedersen *et al.* (1992)

Note. The correlations reported by Loehlin *et al.* (1997) from the Texas Adoption Project are probably attenuated because of a ceiling effect in the Beta IQ test. Some individuals contribute to more than one correlation from the same study.

The argument along these lines against the importance of IQ (or, alternatively, against the evidence for its heritability) was first clearly articulated by Marcus Feldman and Richard Lewontin:

> [A]s selection progresses, the additive genetic variance is "used up" so that the h_N^2 is decreased finally to zero, or nearly so. A consequence of [the Fundamental Theorem] is that, if natural selection has long been in operation on a character, the additive genetic variance for the character

should be small, and the only genetic variance left should be nonadditive (dominance and epistatic variance) …. [W]e would be forced to conclude that whatever it is that IQ measures, it has not been under intense selection for very long. (Feldman and Lewontin, 1975, p. 1167)

This argument concerning the selective depletion of genetic variance has proven to be quite durable. Writing about heritable individual differences in quantitative psychological traits more generally, Tooby and Cosmides argue that

[h]eritable variation in a trait generally signals a *lack* of adaptive significance. The longer selection has operated on a trait and the more intensely it has operated, the less heritable variation is left. Consequently, those traits that have high heritabilities will generally be those traits that are not adaptations, although they may interact in interesting ways with adaptations. Therefore, behavior geneticists tend to be studying phenomena that are not themselves adaptations (however interesting they may be for other reasons) …. Those interested in studying complex psychological adaptations should be most interested in design features that are inherited, but not heritable. (Tooby and Cosmides, 2005, pp. 39–40)

This theme has become an important thread in the articulate and influential writings of Tooby and Cosmides. In the latest broad statement of their views, they write that

selection, interacting with sexual recombination, tends to impose at the genetic level near uniformity in the functional design of our complex neurocomputational machinery … Thus, our important functional machinery tends to be universal at the genetic level, and the heritability statistic associated with this machinery will be close to zero (because there is little variation between individuals caused by genes). In contrast, whenever a mutation fails to make a functional difference, selection will not act on it, and such minor variants can build up at the locus until there is substantial genetic variability for the trait. Hence, its heritability statistic will be high (because most variation between individuals is caused by variation in genes). For this reason, genetic variability is commonly nonadaptive or maladaptive evolutionary noise: neutral variants, negative mutations on their way to being eliminated, and so on. (Tooby and Cosmides, 2005, pp. 39–40)

For these reasons they conclude that "human characteristics that vary due to genetic differences … are unlikely to be evolved adaptations central to human nature" (Tooby and Cosmides, 2005, p. 39).

It has been argued that traits that are highly complex or closely related to fitness in fact show higher levels of genetic variance, which implies that any tendency toward low heritabilities is caused by higher levels of residual or environmental variance (Houle, 1992). However, this view only seems to lend aid to the argument against the evolutionary importance of g, as the question then becomes why the genetic variance in this trait should be so large as to dominate the residual variance in such an atypical manner.

The argument in one form or another seems to have been accepted to some extent even by commentators sympathetic to the notion that the abilities measured by IQ tests have been of adaptive value. Instead of taking the seemingly abundant genetic variability in whatever IQ measures as evidence for the irrelevance of the tests, however, the theoretical biologist William Hamilton viewed this variability as a true evolutionary puzzle: "[I]t is a little hard to see why we are not all selected to the upper limit" (Hamilton, 2001, p. 492).

We now present a counterargument showing that in fact the high heritability of any trait per se cannot be used to rule out its potential evolutionary importance. From our perspective the high heritability of g may be precisely *because* of its positive covariance with fitness over so much of hominid history. Of course, it is necessarily true that upon fixation of all favorable alleles the genetic variance in any trait becomes zero. But the contribution of any given locus to the genetic variance only declines once the frequency of the enhancing allele passes 0.5 (if gene action is purely additive). Before that point the contribution of the locus to the genetic variance actually increases because of symmetry about 0.5 in the genetic variance as a function of allele frequency. The prediction by Feldman and others that the heritability of any trait correlated with fitness should have steadily dwindled until the present day relies implicitly on the assumption that all enhancing alleles have passed from moderate to high frequency. But suppose that the assumption is false. Suppose instead that the reduction in the genetic variance attributable to the increase in frequency of enhancing alleles from moderate to high has been outweighed by new genetic variance attributable to novel variants or the increase in frequency of enhancing alleles from rare to moderate in the standing variation. Then the heritability of the trait should have steadily *increased* until the present day. A bias in the genetic architecture of this kind may even be plausible given two known trends in recent human evolutionary history: (1) the introgression of adaptive alleles from archaic *Homo* lineages, and (2) an exponential increase in population size (Hawks and Cochran, 2006; Hawks et al., 2007). The first mechanism allows the introduction of many more adaptive variants than can arise within a comparable time span by mutation alone for a given population size, while the second increases the number of adaptive mutants that appear per generation in linear fashion. Under *directional selection* these variants are more likely to avoid absorption by the boundary of frequency zero and increasingly contribute to the genetic variance as they become common. These processes biasing the genetic architecture toward initially rare or absent favorable variants increasing in frequency may well make the high heritability of g observed today consistent with a history of intense directional selection.

We now present a somewhat more general framework for this notion. Tooby and Cosmides explicitly state that a trait that has been *selectively neutral* should today exhibit a high heritability, and this is indeed correct. Consider a trait with a purely additive genetic basis in a population with a constant effective size N_e. Each generation a fraction $1/2N_e$ of the genetic variance is lost by drift, while new variance in the amount σ_m^2 is introduced by mutation. The quantity $\sigma_m^2 \approx 2\Sigma_{i=1}^{n} u_i E(a_i^2)$, where $i = 1, \ldots, n$ indexes the loci and u_i denotes the mutation rate at the ith locus, is the *mutational variance*. For the additive genetic variance in generation t, this gives us the simple recursion equation

$$\sigma_A^2(t) = \left(1 - \frac{1}{2N_e}\right)\sigma_A^2(t-1) + \sigma_m^2, \tag{3.1}$$

which has the solution

$$\sigma_A^2(t) \approx 2N_e\sigma_m^2 + \left[\sigma_A^2(0) - 2N_e\sigma_m^2\right]e^{-t/2N_e}. \tag{3.2}$$

Thus, the equilibrium additive genetic variance for a neutral quantitative trait with a purely additive basis is simply

$$\tilde{\sigma}_A^2(N) \approx 2N_e\sigma_m^2 \tag{3.3}$$

(Lynch and Hill, 1986). It turns out that this expression is not much affected by dominance. If the base population is completely homozygous, then the time to 50% of the equilibrium variance is about $1.4N_e$ generations. Since $\sigma_A^2(0)$ is usually not zero, equilibrium can be reached quite rapidly. The equilibrium heritability of a neutral trait is thus

$$\tilde{h}^2(N) \approx \frac{2N_e h_m^2}{2N_e h_m^2 + 1}, \tag{3.4}$$

where $h_m^2 = \sigma_m^2/\sigma_E^2$ is the *mutational heritability*. One can think of this latter quantity as the heritability of a trait in an initially isogamous line after one generation of mutation. Empirically estimated values of h_m^2 tend to fall between 10^{-3} and 10^{-2} (Lynch and Walsh, 1998). The long-term effective population size of *Homo sapiens* is approximately 10^4 (Jobling, Hurles, and Tyler-Smith, 2004), and for such populations it can be seen that nearly all of the phenotypic variation in neutral traits is expected to be genetic. Some plausibly neutral traits in humans, such as fingerprint ridge count, do exhibit heritabilities approaching unity (Holt, 1968). The fact that the heritabilities of most other traits do not approach this magnitude suggests that strict neutrality is exceptional.

Can directional selection produce a heritability less than unity but still as large as that of the g factor? Suppose that a potentially trait-affecting locus is initially fixed for allele B. If the census population size is N, then the frequency of a new mutant B' is $1/2N$. Suppose that BB' and $B'B'$ are augmented in phenotypic value by $a(1+k)$ and $2a$, respectively, relative to BB. Let $p(a,k)$ denote the joint density function of these mutant effects. Also, let $\pi(p_0, a, k)$ denote the probability of fixation for an allele at frequency p_0 and with effects a and k relative to the ancestral allele. The expected contribution from a new mutant initially present in one copy to the total increase in the directionally selected trait over time is thus $2a \cdot \pi(1/2N, a, k)$ – the increment in the mean trait value given the fixation of the new allele times its probability of fixation.

Another way to put it is that if B' is not absorbed by the boundary of frequency zero, then it will eventually increase the mean trait value in the population by $2a$. The asymptotic selection response per generation can then be idealized as the homozygote effect of a mutant times its probability of fixation, summed over all mutants that appear in a generation. Let $\lambda = \Sigma_{i=1}^{n} u_i$ equal the gametic mutation rate. Since $2N\lambda$ new mutants appear in each generation, the asymptotic selection response is thus

$$\tilde{R} = 2N\lambda E\left[2a \cdot \pi\left(\frac{1}{2N}, a, k\right)\right]$$
$$= 2N\lambda \int \int 2a \cdot \pi\left(\frac{1}{2N}, a, k\right) p(a, k) \mathrm{d}a \mathrm{d}k. \tag{3.5}$$

We require the distribution $p(a, k)$ in order to predict the expected asymptotic selection response. This distribution is known for very few traits and organisms. Nevertheless, it is possible to gain some insight into this expression for the expected asymptotic rate by using some simple approximations.

Consider the case where all new mutants are nearly additive ($k \approx 0$). This assumption is empirically and theoretically defensible for alleles of small effect (Simmons and Crow, 1977; Kacser and Burns, 1981). Again, in the case of additive mutants, $\sigma_m^2 = 2\lambda E(a^2)$. We know that the probability of fixation for a favored mutant initially present in one copy is $\pi(1/2N) \approx 2(s+r)(N_e/N)$ for

$2N_es > 1$, where r is the rate of population growth and s is the selective advantage of the heterozygote over the ancestral homozygote (Haldane, 1927; Kimura, 1964; Otto and Whitlock, 1997). For the sake of simplicity, assume that the population is constant in size ($r=0$). For the case where $2N_es \leq 1$, we have $\pi(1/2N) \approx 1/2N + N_es/N$ (Robertson, 1960). For an enhancing additive mutant at a *quantitative trait locus* (QTL), the selection coefficient is $s \approx ia/\sigma_Y$, where i is the standardized differential S/σ_Y between the mean in generation t and the mean of the parents of generation $t+1$ (Kimura and Crow, 1978). As an increase in the additive genetic variance from one to three times the residual variance only increases the phenotypic standard deviation σ_Y by 40%, the distortion introduced by keeping σ_Y constant is tolerable. Making the appropriate substitutions, we find that the asymptotic selection response per generation becomes

$$\tilde{R} \approx \frac{4N_ei\sigma_m^2}{\sigma_Y E(a^2)} \left(\int_{\sigma_Y/2N_ei}^{\infty} a^2 p(a)\mathrm{d}a + \frac{1}{2} \int_0^{\sigma_Y/2N_ei} a^2 p(a)\mathrm{d}a \right) + 2\lambda \int_0^{\sigma_Y/2N_ei} a p(a)\mathrm{d}a$$

(3.6)

(Hill, 1982). We have already assumed that alleles with a depressing effect on the trait have a negligible probability of fixation. We would like to make more assumptions so that this rather opaque expression can be simplified further. One possible assumption is that most of the selection response is attributable to alleles of large effect – "large" depending in this context on the product of population size and the selection coefficient. If this product exceeds unity by a fair margin, then we can neglect the second term inside the parentheses and the last term overall on the right side of Equation (3.6) to obtain

$$\tilde{R} \approx \frac{4N_ei\sigma_m^2}{\sigma_Y} \frac{E^+(a^2)}{E(a^2)} \qquad \text{with} \qquad E^+(a^2) = \int_0^{\infty} a^2 p(a)\mathrm{d}a.$$

(3.7)

We can find the equilibrium additive genetic variance from this expression using the Breeder's Equation, which says that the selection response in any generation is given by

$$R = h^2 S = \sigma_A^2 \frac{i}{\sigma_Y}$$

(3.8)

(Lynch and Walsh, 1998). Thus,

$$\tilde{\sigma}_A^2(S) = 4N_e\sigma_m^2\kappa \qquad \text{with} \qquad \kappa = \frac{E^+(a^2)}{E(a^2)}$$

(3.9)

and

$$\tilde{h}^2(S) = \frac{4N_e h_m^2 \kappa}{4N_e h_m^2 \kappa + 1} \tag{3.10}$$

(Hill and Keightley, 1988). κ can be interpreted more generally as the fraction of the mutational variance appearing each generation that is useable for adaptation. Surprisingly, above a certain threshold, the equilibrium heritability under directional selection does not depend on the strength of selection. It turns out that the selection intensity cancels in the following way. Suppose that selection is very strong. Then a common enhancing allele might be rapidly fixed and no longer contribute to the genetic variance. But then a rare enhancing variant is brought to moderate frequency just as rapidly and replenishes the lost variance. If selection is weak, then a smaller quantity of genetic variance is traded between the alleles heading toward fixation and those departing from the boundary of frequency zero, and the total genetic variance remains unchanged.

If $p(a)$ is such that favorable and unfavorable mutants are equally probable, then $E^+(a^2) = E(a^2)/2$ and the equilibrium heritability reduces to

$$\tilde{h}^2 = \frac{2N_e h_m^2}{2N_e h_m^2 + 1} \tag{3.11}$$

Amazingly, this is the same equilibrium heritability as under complete neutrality. Somehow, in changing fitness regimes from neutrality to directional selection, the inability of trait-depressing mutants to contribute to the genetic variance is exactly canceled by the increased fixation probability of trait-enhancing mutants to leave the equilibrium genetic variance unchanged. The total genetic variance then comes to depend only on the amount of variance generated, which in turn depends on population size.

Keep in mind that the equivalence of neutrality and directional selection assumes equal probability mass on either side of zero for the mutational distribution $p(a)$. Some traits, such as bristle number in *Drosophila*, do seem to satisfy this assumption (Lyman, Lawrence, Nuzhdin, and Mackay, 1996). However, boosting the performance of a complex information-processing device like the brain, even if such performance is unevenly correlated with fitness across time and place, seems much more like the optimization of fitness itself than like a relatively simple morphological change such as moving bristle number up or down. For this reason it is probable that $\kappa < 0.5$. But note that even if $\kappa = 0.01$, setting N_e to 10^4 and h_m^2 to 0.005 produces an equilibrium heritability of roughly 0.67. Also, one might conjecture that weak directional selection in the limit produces the high equilibrium heritability expected under neutrality.

The presented derivations in the cases of neutrality and directional selection have merely scratched the surface of the complex literature devoted to the maintenance of genetic variation in quantitative traits. It may be that *stabilizing selection* in favor of an intermediate value somewhere between the extremes of the phenotypic distribution is a more plausible null model for most traits. However, accounting for even the moderate heritabilities typically observed in nature or in the laboratory is a challenge for available models of stabilizing selection, which attribute standing variation to a balance between new variants introduced by mutation and selection against these variants (Johnson and Barton, 2005).

Our argument has led us to the following conclusion: under a simple model of directional selection where mutation is allowed to contribute to the genetic variance, the equilibrium heritability increases unboundedly with population size. Now consider some quantitative traits in domesticated species with large population sizes. The mean egg weight in chickens is twice as much as in the jungle fowl from which they are descended, yet heritability estimates of chicken egg weight range from 0.50 to 0.70 (Kerje *et al.*, 2003; Zhang *et al.*, 2005). Domesticated rice plants possess both much larger grains than their wild relatives and estimated heritabilities of grain weight ranging from 0.70 to 0.90 (Ahn, 1992; Takeda, 1990; Li *et al.*, 1997). So high heritabilities do cooccur with known histories of very strong directional selection. However, counterexamples also abound, which suggests that the underlying biology of many traits is complex enough that the population-genetic parameters invoked so far cannot adequately predict their heritabilities. For example, it might be that $h_m^2 \kappa$ can decline over time as the space of possible improved genomes for the organism becomes saturated. A limitation of this kind has obviously not prevented our shrewlike ancestor from producing the blue whales among its progeny. But on shorter time scales, especially for a more complex optimization, there may be lulls where the organism must wait for sufficient alteration of its genetic background or environment to allow the appearance of new enhancing mutants that are unencumbered by deleterious pleiotropic effects. We find it interesting that arguments of this kind are rather plausibly countered in the particular case of g. The brain is an extraordinarily complex organ that draws on a large portion of the genome for its development and maintenance. Indeed, a recent report indicates that approximately 80% of mouse genes display some cellular expression above background in the brain (Lein *et al.*, 2007). This large mutational target implies numerous possible quantitative modifications of the brain's performance, which translates in turn to a minimally decaying $h_m^2 \kappa$.

In summary, there is reason to believe that directional selection can sometimes act as a force to increase genetic variation. This may be especially the case in a population that has been disturbed from its equilibrium as a result of introgression or an exponential increase in numbers. In the final chapter of his treatise *The Mathematical Theory of Selection, Recombination, and Mutation*, Reinhard Bürger discusses some models of directional selection, including models of stabilizing selection with a moving optimum, and also concludes that such selection can be a mechanism tending to increase genetic variability. In the final paragraph of the book, he writes:

> Most models designed for explaining the amount of quantitative variation assume that populations are close to equilibrium. However, is this assumption justified? Given the many frequent changes which have continuously occurred in our biosphere, in particular, the rapid and frequent climate changes, it is likely that populations often experience directional selection. During such a period, a substantial increase in genetic variation may occur if there is a sustained supply of favorable mutations (Section 7). (Bürger, 2000, p. 344).

Brain size has increased substantially in the human lineage; IQ is phenotypically and genetically correlated with brain size today; the g factor, the dominant dimension underlying performance on IQ tests, is the most heritable quantitative psychological trait; IQ is the single best predictor of success in the complex mercantile and technological society which has been steadily accreting since early in human prehistory (Striedter, 2005; Posthuma *et al.*, 2002; Bouchard and McGue, 2003; Gottfredson, 2003, 2007). It would be terribly unsatisfying if these facts happened to be strung together by coincidence. We conjecture that directional selection for increased g in the human lineage is responsible for the high heritability of this trait. This proposed solution has a pleasing simplicity to it, and demonstrating its truth would provide a neat illustration of a potentially important evolutionary principle. Far from showing this trait to be a diverting oddity, the substantial heritability of g may justify greater attention to its possible role in human evolution.

Empirical prospects

Although some of our arguments for bringing g and other ability constructs within the fold of human evolutionary studies may depend much on the reader's willingness to acknowledge points of plausibility and reasonableness, we believe that empirical validation of many aspects is much closer than might be immediately apparent.

IQ tests were certainly not designed to measure any anatomical or physiological variables. Moreover, as becomes clear in the review by Matthews, Deary, and Whiteman (2003), there is no guarantee that a psychological trait will show any easily replicable neural correlates. The causal basis of the relevant variation may reside in extremely fine neural microfeatures beyond the relatively low degree of resolution offered by current brain assays. Nevertheless, IQ does show many correlations with rather gross features of the brain that have been reported in multiple studies. See Chabris (2007) and Jung and Haier (2007) for thorough reviews. These multiply replicated neural correlates include overall brain volume, levels of the brain metabolite N-acetylaspartate (NAA), and coherence of white matter fibers as measured by diffusion tensor imaging (DTI).

Of course, correlations do not necessarily imply functional or causal relationships, and efforts to rule out spurious sources of the correlations between IQ and these brain variables have scarcely begun. One powerful method that eliminates many possible confounds is to examine the correlation between two traits within families. As an illustration, take IQ and height. Both traits are highly valued in our society, leading men and women to combine them with other traits in an index of desirability used to evaluate potential mates. Alleles that enhance IQ and height thus tend to be sorted together into the same families, leading to a correlation between these two variables in the population. But this correlation appears to arise entirely as a result of the *gametic disequilibrium* among loci affecting IQ and height induced by the *cross-assortative mating* just described. As the correlation becomes drastically attenuated within families, with the higher-IQ sibling showing little or no tendency to be taller, there seems in general to be no functional relationship between these two variables (Jensen and Sinha, 1993). It is admittedly difficult to imagine that confounds of this kind are what link IQ to its various neural correlates. In the absence of compelling alternative explanations, the presumption that a replicated correlation between IQ and a brain variable represents a functional or causal relationship may well be warranted. It should remain a high priority for future studies, however, to determine whether these correlations hold true within families. If the kind of severe deflation observed for the IQ–height correlation occurs for any of these brain variables, then its status as a possible causal basis of g becomes highly questionable. In contrast, a robust within-family correlation justifies an intensive research effort to dissect the likely mechanistic basis of the relationship.

Of the various correlations referred to above, the most replicated is that between IQ and brain volume. The moderate magnitude of this positive correlation, ranging between 0.30 and 0.40, has been established in dozens of studies collectively enrolling over a thousand subjects (McDaniel, 2005). This correlation is not mediated by overall body size. Efforts to establish a within-family component of the correlation, however, have collectively failed to establish either its presence or absence with much confidence (Jensen and Johnson, 1994; Schoenemann, Budinger, Sarich, and Wang, 2000; Gignac, Vernon, and Wickett, 2003). The much larger samples in the one study by Jensen and Johnson showing a robust within-family correlation between IQ and head circumference (a crude proxy of brain volume) relates to one imaging study by Schoenemann and colleagues showing no correlation does favor the positive result. Combining this pattern with the sheer size of the correlation and the current absence of any plausible competing explanation, we find it more likely than not that the correlation between IQ and brain volume is intrinsic and thus representative of a causal relationship. Obviously, more studies with large samples of sib pairs need to be conducted in order to resolve this issue and others that are raised by the puzzling heterogeneity of results relating to sex moderation, particular brain regions, factorial composition, and other aspects of the relationship between IQ and brain volume.

Greater psychometric sophistication might go some way toward resolving these issues in future studies of the neural correlates of IQ that employ such large samples. *Structural equation modeling* (SEM) is a generalization of Wright's (1921) method of *path analysis* in that the nodes in the diagram of causal relations may stand for either observed variables or latent factors. See Loehlin (2004) for a valuable reference. SEM allows hypotheses specifying the causal influences of various neural variables on particular ability factors such as g to be tested for compatibility with data. In an interesting proposed explanation for the positive manifold. Van der Maas *et al.* (2006) state that the failure to find a neural or cognitive variable that is perfectly correlated with g should count as evidence against its construct validity. Given the numerous correlates of IQ with some plausible claim to causal antecedency, a more reasonable criterion for construct validation might be for a causal path in an SEM from a brain variable to g. Data supporting such a model is consistent with a vector of effects on ability tests that is colinear with their g loadings. It is admittedly difficult, however, to conceive of any quantitative dimension of a system as complex as the central nervous system that might correspond *this* neatly to a high-level abstraction of behavior such as the g factor. But effects of brain volume and NAA levels on diverse indicators of g have indeed been reported (Wickett, Vernon, and Lee, 2000; MacLullich *et al.*, 2002; Jung *et al.*, 2005; Colom, Jung, and Haier, 2006), which tends to support our weaker position attributing the mere fact of substantial correlations among cognitive abilities to diffuse and low-level properties of the neural substrate. Whatever the outcome of studies properly designed to test models of causal relationships between ability factors and their neural correlates, further theoretical psychometric work might be desired to conceptualize the potentially complex and many-to-many mapping between abstractive psychological attributes and their causal bases in the brain.

Once a functional or causal relationship between g and a neural correlate has been firmly established, we can examine the pattern of evolutionary change in this variable implied by extant variation in the primate order and the extent to which this variation tracks an appropriate measure of cognitive abilities. It happens that the question as to what constitutes such a measure has long bedeviled comparative psychology. An interesting approach to this issue, has recently been undertaken by the evolutionary psychologist Robert Deaner, the primatologist Carel van Schaik, and the statistician Valen Johnson. This team compiled 30 different reports comparing the cognitive abilities of different primate genera and performed a meta-analysis encompassing the performance of 24 such genera on nine distinct cognitive paradigms (Johnson, Deaner, and van Schaik, 2002; Deaner, van Schaik, and Johnson, 2006).

If the disqualification of a domain-general dimension were indeed the corollary of the principle that cognitive abilities are narrowly tuned to specific adaptive problems that have arisen in the evolutionary history of a lineage, then it would be surprising to find that the performance of a primate taxon on one cognitive task is strongly predictive of its performance on many others. Yet this is precisely what Deaner and his colleagues found. The authors examined the posterior distributions for the g_i and $s_{i,l}(j)$ and found that the observed rank orders across experiments can be efficiently captured by the ranks of the genera along the postulated single dimension of domain-general ability. The values for the g_i are so predictive that the full model described by Equation (3.12) is barely distinguishable from a reduced model with no paradigm-genus specificities. To put it more simply, we have another positive manifold: a primate genus with a high rank in one experiment or paradigm tends to have high ranks in all of them. The phylogenetic pattern in the results is just as striking. The more recently a genus shares common ancestry with man, the higher its rank on the general factor tends to be. In the words of van Schaik,

When we examined the ranking, it looked as though we had set the
clock back half a century or more: great apes emerged as smarter than
monkeys, who in turn outperformed lemurs and lorises (prosimians).
What professional psychologists had spent decades denouncing as
preconceived notions based on a deeply ingrained cultural bias known
as the Scala Naturae or Great Chain of Being emerges vindicated. (van
Schaik, 2004, p. 130).

The domain generality and predictive power of this primate general factor
gives it some passing resemblance to human g. Indeed, some of the paradigms
serving as indicators of this factor appear to tap g in humans. Tool use,
reversal learning, and oddity problems all distinguish between older and
younger children, between subjects of normal IQ and the mentally retarded,
and the problems within these paradigms preserve their rank order of difficulty regardless of the species to which they are administered (Viaud, 1960).
These points add up to a simple hypothesis: the g factor of cognitive abilities
within the human species and the general factor posited by Deaner's group
both arise from a set of quantitative properties of the brain whose genotypic
distributions have shown a rightward evolutionary trend in the lineage leading to *Homo sapiens*.

Suppose that the general factor among nonhuman primates does indeed
correspond roughly to g itself. What might then be the quantitative neural
variables subserving this factor? It is here that verification of the functional or
causal status of the neural correlates of IQ becomes critical. For instance, if
greater brain size does indeed support higher levels of g, it is then reasonable to
suppose that a correlation between brain size and rank on the general factor
might hold across the primate order. Lee (2007) reported a rank-order correlation of 0.909 between the general factor and *executive brain ratio* (EBR), which is
the sum of the volumes of the neocortex and striatum divided by the sum of the
volumes of the mesencephalon and medulla oblongata. Regrettably, the correlations given by Lee are not quite precise because of a failure to account for their
possible artifactual inflation by phylogenetic inertia. If an ancestral taxon happens to exhibit high standings on two variables for whatever reason, then this
association can persist in its descendant lineages even in the absence of a
functional or causal relationship. A proper analysis by Deaner *et al.* (2007),
however, has confirmed that brain size is indeed strongly correlated with the
general factor.

Given the great promise of these results, their replication and extension
should become a priority for researchers with the relevant expertise. New
data should be fitted to the model, including data on genera and paradigms

not included in the meta-analysis. Further investigation and refinement may lead to a revision of ability rank order leading to a stronger phylogenetic signal and a higher correlation with brain size. If brain size is truly a causal determinant of the g-like factor, then it is not unreasonable to expect an ecological correlation between these two variables approaching unity. It should be kept in mind, however, that there may be spurious reasons for any given taxon to rank similarly in comparisons of performance on distinct behavioral measures. Perhaps a confluence of distinct selection pressures have sculpted narrow proficiencies in both domains such that the taxon does well in each. If the primate general factor is to be construed as a quasi-unitary emergent property of the brain, then the putative indicators of the factor should show positive loadings *within* a given species as well as *among* distinct taxa. Moreover, as does human g, it should emerge in comparisons within biological sibships (Jensen, 1980; Nagoshi, Phillips, and Johnson, 1987). Unfortunately, the frequency of tied ranks in the data analyzed by Deaner and his colleagues indicate that the tasks employed are rather coarse indicators that may not always discriminate well within a species. The demonstration of within-species correlations among cognitive tasks thus demands the expertise of investigators whose familiarity with a model organism will allow them to devise tasks with adequate psychometric properties for that organism. We know of at least one laboratory with the requisite expertise that is currently conducting a multivariate differential study of a primate species. We expect that the results of their study will be available by the time this book goes to press.

Similar studies of non-primate taxa should also prove fruitful, as the same variation in neural parameters giving rise to a general factor in humans and other primates may also cause individual differences within the cognitive repertoires of nonprimates to be positively correlated. Jensen (1998, pp. 148, 163–165) reviews earlier studies of rodents, and the novel research program with laboratory mice described by Galsworthy *et al.* (2005) offers much promise. A cumulative body of positive findings in this vein would prove extremely convenient in that it would justify the use of rodents as model organisms in the search for satisfying mechanistic explanations of the relationship between g and its functional neural correlates.

The emphasis thus far in this section on neural correlates is motivated by the fact that these correlates are empirically well-established. A reconstruction of evolutionary trends in these correlates from extant variation across taxa would thus provide evidence that something akin to the latent traits now measured by IQ tests has been evolving over time. It follows from this rationale that we might also employ the actual genetic variants contributing to differences in cognitive abilities in support of this posited evolutionary trend. Even though evidence of associations between IQ and genetic variants is scanty at present, this approach may be even more compelling to an evolutionist than the study of the intermediate bases of ability factors in the brain because of the obvious centrality of genetics to evolution. We can imagine an abstract chain of genome sequences, each encoding a distinct neural phenotype, each separated from its neighbors by a single discrete step, which binds together the first creature that might be said to have possessed a mind at all – the possession amounting, perhaps, to little more than an enlarged ganglion intervening between sensory and motor channels – to "man noble in reason, infinite in faculty, in apprehension like a god." This image captures a trivial truth that is nevertheless astonishing, and it should inspire efforts toward the ambitious goal of reconstructing at least some links in this chain.

The first step in this endeavor is the discovery of replicable associations between the relevant genotypes and phenotypes. Such associations have been more difficult to come by in the case of mental ability factors than initially anticipated, and convincing results are few (Plomin, Kennedy, and Craig, 2006). This is a problem that can be overcome by brute force. It has now been amply demonstrated that sufficiently dense genome coverage and large sample sizes can uncover reliable genotype-phenotype associations (Easton *et al.*, 2007; Weedon *et al.*, 2007; Scott *et al.*, 2007). No association study of IQ or any non-pathological behavioral trait has approached the genome coverage or sample sizes employed in these studies. Researchers pursuing the genetic basis of cognitive abilities may have no choice but to scale up their efforts and expenditures to the point of supporting multicenter genome-wide association studies individually genotyping many thousands of subjects.

Once a large number of true causal associations between *g* and genetic loci are secured, many important evolutionary inferences become possible. If the methodological developments necessary to measure within-species behavioral differences with sufficient accuracy are in fact made, then we can expect to discover whether polymorphisms in the same genes influencing cognitive abilities in humans also do so in other species. Support for the importance of a *g*-like construct in evolution would grow with the breadth of both the abilities influenced and the taxa in which the influences are operative. See Sabeti *et al.* (2006) for a review of more sophisticated methods for detecting natural selection from genetic data. The one drawback of most of these methods for our purposes, however, is that they are capable of detecting only strong selection. Recalling that the expression for the selection coefficient experienced by a favored allele at a QTL is $s \approx ia/\sigma_Y$, we see that these coefficients should tend to be very small for any trait with an extensive polygenic basis. We conjecture that a multilocus approach, making use of several genes causally associated with the trait, is feasible for the detection of directional selection for a phenotype determined primarily by many loci of small effect. By comparing sequence data from several loci determining a quantitative trait to some theoretical null model of multilocus sequence evolution under stabilizing selection or neutrality, it may be possible to reject a hypothesis that the distribution of the trait has been either stationary or drifting randomly. For example, although the putative selection signature of any given enhancing variant may not stand out from the neutral expectation, those of *all* enhancing variants may clearly come from some distribution other than the null. Another genomic feature of relevance to testing the hypothesis may include the balance of derived and ancestral alleles among enhancing variants.

This problem of detecting directional selection for a trait whose genetic architecture approximates the *infinitesimal model* should become an urgent research priority. Its resolution may allow us the most direct possible glimpse at an evolutionary rise in the general factor as a thread running throughout the tapestry of primate cognitive evolution.

Conclusion

We now present some ruminations that unify the two otherwise distinct issues that have been covered in this chapter: (1) the compatibility of g with a modular structure of cognition, and (2) the implications of the high heritability of g for its evolutionary history.

To our knowledge there are no theories positing innate qualitative differences in cognitive function among normal members of our species – despite the profound differences of *some* type that we do in fact observe. If the differences recorded by IQ tests indeed represent essentially quantitative variation in a species-universal qualitative design, then the observation that so much of the variance in g appears to be accounted for by the additive effects of alleles becomes less surprising. Whereas we might expect allelic variation in qualitative design features of cognition to result in substantial nonadditive *epistasis* for whatever individual differences may exist in overall function, the largely additive nature of the genetic variance in g is tentatively consistent with many loci of small and cumulative effects on quantitative aspects of neural "wetware." On this argument the high narrow-sense heritability of g is potentially relevant to both its evolutionary history and an important aspect of its underlying biology. Perhaps this separation of g from the abstract design of cognition already falls naturally out of our proposal of a dominant dimension of cognitive abilities increasing in its mean over tens of millions of years. If it is truly "one thing" in some sense that has increased over this entire time, then it is hard to see what it might be other than some amalgam of quantitative neural variables of the kind just described. Our suggestions regarding the relationship of g to the design features of the mind and the consistency of a high heritability with past directional selection are thus complementary.

We are cognizant of the warning by the great differential psychologist Cyril Burt that the explanation with the appearance of greatest simplicity – or, at any rate, posing such an appearance to its advocate – is very likely to be wrong in a science with as complex a subject matter as human behavior (Burt, 1940). Of course, at the time Burt had no access to the powerful conceptual tools that have since become available to psychologists (Pinker, 1997). But the fate of the g factor in an overall framework of cognition (regardless of whether this fate is destined to be banishment, our own proposal, or something else entirely) seems to depend ultimately on more powerful empirical methods and models of neural computation than now exist. For this reason it is probable that Burt would not withdraw his admonition with respect to this issue. However, if the arguments given here have weakened the apparent a-priori considerations against including the g factor among the phenomena to be encompassed by a complete account of human cognitive evolution, then this chapter will have succeeded in its avowedly negative goals.

References

Ahn, S. M. (1992). *Origin and Differentiation of Domesticated Rice in Asia – A Review of Archaeological and Botanic Evidence.* Unpublished doctoral dissertation, University College London.

Alarcón, M., Plomin, R., Fulker, D. W., Corley, F., and DeFries, J. C. (1999). Multivariate genetic analyses of specific cognitive abilities in parents and their 16-year-old children in the Colorado Adoption Project. *Cognitive Development*, **14**, 175–193.

Bartholomew, D. J. (2004). *Measuring Intelligence: Facts and Fallacies.* Cambridge: Cambridge University Press.

Bloom, P. (2000). *How Children Learn the Meanings of Words.* Cambridge, MA: MIT Press.

Bouchard, T. J., Lykken, D. T., McGue, M., Segal, N. L., and Tellegen, A. (1990). Sources of human individual differences: The Minnesota Study of Twins Reared Apart. *Science*, **250**, 223–228.

Bouchard, T. J. and McGue, M. (2003). Genetic and environmental influences on human psychological differences. *Journal of Neurobiology*, **54**, 4–45.

Brand, C. (1987). The importance of general intelligence. In S. Modgil and C. Modgil (Eds.), *Arthur Jensen: Consensus and Controversy* (pp. 251–265). New York: Falmer.

Brand, C. (1996). *The g Factor: General Intelligence and its Implications*. Chichester, UK: Wiley.

Bürger, R. (2000). *The Mathematical Theory of Selection, Recombination, and Mutation*. Chichester, UK: Wiley.

Burt, C. (1940). *The Factors of the Mind*. London: University of London Press.

Capron, C. and Duyme, M. (1996). Effect of socioeconomic status of biological and adoptive parents on WISC-R subtest scores of their French adopted children. *Intelligence*, **22**, 259–275.

Carroll, J. B. (1993). *Human Cognitive Abilities: A Survey of Factor-Analytic Studies*. Cambridge: Cambridge University Press.

Carroll, J. B. (2003). The higher-stratum structure of cognitive abilities: Current evidence supports g and about ten broad factors. In H. Nyborg (Ed.), *The Scientific Study of General Intelligence: Tribute to Arthur R. Jensen* (pp. 5–21). Oxford: Elsevier.

Chabris, C. F. (2007). Cognitive and neurobiological mechanisms of the Law of General Intelligence. In M. J. Roberts (Ed.), *Integrating the Mind* (pp. 449–491). Hove, UK: Psychology Press.

Chabris, C. F., *et al.* (1998). Does IQ mattter? *Commentary*, **106**, 13–23.

Chomsky, N. (1959). A review of B. F. Skinner's *Verbal Behavior*. *Language*, **35**, 26–58.

Colom, R., Jung, R. E., and Haier, R. J. (2006). Distributed brain sites for the g-factor of intelligence. *NeuroImage*, **31**, 1359–1365.

Cosmides, L. (1989). The logic of social exchange: Has natural selection shaped how humans reason? Studies with the Wason selection task. *Cognition*, **31**, 187–276.

Deaner, R. O., Isler, K., Burkart, J., and van Schaik, C. P. (2007). Overall brain size, and not encephalization quotient, best predicts cognitive ability across non-human primates. *Brain, Behavior and Evolution*, **70**, 115–124.

Deaner, R. O., van Schaik, C. P., and Johnson, V. E. (2006). Do some taxa have better domain-general cognition than others? A meta-analysis of nonhuman primate studies. *Evolutionary Psychology*, **4**, 149–196.

Deary, I. J. (2000). *Looking Down on Human Intelligence: From Psychometrics to the Brain*. Oxford: Oxford University Press.

Dehaene, S. (1997). *The Number Sense: How the Mind Creates Mathematics*. New York: Oxford University Press.

Easton, D. F., Pooley, K. A., Dunning, A. M., Pharoah, P. D. P., Thompson, D., Ballinger, D. G., *et al.* (2007). Genome-wide association study identifies novel breast cancer susceptibility loci. *Nature*, **447**, 1087–1093.

Feldman, M. W. and Lewontin, R. C. (1975). The heritability hang-up. *Science*, **190**, 1163–1168.

Flanagan, J. C., Dailey, J. T., Shaycoft, M. F., Gorham, W. A., Orr, D. B., and Goldberg, I. (1962). *Design for a Study of American Youth*. Boston: Houghton Mifflin.

Fodor, J. A. (1983). *The Modularity of Mind: An Essay on Faculty Psychology*. Cambridge, MA: MIT Press.

Geary, D. C. (2005). *The Origin of Mind: Evolution of Brain, Cognition, and General Intelligence*. Washington, DC: American Psychological Association.

Gignac, G., Vernon, P. A., and Wickett, J. C. (2003). Factors influencing the relationship between brain size and intelligence. In H. Nyborg (Ed.), *The Scientific Study of General Intelligence: Tribute to Arthur R. Jensen* (pp. 93–106). Oxford: Elsevier.

Gottfredson, L. S. (2003). g, jobs, and life. In H. Nyborg (Ed.), *The Scientific Study of General Intelligence: Tribute to Arthur R. Jensen* (pp. 293–342). Oxford: Elsevier.

Gottfredson, L. S. (2007). Innovation, fatal accidents, and the evolution of general intelligence. In M. J. Roberts (Ed.), *Integrating the Mind* (pp. 387–425). Hove, UK: Psychology Press.

Gottfredson, L. S. and Deary, I. J. (2004). Intelligence predicts health and longevity, but why? *Current Directions in Psychological Science*, **13**, 1–4.

Gould, S. J. (1980). *The Panda's Thumb: More Reflections in Natural History*. New York: Norton.

Haldane, J. B. S. (1927). A mathematical theory of natural and artificial selection, part V: Selection and mutation. *Proceedings of the Cambridge Philosophical Society*, **23**, 838–844.

Hamilton, W. D. (1964). The genetical evolution of social behaviour I and II. *Journal of Theoretical Biology*, **7**, 1–52.

Hamilton, W. D. (2001). *Narrow Roads of Gene Land vol. 2 : The Evolution of Sex*. Oxford: Oxford University Press.

Hawks, J. and Cochran, G. M. (2006). Dynamics of adaptive introgression from archaic to modern humans. *PaleoAnthropology*, 101–115.

Hawks, J., Wang, E. T., Cochran, G. M., Harpending, H. C., and Moyzis, R. K. (2007). Recent acceleration of human adaptive evolution. *Procedings of the National Academy of Sciences, USA*, **104**, 20753–20758.

Herrnstein, R. J. and Murray, C. (1994). *The Bell Curve: Intelligence and Class Structure in American Life*. New York: Free Press.

Hill, W. G. (1982). Rates of change in quantitative traits from fixation of new mutations. *Proceedings of the National Academy of Sciences, USA*, **79**, 142–145.

Hill, W. G. and Keightley, P. D. (1988). Interrelations of mutation, population size, artificial and natural selection. In B. S. Weir, E. J. Eisen, M. M. Goodman, and G. Namkoong (Eds.), *Proceedings of the Second International Conference on Quantitative Genetics* (pp. 57–70). Sunderland, MA: Sinauer Associates.

Holt, S. B. (1968). *The Genetics of Dermal Ridges*. Springfield, IL: Charles Thomas.

Houle, D. (1992). Comparing evolvability and variability of quantitative traits. *Genetics*, **130**, 195–204.

Humphreys, L. G. (1994). Intelligence from the standpoint of a (pragmatic) behaviorist. *Psychological Inquiry*, **5**, 179–192.

Jensen, A. R. (1980). Uses of sibling data in educational and psychological research. *American Educational Research Journal*, **17**, 153–170.

Jensen, A. R. (1998). *The g Factor: The Science of Mental Ability*. Westport, CT: Praeger.

Jensen, A. R. (2000). The g factor is about variance in human abilities, not a cognitive theory of mental structure. *Psycholoquy*, **11**, (041).

Jensen, A. R. and Johnson, F. W. (1994). Race and sex differences in head size and IQ. *Intelligence*, **18**, 309–333.

Jensen, A. R. and Sinha, S. N. (1993). Physical correlates of human intelligence. In P. A. Vernon (Ed.), *Biological Approaches to the Study of Human Intelligence* (pp. 139–242). New York: Ablex Publishing.

Jobling, M. A., Hurles, M., and Tyler-Smith, C. (2004). *Human Evolutionary Genetics: Origins, Peoples and Disease*. New York: Garland Science.

Johnson, T. and Barton, N. H. (2005). Theoretical models of selection and mutation on quantitative traits. *Philosophical Transactions of the Royal Society, Series B*, **360**, 1411–1425.

Johnson, V. E., Deaner, R. O., and van Schaik, C. P. (2002). Bayesian analysis of rank data with application to primate intelligence experiments. *Journal of the American Statistical Association*, **97**, 8–17.

Johnson, W., Bouchard, T. J., McGue, M., Segal, N. L., Tellegen, A., Keyes, M., *et al.* (2007). Genetic and environmental influences on the Verbal-Perceptual-Image Rotation (VPR) model of the structure of mental abilities in the Minnesota Study of Twins Reared Apart. *Intelligence*, **35**, 542–562.

Jung, R. E. and Haier, R. J. (2007). The parieto-frontal integration theory (P-FIT) of intelligence: Converging neuroimaging evidence. *Behavioral and Brain Sciences*, **30**, 135–154.

Jung, R. E., Haier, R. J., Yeo, R. A., Rowland, L. M., Petropoulos, H., Levine, A. S., *et al.* (2005). Sex differences in N-acetylaspartate correlates of general intelligence: An 1H-MRS study of normal human brain. *NeuroImage*, **26**, 965–972.

Kacser, H. and Burns, J. A. (1981). The molecular basis of dominance. *Genetics*, **97**, 639–666.

Kanazawa, S. (2004). General intelligence as a domain-specific adaptation. *Psychological Review*, **111**, 512–523.

Kanwisher, N. (2000). Domain specificity in face perception. *Nature Neuroscience*, **3**, 759–763.

Kennerknecht, I., Grueter, T., Welling, B., Wentzek, S., Horst, J., Edwards, S., *et al.* (2006). First report of prevalence of non-syndromic hereditary prosopagnosia (HPA). *American Journal of Medical Genetics Part A*, **140A**, 1617–1622.

Kerje, S., Carlborg, O., Jacobsson, L., Schutz, K., Hartmann, C., Jensen, P., *et al.* (2003). The twofold difference in adult size between the red junglefowl and White Leghorn chickens is largely explained by a limited number of QTLs. *Animal Genetics*, **34**, 264–274.

Kimura, M. (1964). Diffusion models in population genetics. *Journal of Applied Probability*, **1**, 177–232.

Kimura, M. and Crow, J. F. (1978). Effect of overall phenotypic selection on genetic change at 50 individual loci. *Proceedings of the National Academy of Sciences, USA*, **75**, 6168–6171.

Klein, R. G. and Edgar, B. (2002). *The Dawn of Human Culture*. New York: Wiley.

Lee, J. J. (2007). A *g* beyond *Homo sapiens?* Some hints and suggestions. *Intelligence*, **35**, 253–265.

Lein, E. S., Hawrylycz, M. J., Ao, N., Ayres, M., Bensinger, A., Bernard, A., *et al.* (2007). Genome-wide atlas of gene expression in the adult mouse brain. *Nature*, **445**, 168–176.

Li, Z., Pinson, S. R. M., Park, W. D., Paterson, A. H., and Stansel, J. W. (1997). Epistasis for three grain yield components in rice *(Oryza sativa L.)*. *Genetics*, **145**, 453–465.

Loehlin, J. C. (2004). *Latent Variable Models: An Introduction to Factor, Path, and Structural Equation Analysis.* Mahwah, NJ: Lawrence Erlbaum Associates.

Loehlin, J. C., Horn, J. M., and Willerman, L. (1997). Heredity, environment, and IQ in the Texas Adoption Project. In R. J. Sternberg and E. Grigorenko (Eds.), *Intelligence, Heredity and Environment* (pp. 105–125). Cambridge: Cambridge University Press.

Lubinski, D. (2004). Introduction to the special section on cognitive abilities: 100 years after Spearman's 1904 " 'General intelligence,' objectively determined and measured". *Journal of Personality and Social Psychology*, **86**, 96–111.

Luo, D., Petrill, S. A., and Thompson, L. A. (1994). An exploration of genetic g: Hierarchical factor analysis of cognitive data from the Western Reserve Twin Project. *Intelligence*, **18**, 335–347.

Lyman, R. F., Lawrence, F., Nuzhdin, S. V., and Mackay, T. F. C. (1996). Effects of single *P-* element insertions on bristle number and viability in *Drosophila melanogaster*. *Genetics, US*, 277–292.

Lynch, M. and Hill, W. G. (1986). Phenotypic evolution by neutral mutation. *Evolution*, **40**, 915–935.

Lynch, M. and Walsh, B. (1998). *Genetics and Analysis of Quantitative Traits*. Sunderland, MA: Sinauer Associates.

Mackintosh, N. J. (1998). *IQ and Human Intelligence*. New York: Oxford University Press.

MacLullich, A. M. J., Ferguson, K. J., Deary, I. J., Seckl, J. R., Starr, J. M., and Wardlaw, J. M. (2002). Intracranial capacity and brain volumes are associated with cognition in healthy elderly men. *Neurology*, **59**, 169–174.

Markman, E. (1992). Constraints on word learning: Speculations about their nature, origins, and domain specificity. In M. R. Gunnar and M. M. P (Eds.), *Modulary and Constraints on Language and Cognition: The Minnesota Symposium on Child Psychology* (pp. 59–101). Hillsdale, NJ: Lawrence Erlbaum Associates.

Matthews, G., Deary, I. J., and Whiteman, M. C. (2003). *Personality Traits*. Cambridge: Cambridge University Press.

McDaniel, M. A. (2005). Big-brained people are smarter: A meta-analysis of the relationship between in vivo brain volume and intelligence. *Intelligence*, **33**, 337–346.

McDonald, R. P. (1985). *Factor Analysis and Related Methods*. Hillsdale, NJ: Lawrence Erlbaum Associates.

McGue, M., Bouchard, T. J., Iacono, W. G., and Lykken, D. T. (1993). Behavioral genetics of cognitive ability: A life-span perspective. In R. Plomin and G. E. McClearn (Eds.), *Nature, Nurture, and Psychology* (pp. 59–76). Washington, DC: American Psychological Association.

Miller, G. (2000). *The Mating Mind: How Sexual Choice Shaped the Evolution of Human Nature*. New York: Doubleday.

Mousseau, T. A. and Roff, D. A. (1987). Natural selection and the heritability of fitness components. *Heredity*, **59**, 181–197.

Murray, C. (1998). *Income Inequality and IQ*. Washington, DC: AEI Press.

Nagoshi, C. T., Phillips, K., and Johnson, R. C. (1987). Between- versus within-family factor analyses of cognitive abilities. *Intelligence*, **11**, 305–316.

Otto, S. P. and Whitlock, M. C. (1997). The probability of fixation in populations of changing size. *Genetics*, **146**, 723–733.

Pedersen, N. L., Plomin, R., Nesselroade, J. R., and McClearn, G. E. (1992). A quantitative genetic analysis of cognitive abilities during the second half of the life span. *Psychological Science*, **3**, 346–353.

Petrill, S. A., Lipton, P. A., Hewitt, J. K., Plomin, R., Cherny, S. S., Corley, R., *et al.* (2004). Genetic and environmental contributions to general cognitive ability through the first 16 years of life. *Developmental Psychology*, **40**, 805–812.

Pinker, S. (1994). *The Language Instinct: How the Mind Creates Language*. New York: Harper-Collins.

Pinker, S. (1997). *How the Mind Works*. New York: Norton.

Plomin, R., Fulker, D. W., Corley, R., and DeFries, J. C. (1997). Nature, nurture, and cognitive development from 1 to 16 years: A parent-offspring adoption study. *Psychological Science*, **8**, 442–447.

Plomin, R., Kennedy, J. K. J., and Craig, I. W. (2006). The quest for quantitative trait loci associated with intelligence. *Intelligence*, **34**, 513–526.

Posthuma, D., de Geus, E. J. C., Baare, W. F. C., Pol, H. E. H., Kahn, R. S., and Boomsma, D. I. (2002). The association between brain volume and intelligence is of genetic origin. *Nature Neuroscience*, **5**, 83–84.

Raab, M. and Gigerenzer, G. (2004). Intelligence as smart heuristics. In R. J. Sternberg and J. E. Pretz (Eds.), *Cognition and Intelligence: Identifying the Mechanisms of Mind* (pp. 188–207). Cambridge: Cambridge University Press.

Richardson, K. (1999). Demystifying *g*. *Psycholoquy*, **11**, (048).

Rijsdijk, F. V., Vernon, P. A., and Boomsma, D. I. (2002). Application of hierarchical genetic models to Raven and WAIS subtests: A Dutch twin study. *Behavior Genetics*, **32**, 199–210.

Robertson, A. (1960). A theory of limits in artificial selection. *Proceedings of the Royal Society of London, Series B*, **153**, 234–249.

Roff, D. A. (1997). *Evolutionary Quantitative Genetics*. New York: Chapman and Hall.

Sabeti, P. C., Schaffner, S. F., Fry, B., Lohmueller, J., Varilly, P., Shamovsky, O., *et al.* (2006). Positive natural selection in the human lineage. *Science*, **312**, 1614–1620.

Schoenemann, P. T., Budinger, T. F., Sarich, V. M., and Wang, W. S. (2000). Brain size does not predict general cognitive ability within families. *Proceedings of the National Academy of Sciences, USA*, **97**, 4932–4937.

Schull, W. J. and Neel, J. V. (1965). *The Effects of Inbreeding on Japanese Children*. New York: Harper and Row.

Scott, L. J., Mohlke, K. L., Bonnycastle, L. L., Willer, C. J., Li, Y., Duren, W. L., *et al.* (2007). A genome-wide association study of type 2 diabetes in Finns detects multiple susceptibility variants. *Science*, **316**, 1341–1345.

Shaycoft, M. F. (1967). *The High School Years: Growth in Cognitive Skills*. Pittsburgh: American Institutes for Research and School of Education, University of Pittsburgh.

Simmons, M. J. and Crow, J. F. (1977). Mutations affecting fitness in *Drosophila* populations. *Annual Review of Genetics*, **11**, 49–78.

Skinner, B. F. (1957). *Verbal Behavior*. New York: Appleton-Century-Crofts.

Spearman, C. (1904). General intelligence: Objectively determined and measured. *American Journal of Psychology*, **15**, 201–293.

Stanovich, K. E. and West, R. F. (2000). Individual differences in reasoning: Implications for **54** the rationality debate? *Behavioral and Brain Sciences*, **23**, 645–726.

Sternberg, R. J. (1987). Most vocabulary is learned from context. In M. G. McKeown and M. E. Curtis (Eds.), *The Nature of Vocabulary Acquisition* (pp. 89–105). Hillsdale, NJ: Lawrence Erlbaum Associates.

Stone, V. E., Cosmides, L., Tooby, J., Kroll, N., and Knight, R. T. (2002). Selective impairment of reasoning about social exchange in a patient with bilateral limbic system damage. *Proceedings of the National Academy of Sciences, USA*, **99**, 11531–11536.

Striedter, G. F. (2005). *Principles of Brain Evolution*. Sunderland, MA: Sinauer Associates.

Takeda, K. (1990). Heritability for grain size estimated from parent-offspring correlation and selection response. *Japanese Journal of Breeding*, **40**, 313–320.

Tooby, J. and Cosmides, L. (2005). Conceptual foundations of evolutionary psychology. In D. M. Buss (Ed.), *The Handbook of Evolutionary Psychology* (pp. 5–67). Hoboken, NJ: Wiley.

Trivers, R. L. (1971). The evolution of reciprocal altruism. *Quarterly Review of Biology*, **46**, 35–57.

van der Maas, H. L. J., Dolan, C. V., Grasman, R. P. P. P., Wicherts, J. M., Huizenga, H. M., and Raijmakers, M. E. J. (2006). A dynamical model of general intelligence: The positive manifold of intelligence by mutualism. *Psychological Review*, **113**, 842–861.

van Schaik, C. P. (2004). *Among Orangutans: Red Apes and the Rise of Human Culture*. Cambridge, MA: Harvard University Press.

Viaud, G. (1960). *Intelligence: Its Evolution and Forms*. London: Hutchinson.

Wainwright, M., Wright, M. J., Geffen, G. M., Geffen, L. B., Luciano, M., and Martin, N. G. (2004). Genetic and environmental sources of covariance between reading tests used in neuropsychological assessment and IQ subtests. *Behavior Genetics*, **34**, 365–376.

Weedon, M. N., Lettre, G., Freathy, R. M., Lindgren, C. M., Voight, B. F., Perry, J. R. B., *et al.* (2007). A common variant of *HMGA2* is associated with adult and childhood height in the general population. *Nature Genetics*, **39**, 1245–1250.

Wickett, J.C., Vernon, P.A., and Lee, D.H. (2000). Relationships between factors of intelligence and brain volume. *Personality and Individual Differences*, **29**, 1095–1122.

Willerman, L. and Bailey, J.M. (1987). A note on Thomson's sampling theory for correlations among mental tests. *Personality and Individual Differences*, **8**, 943–944.

Wright, S. (1921). Correlation and causation. *Journal of Agricultural Research*, **20**, 557–585.

Zhang, L.C., Ning, Z.H., Xu, G.Y., Hou, Z.C., and Yang, N. (2005). Heritabilities and genetic and phenotypic correlations of egg quality traits in brown-egg dwarf layers. *Poultry Science*, **84**, 1209–1213.

4

Where there is an adaptation, there is a domain: The form-function fit in information processing

H. CLARK BARRETT

Introduction

The study of domain specificity is the study of the fit between the properties of information processing systems and the properties of information that they process. Critical to this enterprise is the fact that information processing systems do not process information randomly. This gives rise to an inevitable relationship: every information processing system does something systematic with information, and that, in turn, delineates a domain. The question of what kind of information a system operates on therefore depends critically on what it does with that information, which in turn depends on its function. This is a version of the idea of "form-function fit" in biology, applied specifically to the realm of information processing, and it is the central tenet of the study of domain specificity as I will define it here.

The rest is in the details. Those details, however, are so critically important in any given case that they make the central tenet almost useless by itself. It is true that mechanisms entail domains. However, nothing follows specifically from this fact about how many adaptations the mind must contain "how specialized" they must be. The answers to those questions depend on particular details of evolutionary history. However, when knowledge of that history is combined with principles of cognitive engineering, the central principle of domain specificity is a powerful tool for the empirical exploration of mind design. The rest of the chapter will be devoted to explaining this principle, showing how it manifests in actual cognitive architecture, and exploring how it can be used as a tool for research.

Foundations in Evolutionary Cognitive Neuroscience, ed. Steven M. Platek and Todd K. Shackelford.
Published by Cambridge University Press. © Cambridge University Press 2009.

The processes that shape organismic architecture

A fundamental fact about evolution is that it is a historical process. "Historical" does not refer to history in the sense that historians use the word but means, at its simplest, that events in evolution are dependent on events that came before. For example, it is a basic fact about natural selection that it can only operate on variation that is present in a population. This might be part of the explanation for why we don't have X-ray vision: no variant of that kind has arisen in evolutionary history, so there was nothing for natural selection to act upon.

More broadly, the historicity of the evolutionary process means that the present state of an organism (like any present physical state) depends on an infinite number of prior events and processes, including but not limited to natural selection. Therefore we, like any organism, have an indefinite number of properties that are due to "accidents," events that were random with respect to the designing process of selection. And a large number of properties of any species exist because of events (selective or not) that happened long before the origin of that species. Our having four limbs is such a property.

There are many processes, then, that shape the course of evolutionary history. Only one process, however, is a *designing process*: natural selection. This is the only process that systematically produces phenotypes, or architectures, that are better designed[1] with respect to fitness than the phenotypes that existed prior to its operation. Other processes contribute to and shape the variation that natural selection acts upon, but do not themselves cause design to evolve. For example, mutation introduces variation into populations – and must therefore be part of the explanation for what exists – but does not systematically introduce *better* variants.

This means that there are many features of organisms, including features of cognitive architecture, that we would not want to invoke selection to explain. But, importantly, all aspects of information processing that exhibit design (that process information in a systematic, functional, goal-directed manner) are either adaptations, parts of adaptations, comprised of adaptations, or the result of adaptations. For example, aspects of the phenotype that are due to learning or adaptive plasticity, such as the ability to play chess, fall into the latter category.

It is important, then, to be clear that when we see information processing that is systematic and well-designed, we are looking at the product of an adaptation. However, this does not answer the question of *what* adaptation is responsible. We might see, for example, well-organized processing of information about chess, but this does not mandate that the adaptation involved is an adaptation *for* chess. To answer the question of what underlying adaptation or adaptations are involved – and what their domain is – we must go deeper into questions of design and the relationship between information-processing design and information structure.

Adaptations imply domains

The central principle of domain specificity is that adaptations imply domains. This is true in two conceptually distinct ways and it is important to distinguish between them, though they will both turn out to be important for a complete understanding of domain specificity.

The first sense is that all adaptations are adaptations *to* something. We should be careful in framing this statement in a proper causal/historical sense, to avoid overly naive interpretations about what an adaptation is "for." Natural selection is a systematic sampling process that involves a large number of events, or design tests. Each of these tests is an interaction between the design, as it currently is, and the environment. The design is put into the environment, like a test vehicle into a wind tunnel, and has a particular amount of success (paid out in the currency of fitness: reproductive success). This success depends on how well the design performs in the environment, which depends on its design features, or relevant properties, interacting with the particulars of the environment in the individual test. Crucially, only some of the properties of the testing environment impact the performance of the tested design, through interaction with it. For example, the density of air in a wind tunnel can affect how well a particular wing design performs.

The fitness results of each of these tests are added up over time, and the result is the outcome of natural selection. The resulting design, then, is *adapted to* a particular set of circumstances, namely, those properties of the test environments, statistically summed, that shaped the eventual design. If we designed airplane wings using wind tunnels that had an average air density and speed, for example, we could say that the resulting wings were *adapted to* air, and in particular, to air of that density and speed (or a statistical distribution around it). This is one meaning of the statement that every adaptation has a domain: every adaptation is tailored to a particular set of circumstances and not others. In this sense, for example, the domain of a dolphin's fin includes certain properties of seawater. It does not include tree branches, and does not include *all* properties of seawater (for example, seawater's light-reflecting properties might not have influenced the evolution of fin shape). Note that the domain, in this sense, is intimately related to, but not the same as, the fin's function, namely, propelling the dolphin through seawater.[2]

There is a second related, but causally much different, sense in which every adaptation entails a domain. The first sense of *domain* defined domains in a causal-historical sense, by referring to the set of circumstances that shaped design. The second sense of *domain* defines it in terms of present properties. This is because the current properties of any object determine how it will interact with the environment, and in the specific case of information-processing mechanisms, the properties of the mechanism determine how it will interact with information, and what kind of information it can interact with.

Some of this will be due to how information is routed to the mechanism by the brain, and some of this will be due to features of the mechanism itself that determine what information it accepts. Barrett (2005) defined these two different ways that information can be selected for processing as access specificity and processing specificity, respectively. For example, auditory mechanisms presumably process auditory information and not other kinds of information at least in part because this information is selectively routed to them by the hearing system (access specificity). But it can also be the case that some mechanisms are selectively sensitive to, or perhaps only capable of processing, information of a certain kind, even when exposed to many kinds (processing specificity). One can imagine, for example, a mechanism that is exposed to all kinds of auditory information, but is only sensitive to information that has certain properties that are characteristic of speech. Marcus, Fernandes, and Johnson (2007), for example, have found evidence for a mechanism in infants that detects statistical regularities in sound patterns, but only when they learn those patterns from speech and not, for example, sequences of musical tones.

It is not difficult to see how the same physical properties of a mechanism that cause it to perform its computations also determine what it will and won't process. A coin-sorting machine computes in a causally transparent fashion, using a system of chutes and holes of different sizes. Because of how it sorts coins, the sorter can't sort oranges or footballs, and indeed, won't even accept them. A property that is less often noticed is that it will also "carry through" certain information without changing it (Barrett, 2005). For example, if it is designed to sort dimes from nickels by size, it might treat dimes the same as similarly sized non-dime objects, such as dime-sized washers or coins from another country. In other words, it does not discriminate between dimes and pseudo-dimes: the outputs with regard to dimes and pseudo-dimes are unchanged from the inputs. In this very important sense, the sorter *has not processed* the dime vs. pseudo-dime information at all. It is as if the mechanism wasn't there. In a precise technical sense, the dime/pseudo-dime distinction is not within its domain.[3]

The important point here is that the nature of the information the mechanism processes is a direct consequence of how it does its computations, "… computations – it is determined by the causal properties of the machinery involved – and …" and this is true of any mechanism of any kind. This is the second, important meaning of the statement that every mechanism inevitably has a domain.

Proper vs. actual domains

The two senses of domain described above map closely onto what is perhaps the most important distinction to be made in understanding domain specificity: the distinction between *proper* and *actual* domains (Sperber, 1994).

The proper domain of an evolved mechanism is the domain of information that the mechanism was designed, by selection, to process. For example, there is evidence for a mechanism in the visual system designed to detect snakes (Öhman, Flykt, and Esteves, 2001). The proper domain of this mechanism is snakes, and this maps onto the first, causal-historical, sense of domains described above.[4]

The actual domain of an evolved mechanism is the domain of information that the mechanism will actually process. This maps onto the second sense of domain described above, the domain delineated by the physical properties of the mechanism. When the properties of information cause that information to be processed by a mechanism – whether or not that information is of a type the mechanism was designed to process – it is said to satisfy the mechanism's input conditions. The design features of a mechanism *entail* that it will process some kinds of information that it was not designed to process. This is an inevitable consequence of the causal nature of computational devices: their actual domains will be broader than their proper domains.

For example, a coin sorter might sort nickels from dime-sized washers even though it wasn't designed to deal with dime-sized washers. In the case of a snake detection mechanism, it might be triggered by objects that sufficiently resemble snakes; for example, horses are commonly startled by objects such as twisted branches or garden hoses. The fact that the actual domain of a mechanism is broader than its proper domain will inevitably result in phenomena such as false positives, as in the snake/garden hose case. If these mistakes impact fitness, then selection will begin to tune the parameters of the mechanism (Haselton and Buss, 2000). However, every mechanism entails a class of potential stimuli that it would process, but that have not yet been encountered by selection.

The distinction between proper and actual domains is of critical importance in discussions about what a mechanism is "for." In some debates about domain specificity these two meanings have been conflated (is a coin sorter for sorting coins, or for discriminating between discs of diameter X and diameter Y?), and this has resulted in unnecessary confusion.

Content domains and formal domains

Sometimes domain specificity is defined as specialization to deal with particular information "content" (e.g., see Hirschfeld and Gelman, 1994). The word "content" itself is typically not defined, but it often refers, roughly, to the "meaning" of the information, what it is "about," or what category of thing in the world it pertains to. For example, mechanisms designed to handle information about faces (Kanwisher, McDermott, and Chun, 1997), mental states (Baron-Cohen, 1995; Leslie, 1994), and social contracts (Cosmides, 1989) are often given as paradigm cases of domain-specific mechanisms.

From the strict functionalist/computational view I am advocating here, however, "content," in the sense I have glossed above, is invisible to any mechanism. Mechanisms simply operate causally, on the properties of information presented to them, and do not know what it is about. As described above, the process of natural selection engineers the properties of mechanisms so that they are sensitive to features of information that impacted fitness in past environments. Some mechanisms become tailored to particular "content" domains in the way we think of them, for example, faces, or animals, or food. However, "tailored to" has a very specific meaning here: the mechanism might have a perceptual interface that causes it to *reliably pick out* items of a particular category, such as faces or food, but it still must use some formal property to do so (e.g., a particular configuration of features in the case of faces; Morton and Johnson, 1991). If we had a complete causal account of the actual domain of any mechanism, it would be specified in terms of formal properties, not content.

A metaphor might be useful here. A person who designs a coin sorter might design it to sort nickels from dimes. The "content" that it is designed for is therefore nickels and dimes, and not dime-sized washers. A human observer who uses the device to sort coins knows this too. But does the coin sorter itself "know" that it is designed for coins? Of course not. And this has a functional manifestation: because it can't distinguish dimes from pseudo-dimes, it will treat them the same way, as a consequence of its computational design features. So facts about the "content" that the machine was designed for are historical facts about the designing process, not properties of the machine itself. The resulting machine bears an *imprint* of the content it was designed to process, in the form of design features that leverage or exploit features of the proper domain, coins. But these leveraged features are, and must be, formal properties.

This is not to say that evolved mechanisms cannot be extremely precise at picking out particular types of thing in the world. There is evidence, for example, that the face recognition mechanism is very successful at picking out just faces, even when presented with stimuli that are similar to faces on various formal dimensions (Duchaine *et al.*, 2006). This suggests that it is using some combination of formal properties in a way that we have not yet fully discovered.

But even the simple case of the coin sorter, which uses only size and shape, illustrates an important point about the form-function fit between evolved formal input conditions and the properties of real-world "content" domains. This fit is a "leveraging" relationship in which the input conditions are tuned so that they select the right information when the current environment is sufficiently similar to the historical environment along the right dimensions. Some dimensions, and some information properties, matter more than others. In fact, two general principles can be inferred from the way input conditions are shaped.

First, dimensions of variation that were not important in fitness terms, or that did not exist, in ancestral environments are often invisible to the mechanism. For example, if dime-sized washers were sufficiently common in environments where coin sorters might be deployed – such as vending machines – one might expect engineers to design some mechanism for excluding them. If they are not common, however, then the dime/washer distinction is not engineered into the system.

Second, if in historical environments multiple types of information were available that the mechanism could leverage to do its job, and if these types of information were in some way redundant, the mechanism might evolve to use an efficient *subset* of the available information. This follows from the fact that evolution entails tradeoffs, and if use of lots of information involves costs that are not offset by corresponding fitness benefits, less information will be used (Gigerenzer and Todd, 1999). For example, our coin sorter uses a simple heuristic, size, to discriminate between coins, and ignores other properties. It turns out that another property – which President's face is on the coin – is 100% correlated with the size difference between nickels and dimes, but this information is not only entirely redundant, it is harder to engineer a system to detect it than to simply detect diameter.

The fact that evolved mechanisms use formal properties that have been tuned by selection to leverage features of their proper domain matters for how evolved mechanisms actually operate, and for how we interpret data about them. Consider, for example, mechanisms for kin detection in humans. There is evidence that such mechanisms exist, and that they use coresidence during childhood as a cue to "detect" genetic relatives (Fessler and Navarrete,

2004; Lieberman, Tooby, and Cosmides, 2007).[5] I use "detect" in quotes here because this design feature is thought to leverage a property of ancestral environments, namely, that children tended to live with genetic relatives. Using coresidence as a cue is a good bet – it was a valid cue to kinship in ancestral environments. The kinship detection mechanism, in turn, causes certain changes in disposition with regard to detected kin: for example, it causes them to become unappealing as sexual partners (Wolf, 1995). There are two important points that follow from the fact that the mechanism uses formal properties and not "content" in the sense of *actual* kinship. The first is that the mechanism can make mistakes: sexual attraction is also downregulated towards coresiding non-kin (technically, a fitness mistake, since the device is designed to exclude kin only). The second is that the mechanism does not "know" that it is about kinship, and the individuals whose behavior it regulates need not know this either.

Are there domain-general adaptations?

In discussions of domain specificity, questions often arise about the relationship between domain-specific and domain-general adaptations. Do domain-general adaptations exist? If so, how much of the mind is domain specific, and how much is domain general?

The answer depends on what definition of domain one is using. By "domain general," most psychologists are referring to mechanisms that can be applied to a wide range of problems. In this sense, domain-general adaptations clearly exist, and the mind is therefore a mixture of domain-specific and domain-general mechanisms. However, even on this construal of domain generality, the question of just "how specialized" or "how generalized" the mind is overall is an empirical question that we still don't have the answer to, because the work of discovering and describing all of the mind's mechanisms is not yet done.

I have advocated a view of domain specificity according to which all mechanisms have a proper domain, by virtue of their evolutionary history, and an actual domain, by virtue of the information processing properties they have. In this sense, all evolved mechanisms are domain specific. This usage differs from conventional usage by psychologists, for two reasons: first, as I have stressed, mechanisms do not possess domains to varying degrees; and second, the notion that "narrowness" of domains can be arrayed along a single dimension is misleading.

How do we reconcile the formal definition of domains I have proposed, in which every mechanism has a domain, with the observation that some adaptations seem to be more narrowly "targeted" than others? In doing so it is important to be clear about a key distinction: the distinction between the breadth of information for which a mechanism might be deployed, and the fit between the properties of the information and the nature of the processing. One mechanism might use a wider "breadth" of possible information than another, on some criterion, but this does not necessarily mean that the one mechanism is less specialized than the other. To take just one example, a camera that can film in both visible and infrared light is not necessarily less specialized than one that can only film in visible light, though its domain is broader.

The evolution of traits always entails tradeoffs. As described above, natural selection is a kind of titration or tuning process that selects between available designs based on their different fitness effects. In information processing and the regulation of behavior, particular kinds of tradeoffs will be involved depending on the function of the mechanism. For example, in problems of signal detection, there will be tradeoffs involved in tuning the parameters of the mechanism to minimize different types of error. Decreasing one type of error will result in increasing others. The balance that is selected will depend on the fitness effects of these different types of error (Haselton and Buss, 2000).

Similarly, evolutionists often speak of tradeoffs between specialization and generalization. Broadly, being a generalist means that more problems can be handled, but particular problems are usually handled less well than specialists tailored to each problem could handle them.

Given such tradeoffs, what determines where the break-even point of fitness will lie, along the specialization-generalization continuum? Clearly, it depends on the details of the case. But one can imagine various general principles. For example, if there is a common solution that holds across a range of problem types, it is possible for a mechanism to evolve that implements the solution, but that does not have, as part of its proper domain, something that distinguishes *between* the different problem types to which it applies. It would, however, still need to have properties that cause it to detect the class of problems where it applies.

There are a variety of information-processing solutions that have been proposed that solve problems that are specific in nature, but that hold across a variety of problem types. There are learning algorithms, for example, that might have broad applicability. Gallistel and Gibbon (2000), for example, proposed that many learning problems in behavioral decision-making that were thought to be solved by an associative learning mechanism might actually be solved by a more computationally specialized time series learning algorithm. Gigerenzer, Todd, and colleagues (Gigerenzer and Todd,1999; Gigerenzer and Goldstein, 1996) have proposed a variety of decision-making heuristics or algorithms, such as "Take The Best," which depend on the cue structure of information that might hold widely across many information types (in the case of Take The Best, noncompensatory cue structures; Gigerenzer and Goldstein, 1996).

Such mechanisms are "domain general" in the sense that they can be applied across many information types. They also seem to disregard "content" in the intuitive sense, because they can handle information that is "about" a wide range of things. But these mechanisms are specialized, have algorithms that are precisely tailored to handle a specific information-processing problem, and do have both proper and actual domains. If Take The Best is an evolved mechanism, for example, then there was a set of evolutionary circumstances, all of which involved non-compensatory cue structures, that caused the mechanism to evolve. Its procedures are tailored to the structure of its proper domain, namely, non-compensatory cue structures. And if it is actually deployed in cognition, it must have an actual domain: there must be some set of properties that determine when it will be applied and when it will not be.

The nature of specialization, then, is heterogeneous. Different adaptations are specialized in different ways, some of which cause them to deal with "broad" swaths of information, and others narrower, depending on what kinds of problems they are designed to solve. However, it is a mistake to think of specialization vs. generalization as a single dimension along which mechanisms can be arrayed. Think of the organs of the body: heart, kidney, liver, spleen, lungs are all specialized, but it is difficult to say which has a "broader" or "narrower" domain. Is pumping blood narrower or broader than detoxifying it? Problem space has high dimensionality, and the dimensions of specialization of different systems are often orthogonal rather than overlapping. Only when there is a shared dimension does it really make sense, conceptually, to talk about broader or narrower domains.

As Barrett and Kurzban (2006) have argued, once the domain of a mechanism or system has been properly defined in formal terms, debates about whether it is "domain specific" or "domain general" become moot. Edge detectors in the visual system have the domain of visual edges, and speech parsers in the auditory system have the domain of language features in the speech signal. There is no reason why we need to try to line up these apples and oranges along a single dimension of specificity/generality.

On the issue of domain-general mechanisms there is one final distinction that is of critical importance: the distinction between domain-general *mechanisms* and domain-general *principles*. It is important to remember that the concept of domains as evolutionary psychologists use it applies to evolved information-processing mechanisms, not just "psychological phenomena" in general. There may be elements of information-processing design – for example, information-processing principles – that are shared across systems, without being the same *mechanism* per se. For example, many processes, such as visual processes, motor control, and inductive learning and reasoning, may use some form of Bayesian updating (Körding and Wolpert, 2006; Tenenbaum, Griffiths, and Kemp, 2006; Yuille and Kersten, 2006). However, this does not mean that there is a single Bayesian "mechanism" that operates across these domains. Rather, Bayesian updating could be a principle or solution that has been engineered into multiple systems. If we called Bayesian updating "domain general," then we would want to be clear that we do not mean it in the sense of a domain-general *mechanism*.

Reconciling flexibility with domain specificity

Living things are clearly flexible, in a biologically relevant way. Not only do they do different things depending on the circumstances, but the things they do in a particular circumstance are often better suited to that circumstance, in fitness terms, than what they might have done in other circumstances. It has been argued that humans, in particular, are masters of flexibility, and that there are features of our brains that make us more flexible than any other organism.

It is sometimes held that domain specificity is incompatible with flexibility. Sometimes this is even framed as a kind of tradeoff: to the degree that an organism or mechanism is specialized, then it is inflexible to that same degree.

Hopefully it is clear by now that on the view of domain specificity I have described here, this does not follow. To take a simple example, even a mechanism that has been selected for flexibility as a main part of its design, such as a learning algorithm, can only succeed if its information processing features are tailored to the learning problem at hand (e.g., time series learning, Bayesian updating). Beyond that, however, flexibility of some kind or other is part of the solution to almost every adaptive problem, from foraging to finding mates to learning language, and so there will be few evolved mechanisms that do not have flexibility as part of their design. Finally, it is the case that mechanisms that have not been selected "for" flexibility per se will nevertheless inevitably have a degree of flexibility that is afforded by their design features and the nature of their proper domain.

In discussions of flexibility it is important to keep in mind that flexibility is not a "thing." It is not like a substance that mechanisms can possess to varying degrees. Instead, it is a property that is *afforded* by the design features of a mechanism, and can be afforded in many different ways. For example, the Take The Best algorithm is "flexible" in just the same sense that it is domain general: it can be deployed across a wide range of information types, as long as they have noncompensatory cue structure (Gigerenzer and Goldstein, 1996). A learning algorithm, such as a Bayesian updating algorithm, is flexible in the sense that it is designed to modify the weights on some other, decision-making algorithm in a systematic way. Finally, even a classic domain-specific mechanism like the mechanism that determines diet breadth in foraging has flexibility as an intrinsic part of its design in the sense that it must learn particular parameters such as caloric value of specific foods and their encounter rates in the environment (Stephens and Krebs, 1986).[6] In each of these cases, flexibility comes as a result of how the mechanism is designed. This is always the case: flexibility in the biologically relevant sense, e.g., fitness-promoting as opposed to fitness-random flexibility, can only be the result of design features that have been shaped by natural selection. There are many kinds of flexibility, each tailored to a particular kind of problem, even if the problem is very "broad," such as learning time series (Gallistel and Gibbon, 2000).

An important question is how evolved mechanisms can deal with "novel" stimuli. In its most relevant sense, this means stimuli that have not been encountered over evolutionary time.

Here we must revisit the concept of a proper domain, and of the relationship between a mechanism's design features (and, therefore, its actual domain) and its proper domain. Recall that strictly speaking, the proper domain of a mechanism is never a type or class of stimuli or events, but rather, a historical set of circumstances that shaped the mechanism. To make this clear, we might say that the proper domain of a face recognition mechanism is faces, but we should remember that any particular face that the mechanism handles, now, is, technically, evolutionarily novel. George W. Bush's face, for example, is unique, and did not exist prior to his birth. When recognizing Bush's face, then, my face recognition system is handling an evolutionarily novel stimulus. In fact, *all* stimuli that my brain handles are evolutionarily novel. If my brain is composed entirely of mechanisms that evolved in past environments, how is this possible?

The answer, which is the general answer to how all adaptive flexibility is possible, is that there were regularities in the structure of past environments which continue to be true today. Face recognition mechanisms evolved because human faces existed in ancestral environments and there was a fitness advantage in being able to distinguish between them. A system evolved with at least two properties: first, it leveraged the *common* features of faces to be able to detect them, and second, it leveraged the dimensions along which faces *vary* to build a system that could use the relevant dimensions of variation to learn to discriminate between individual faces. Bush's face both shares the relevant common features of other faces and falls within the system's range of variation that allows his face to be learned and discriminated.[7]

The case with other systems that deal adaptively with evolutionarily novel stimuli is no different in principle, though the details of course vary, as they do with all adapted systems. If a learning system is capable of learning the "right" thing in an evolutionarily novel circumstance, it is because the structure of that learning environment matches the structure of ancestral learning environments along the relevant dimensions.

This is why, for example, it is not problematic that forks can be handled by our visual system, even though forks did not exist in ancestral environments. The visual system is composed of many adaptations, and for each adaptation that can handle forks, it is true that forks have properties that match the properties of that adaptation's proper domain along the relevant dimensions, and the dimensions along which forks vary from ancestral objects are within the range of variation that the system can handle. This is true for mechanisms with diverse proper domains that handle forks: the edge of a fork tine can be handled by the edge detectors in early visual processing, and properties of a fork cause it to be handled by systems designed to represent the properties of hand-held objects for motor processing.

Evolutionarily novel stimuli, then, are the norm rather than the exception for evolved systems: every object or situation encountered is new in its details. Environmental variability is therefore something that evolution inevitably has to deal with. The relevant questions are, along what parameters does the environment vary and not vary, and how does this permit the engineering of mechanisms that systematically exploit the variances and invariances? Contrary to some arguments, variable environments do not render impossible the evolution of domain-specific mechanisms, be they mechanisms for finding food or mates, recognizing conspecifics, or learning skills. The relevant question for psychological research is how the design features of the mechanism help it to solve its adaptive problem in a flexible way. In every case that is solved by an evolved system, there must be a mapping between the present problem structure and the ancestral problem structure that makes the solution possible.

I have suggested that the only processes that find solutions to problems are either natural selection itself, or cognitive processes shaped by natural selection to do so. While this is broadly true, there is an important, solution-finding subcategory of the evolutionary process that is important to mention: cultural evolution (Boyd and Richerson, 1985). Among the processes of cultural evolution is a cultural analog of genetic natural selection which has the same hill-climbing property as genetic natural selection, in that it selects between cultural variants and, in a ratchet-like fashion, results over time in the evolution of complex cultural solutions to problems. Cultural artifacts like tools, houses, and food preparation techniques are examples (Richerson and Boyd, 2005). It is important to take into account this potential source of solutions to problems. Clearly, these solutions will depend on some interaction between culturally transmitted information and evolved mechanisms that acquire and use it. How this interaction works in specific cases is a growing area of research (Tomasello *et al.*, 2005).

Directions for future research

This chapter has presented some basic principles and a framework for understanding domain specificity. On this view, the nature of adaptive speciali-zation, and therefore of domains, is heterogeneous. Nevertheless, every adapta-tion has both a proper domain and an actual domain. These two ideas point to several complementary avenues of future research on domain specificity.

The first is that the work of describing the heterogeneous assemblage of adaptations that comprise the mind is far from done. In fact, we probably know far more about it than is generally considered to be the case, because many researchers are studying domain-specific adaptations either without knowing that they are doing so or without explicitly representing that they are doing so in the presentation of their work. Moreover, for various reasons, including sociological factors and intuitions about what counts as "content," a circumscribed set of phenomena has become associated with the label "domain specific," but the actual set, according to the criteria I have offered here, is probably much larger.

If one were to ask a psychologist to list the domain-specific adaptations they know about, they might mention a list that would include mate choice mechan-isms (Buss, 1989), mechanisms involved in cheater detection and other aspects of cooperation (Cosmides, 1989), face recognition mechanisms (Duchaine *et al.*, 2006; Kanwisher *et al.*, 1997), mechanisms involved in mindreading, or "theory of mind" (Baron-Cohen, 1995; Leslie, 1994), mechanisms underlying intuitive physics (Baillargeon, 2004; Spelke, 2000), language acquisition and production mechanisms (Pinker, 1994), kin detection mechanisms (Fessler and Navarrete, 2004; Lieberman *et al.*, 2007), and mechanisms related to specific emotions like disgust, fear, and jealousy (Buss *et al.*, 1992; Öhman and Mineka, 2001; Rozin, Haidt, and McCauley, 1993).

However, I have pointed to other mechanisms that are likely to have an evolved function and to have specific input conditions for the type of informa-tion that they process. Gallistel and Gibbon (2000), for example, have suggested that many phenomena thought to be explained by a very general "associative learning" mechanism are in fact better accounted for by a mechanism dedicated specifically to time series learning, and that has specific input criteria. Another phenomenon that is also thought of by psychologists as a paradigm case of domain generality is working memory. Baddeley (1986) has proposed that working memory is comprised of distinct subsystems, each of which is functionally specialized to handle a particular information format, and all of which have formal constraints on information processing. Repovs and Baddeley (2006) present evidence that working memory contains at least three subsystems, the visuospatial sketchpad, the phonological loop, and the episodic buffer. These are specialized to handle visuospatial information, phonological information, and an integrated representation of both types, respectively. They have buffers that impose limits on the amount and format of information they can handle. The existence of such constraints has been known for some time, for example, in Miller's (1956) classic finding that "seven plus or minus two" chunks of information can be handled at a time. While this finding has been revised, and "content" effects have been shown in that how items are chunked matters – the basic finding that working memory has substantial format constraints that are related to its function is still valid (Cowan, 2001).

There are many other examples of such findings that are not often considered under the rubric of evolved specializations whose design features delineate a domain. Another example is substantial work showing two pathways in the visual system, one for information about *what* an object is and another for information about *where* it is, two clearly functionally specialized subsystems with proprietary information formats (Haxby *et al.*, 1991; Ungerleider and Haxby, 1994). Existing data on brain systems alone would be enough to greatly expand our catalog of specialized brain systems. However, there is also much – arguably, more – that we don't yet know. Expanding our catalog of the specialized information-processing adaptations of which the brain is comprised should therefore be a major goal for future research.

Another major goal follows from the observation that every evolved cognitive mechanism has both a proper and an actual domain. Currently, even for mechanisms that are relatively well-studied, one or both of these is underspecified. Often, it is the actual domain that is more poorly understood, because the task of coming up with the correct description of the properties of information that cause it to be processed by a mechanism is a difficult one. This has perhaps been done most rigorously in the study of vision, from low-level mechanisms such as edge detectors to higher-level mechanisms such as object recognition mechanisms (Palmer, 1999). Here, the properties of actual domains are often discovered empirically, and the proper domain is inferred from that (e.g., edges).

In other cases, we have a good bet about the proper domain of a mechanism, but the properties of the actual domain – what properties cause information to be processed – have not been fully described. Face recognition is a good example. It has long been known that faces are processed by the facial fusiform area of the fusiform gyrus, or FFA (Kanwisher *et al.*, 1997), but there has been much debate and empirical work on whether the area processes faces alone, or some broader set of stimuli that includes faces (Gauthier *et al.*, 2000;). There is now mounting evidence that the FFA is indeed specialized for faces alone (McKone, Kanwisher, and Duchaine, 2007; Duchaine *et al.*, 2006). However, while we know about some of the cues that are important in face processing (e.g., Morton and Johnson, 1991), we still do not have a complete description of the formal properties that allow the system to recognize faces in particular. The same is true for many other systems where we have some evidence about the proper domain: for example, there are mechanisms that appear specific to speech processing (Marcus *et al.*, 2007), but we often do not have a complete description of the properties that cause the mechanism to recognize a particular sound pattern as speech. This can be a difficult task, because an accurate informational description of the actual domain might be quite complex.

A final and important avenue for future work on domain specificity will be to elucidate not only the formal description of the input domain of a system, but also a complete formal description of its procedures, or what it does with the information that is being processed. Again, this is known in certain cases, such as in vision, and there are also good models of the actual algorithms used in area of "higher" cognition like categorization and decision-making. But in many cases, research on domain specificity is considered complete once it has been established that the phenomenon is specific to a particular domain. However, as I have tried to stress here, *what* information is used by a mechanism is intimately related to *how* it uses that information. By studying in tandem both the input domains and procedures of evolved mechanisms, we will come much closer to a fuller understanding of the form-function fit in cognition.

Conclusion

In this chapter I have attempted to sketch an account of domain specificity that is based on logical rather than intuitive principles. In so doing, I am aware that I am using the term "domain specific" in ways that differ from how it is frequently used by many psychologists. I have tried to show where these different usages overlap and diverge, especially in the section on the domain-specific/domain-general distinction, and to acknowledge that there are elements of the domain-specific/domain-general distinction that make sense. However, I have also tried to argue that treating specificity/generality as a single linear dimension is a mistake that does not map well onto the heterogeneity of adaptive specialization that we see in the mind and in other aspects of the phenotype. To some extent, our strong intuition that some things are specialized and others not is an illusion that reflects our ignorance about the specific structural properties that are necessary for a mechanism to do its job. A mechanism that recognizes only elephants would certainly seem intuitively and obviously narrowly specialized. A mechanism that does a Fourier transform or a time series analysis might seem more "general" to us, but that is more a matter of intuition or definition than some actual property of the world or the mechanism, since a mechanism that carries out Fourier transforms must presumably be a specialized and well-tuned piece of cognitive equipment indeed.

In discussions about domain specificity it is important to remember that some issues are issues of definition, and disagreements that come down to differing opinions about how words should be defined are, in the long run, trivial and unnecessary. The establishment of conventions of word use solves this easily. However, when there are real underlying conceptual issues that are being obscured, that is a genuine problem. The main conceptual misunderstanding that I have hoped to address here is the mistaken notion that some mechanisms are "general" in either the sense that they don't have a specific function, or that they have no domain (or that their domain includes "everything"). Mechanisms are specialized to do different things, but if they are adaptations, then our goal should be to come up with a description of their function and of the structure that allows them to carry out that function. Once we have done this, we will have an exact description of where they fall in the high-dimensional space of cognitive specialization, and placing them on a one-dimensional specialized/generalized continuum will then be unnecessary.

Notes

1. Here I use the concept of *design* in the shorthand sense often used by biologists and described by Dawkins (1986), not in the sense of design by an intentional agent.

2. It is a logical necessity that every adaptation must have a historical domain, or set of conditions to which it was adapted. Whether we can come up with the correct description of those conditions is another matter. These have been conceptually folded together in some arguments about domain specificity, and it is important to keep them distinct.

3. This example shows how important it is to think rigorously about the *computational* properties of a system, and not to fixate on spatial metaphors for modules as boxes or pipes. For example, dimes and pseudo-dimes "pass through" a coin sorter, so they literally "enter" as inputs, but because the distinction is invisible to the mechanism, it is not computed. The point is that whether the information "gets into" the module is not relevant: it is that the dime/pseudo-dime distinction is not part of the computational domain of the mechanism.

4. Note that if we are being rigorous, the proper domain is a historically encountered set of events or properties of events, not

a "type." In other words, technically the proper domain is not just "snakes" or "information about snakes," but a specific set of snakes encountered in the past. In practice, however, this is usually glossed and described as a type of some kind, e.g., "snakes," and so might include snake species that humans never encountered. This usually doesn't matter much except, as we will see, in discussions about mechanisms that deal with evolutionarily "novel" stimuli.

5. In fact, there is evidence for kinship detection mechanisms in other mammal species that also use coresidence as a cue, e.g., in mice (Yamazaki et al., 1988). The system might therefore have been present in the common ancestor of humans and mice, and both species possess modified forms of this ancestral system. Interestingly, coresidence is not the only cue that is used to detect kinship: for example, the major histocompatibility complex, MHC, appears to play a role, and MHC has formal properties that make it diagnostic of kinship (Penn and Potts, 1999). However, use of the MHC system itself appears to be tuned by the initial cue of coresidence (Yamazaki et al., 1988).

6. Foraging mechanisms are also flexible in that there is evidence that they can be applied in situations other than food foraging when the formal properties of those situations are similar enough to food foraging, e.g., foraging for information on the internet (Pirolli and Card, 1999), or in a computer game (Hutchinson, Wilke, and Todd, in press).

7. In fact, the system's design features will make it so that it is "flexible" enough to handle non-face items that fall within its actual domain because they are similar enough to faces along the relevant dimensions, e.g., computer-generated faces, wooden masks, etc.

References

Baddeley, A. D. (1986). *Working Memory*. Oxford, UK: Clarendon Press.

Baillargeon, R. (2004). Infants' physical world. *Current Directions in Psychological Science*, **13**, 89–94.

Baron-Cohen, S. (1995). *Mindblindness*. Cambridge, MA: MIT Press.

Barrett, H. C. (2005). Enzymatic computation and cognitive modularity. *Mind and Language*, **20**, 259–287.

Barrett, H. C. and Kurzban, R. (2006). Modularity in cognition: Framing the debate. *Psychological Review*, **113**, 628–647.

Boyd, R. and Richerson, P. (1985). *Culture and the Evolutionary Process*. Chicago: University of Chicago Press.

Buss, D. M. (1989). Sex differences in human mate preferences: Evolutionary hypotheses tested in 37 cultures. *Behavioral and Brain Sciences*, **12**, 1–49.

Buss, D. M., Larsen, R. J., Westen, D., and Semmelroth, J. (1992). Sex differences in jealousy: Evolution, physiology, and psychology. *Psychological Science*, **3**, 251–255.

Cosmides, L. (1989). The logic of social exchange: Has natural selection shaped how humans reason? Studies with the Wason selection task. *Cognition*, **31**, 187–278.

Cowan, N. (2001). The magical number 4 in short-term memory: A reconsideration of mental storage capacity. *Behavioral and Brain Sciences*, **24**, 87–185.

Dawkins, R. (1986). *The Blind Watchmaker*. New York: Norton.

Duchaine, B., Yovel, G., Butterworth, E., and Nakayama, K. (2006). Prosopagnosia as an impairment to face-specific mechanisms: Elimination of the alternative hypotheses in a developmental case. *Cognitive Neuropsychology*, **23**, 714–747.

Fessler, D. M. T. and Navarrete, C. D. (2004). Third-party attitudes toward sibling incest: Evidence for Westermarck's hypotheses. *Evolution and Human Behavior*, **25**, 277–294.

Gallistel, C. R. and Gibbon, J. (2000). Time, rate and conditioning. *Psychological Review*, **107**, 289–344.

Gauthier, I., Skudlarski, P., Gore, J. C., and Anderson, A. W. (2000). Expertise for cars and birds recruits brain areas involved in face recognition. *Nature Neuroscience*, **3**, 191–197.

Gigerenzer, G. and Goldstein, D. G. (1996). Reasoning the fast and frugal way: Models of bounded rationality. *Psychological Review*, **103**, 650–669.

Gigerenzer, G. and Todd, P. M. (1999). Fast and frugal heuristics: The adaptive toolbox. In Gigerenzer, G., Todd, P. M., and the ABC Research Group (Eds.), *Simple Heuristics That Make Us Smart* (pp. 3–34). New York: Oxford University Press.

Haselton, M. G. and Buss, D. M. (2000). Error management theory: A new perspective on biases in cross-sex mind reading. *Journal of Personality and Social Psychology*, **78**, 81–91.

Haxby, J. V., Grady, C. L., Horwitz, B., Ungerleider, L. G., Mishkin, M., Carson, R. E., Herscovitch, P., Schapiro, M. B., and Rapoport, S. I. (1991). Dissociation of object and spatial visual processing pathways in human extrastriate cortex. *Proceedings of the National Academy of Sciences*, **88**, 1621–1625.

Hirschfeld, L. A. and Gelman, S. A. (1994). Toward a topography of mind: An introduction to domain specificity. In L. A. Hirschfeld and S. A. Gelman (Eds.), *Mapping the Mind: Domain Specificity in Cognition and Culture*. New York: Cambridge University Press.

Hutchinson, J. M. C., Wilke, A., and Todd, P. M. (in press). Patch leaving in humans: Can a generalist adapt its rules to dispersal of items across patches? *Animal Behaviour*.

Kanwisher, N., McDermott, J., and Chun, M. M. (1997). The fusiform face area: A module in human extrastriate cortex specialized for face perception. *Journal of Neuroscience*, **17**, 4302–4311.

Körding, K. P. and Wolpert, D. M. (2006). Bayesian decision theory in sensorimotor control. *Trends in Cognitive Sciences*, **10**, 319–326.

Lieberman, D., Tooby, J., and Cosmides, L. (2007). The architecture of human kin detection. *Nature*, **445**, 727–731.

Leslie, A. M. (1994). ToMM, ToBy, and agency: Core architecture and domain specificity. In Hirschfeld, L. A. and Gelman, S. A., (Eds.), *Mapping the Mind: Domain Specificity in Cognition and Culture* (pp. 119–148). Cambridge, UK: Cambridge University Press.

Marcus, G. F., Fernandes, K. J., and Johnson, S. P. (2007). Infant rule learning facilitated by speech. *Psychological Science*, **18**, 387–391.

McKone, E., Kanwisher, N., and Duchaine, B. C. (2007). Can generic expertise explain special processing for faces? *Trends in Cognitive Sciences*, **11**, 8–15.

Miller, G. A. (1956). The magical number seven, plus or minus two: Some limits on our capacity for processing information. *Psychological Review*, **63**, 81–97.

Morton, J. and Johnson, M. H. (1991). CONSPEC and CONLERN: A two-process theory of infant face recognition. *Psychological Review*, **98**, 164–181.

Öhman, A., Flykt, A., and Esteves, F. (2001). Emotion drives attention: Detecting the snake in the grass. *Journal of Experimental Psychology: General*, **130**, 466–478.

Öhman, A. and Mineka, S. (2001). Fear, phobias and preparedness: Toward an evolved module of fear and fear learning. *Psychological Review*, **108**, 483–522.

Palmer, S. E. (1999). *Vision Science: From Photons to Phenomenology*. Cambridge, MA: MIT Press.

Penn, D. J. and Potts, W. K. (1999). The evolution of mating preferences and major histocompatibility complex genes. *American Naturalist*, **153**, 145–164.

Pinker, S. (1994). *The Language Instinct: How the Mind Creates Language*. New York: Harper Collins.

Pirolli, P. L. and Card, S. K. (1999). Information foraging. *Psychological Review*, **106**, 643–675.

Repovs, G. and Baddeley, A. (2006). The multi-component model of working memory: Explorations in experimental cognitive psychology. *Neuroscience*, **139**, 5–21.

Richerson, P. and Boyd, R. (2005). *Not by Genes Alone: How Culture Transformed Human Evolution*. Chicago: University of Chicago Press.

Rozin, P., Haidt, J., and McCauley, C. R. (1993). Disgust. In M. Lewis and J. Haviland (Eds.), *Handbook of Emotions*, pp. 575–594. New York: Guilford.

Spelke, E. S. (2000). Core knowledge. *American Psychologist*, **55**, 1233–1243.

Sperber, D. (1994). The modularity of thought and the epidemiology of representations. In L. A. Hirschfeld and S. A. Gelman (Eds.), *Mapping the Mind: Domain Specificity in Cognition and Culture* (pp. 39–67). New York: Cambridge University Press.

Stephens, D. W. and Krebs, J. R. (1986) *Foraging Theory*. Princeton: Princeton University Press.

Tenenbaum, J. B., Griffiths, T. L., and Kemp, C. (2006). Theory-based Bayesian models of inductive learning and reasoning. *Trends in Cognitive Sciences*, **10**, 309–318.

Tomasello, M., Carpenter, M., Call, J., Behne, T., and Moll, H. (2005). Understanding and sharing intentions: The origins of cultural cognition. *Behavioral and Brain Sciences*, **28**, 675–691.

Ungerleider, L. G. and Haxby, J. V. (1994). "What" and "where" in the human brain. *Current Opinion in Neurobiology*, **4**, 157–165.

Wolf, A. P. (1995) *Sexual Attraction and Childhood Association: A Chinese Brief for Edward Westermarck*. Stanford, CA: Stanford University Press.

Yamazaki, K., Beauchamp, G. K., Kupniewski, D., Bard, J., Thomas, L., and Boyse E. A. (1988). Familial imprinting determines H-2 selective mating preferences. *Science*, **240**, 1331–1332.

Yuille, A. and Kersten, D. (2006). Vision as Bayesian inference: analysis by synthesis? *Trends in Cognitive Sciences*, **10**, 301–308.

5

Invention and community in the emergence of language: Insights from new sign languages

MICHAEL A. ARBIB

Conceptual frameworks

What was the interplay of biological and cultural evolution in yielding modern humans with their rich, flexible, and diverse languages? What has biological evolution contributed to the innate capabilities of the human brain that allow human children to master language and how has society evolved to develop those capabilities? I approach these questions through analysis of the recent development of two new sign languages: Nicaraguan Sign Language (NSL), which developed in just 25 years within a community of deaf Nicaraguans, and Al-Sayyid Bedouin Sign Language (ABSL), which developed over a period of at most 70 years in a community of deaf and speaking Bedouin. Understanding the tradeoff between innate capabilities and social influences in the emergence of NSL and ABSL will ground an understanding of how these modern social influences may differ from those available to early humans at the dawn of language.

The mirror system hypothesis (MSH) is a specific theory of the evolution of the human "language-ready brain." It is informed by the view that language is a multimodal system of production and performance that involves voice, hands, and face. Speaking humans accompany their speech with facial expressions and cospeech gestures of the hands (Kendon, 2004; McNeill, 1992, 2005), while many deaf people employ signed languages that are very different from spoken languages – with specific signs (which may integrate arm, hand, and face movements) that are part of a conventionalized system with limited resemblance to cospeech gestures. Details of MSH are set forth in Arbib (2005a, developing the insights of Arbib and Rizzolatti, 1997; Rizzolatti and Arbib, 1998), with commentaries and a response. Here a brief summary will set the stage for the rest of this

Foundations in Evolutionary Cognitive Neuroscience, ed. Steven M. Platek and Todd K. Shackelford.
Published by Cambridge University Press. © Cambridge University Press 2009.

chapter. MSH provides a theory which offers a strong role for gesture in the origins of language (cf. Armstrong *et al.*, 1995; Armstrong and Wilcox, 2007; Corballis 2002; Hewes, 1973; Kendon, 2002) with a neurological twist – it suggests that the brain mechanisms which support language evolved atop a mirror system for grasping (i.e., a brain system active both when the subject is grasping and when the subject observes another grasping) which is similar in the brains of monkeys, apes, and humans.

From simple to complex imitation and the evolution of protolanguage

Monkeys have little or no capacity for imitation (Visalberghi and Fragaszy, 1990, 2001), apes (chimpanzees, gorillas, bonobos, orangutans) have a capacity for *simple imitation*, whereas humans are the only primates capable of *complex imitation*. We thus argued that the mirror system shared by the common ancestor of monkeys, apes, and humans then evolved in human ancestors as part of successively larger, more competent systems.

- First, an enlarged system to support *simple imitation*, the ability to acquire some novel actions by extensive observation and repetition, but only on a limited basis, evolved in the common ancestor of humans and apes. For example, Byrne and Byrne (1993) found that gorillas learn complex feeding strategies but may take months to do so. Consider eating nettle leaves. Skilled gorillas grasp the stem firmly, strip off leaves, remove petioles bimanually, fold leaves over the thumb, pop the bundle into the mouth, and eat. Teaching is virtually never observed in apes (Caro and Hauser, 1992) and the challenge is compounded because the sequence of "atomic actions" varies greatly from trial to trial.
- Further evolution in the human line since the divergence of the great apes yielded brain mechanisms to support *complex imitation* – the ability (i) to observe a novel performance and see, to a first approximation, the key subgoals it involves and the actions which appear to achieve them, and (ii) to use this to reproduce novel behaviors on the basis of very few observations, so long as the constituents are familiar (Arbib, 2002; Wohlschläger *et al.*, 2003). Nonetheless, much practice may be required to hone a novel skill so acquired.

Note that the above discussion says nothing about communication. Rather, we suggest that the ability to imitate praxic skills may confer selective advantage for those who can learn from the successful goal achievements of others. Figure 5.1 goes further, showing how these new forms of imitation may have made new forms of manual communication possible. Arbib, Liebal, and Pika (in

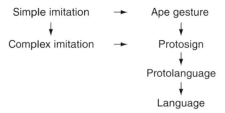

Figure 5.1 A sketch of key elements of the Mirror System Hypothesis. The left hand column suggests that the capability for simple imitation allows apes (and, presumably, the common ancestor of apes and humans) to acquire a small repertoire of communicative manual gestures, but it required the evolution of mechanisms for complex imitation (in the hominim line) to support the open-ended symbol creation of pantomime and, through extensive conventionalization, protosign and then (adding protospeech to expand upon protosign) protolanguage. It is argued (controversially) that the transition from protolanguage to language was then a matter of cultural rather than biological evolution. See text for details.

press), summarizing data on primate communication, note that monkey vocalizations are innately specified (though occasions for using a call may change with experience), whereas a group of apes can develop in the order of 10 novel gestures for communicative purposes, perhaps acquired by *ontogenetic ritualization* whereby reduced forms of actions may yield gestures that serve to request the action (Tomasello *et al.*, 1997) and further shared by simple imitation. This supports the hypothesis that it was gesture, rather than vocalization (Seyfarth *et al.*, 2005), that created the opening for greatly expanded communication once complex imitation had evolved for practical manual skills. Arbib (2005a) argues that complex imitation supported the spontaneous use of pantomime (cf. Stokoe, 2001) to dramatically expand the semantics of gestural communication (Figure 5.1).

The current version of MSH then posits that:

- Further evolution yielded novel brain mechanisms which allowed protohuman groups to move from pantomimes – which, while expressive, may require much time to produce yet still be ambiguous – to a system of conventionalized gestures which were easier both to produce and interpret. The result was a rudimentary form of *protosign*.
- In due course, the brain and vocal apparatus evolved, in an expanding spiral (Arbib, 2005b; cx. MacNeilage and Davis, 2005), the mechanisms to integrate protosign with *protospeech*, a new open system of communicative vocalizations. At this stage, then, (proto)humans had a *protolanguage* – in the sense of a system of utterances which served as a precursor to human language in that it was open-ended in a manner denied to the

morphemes and larger forms to the combination of their meanings). What needs remarking here, though, is that the features of *discreteness* and *combinatorial patterning* are not restricted to language. For example, a frog's behavior may be dissected into a set of basic motor schemas such as orient, jump, lunge, and snap. However, there is a crucial parametric aspect there as well – e.g., in determining the appropriate angle of orientation to approach the prey or escape the predator. What the frog lacks, and what complex imitation provides, is the ability to analyze another's behavior in these terms and respond accordingly. Thus the crucial point is raised that some of Hockett's features hold for proto-language more generally, and in some cases even for praxis once it is wedded to complex imitation (Roy and Arbib, 2005).

Hockett (1987) also lists *duality of patterning*, in which *meaningful* units are composed from a smaller set of *meaningless* units as when discrete sounds combine to form words. Stokoe (1960) demonstrated that a sign language also has duality of patterning – meaningless handshapes, locations, and movements combine to form a large set of lexical items. This provides the basis for "sign phonology." However, Aronoff *et al.* (2008) find an unexpectedly high degree of intersigner variation in Al-Sayyid Bedouin Sign Language, suggesting that lin-guistic proficiency *can* occur without duality of patterning. For example, the second generation uses signs for "tree" which remain close to pantomime and thus vary greatly, though the signs used by members of the same family may be similar.

Describing languages; learning a language

It will be worth briefly considering how a language may be character-ized and how a modern child normally acquires a language. This may then be contrasted with what happens when the language model available to the child is incomplete. Each language is generative or productive, being made up of words and grammatical markers that can be combined in diverse ways to yield an essentially unbounded stock of sentences. In almost all human languages, the ability to build utterances includes processes that can be described by recursive rules, e.g., "a noun phrase is still a noun phrase if you insert an(other) adjective," in which the generic construct – here noun phrase – appears as a term in its own definition. Given the view, noted above, that recursion of action (but not of communication) is part of language readiness, the key transition here is the compositionality that allows cognitive structure to be reflected in symbolic structure, as when perception (not uniquely human) grounds linguistic descrip-tion (uniquely human) so that, e.g., the noun phrase describing a part of an object may optionally form part of the noun phrase describing the overall object. From this point of view, recursion in language is a corollary of the essentially recursive nature of action and perception *once symbolization becomes compositional.*

For reasons summarized elsewhere (Arbib, 2007; Arbib and Hill, 1988), I reject the view that a Universal Grammar is genetically encoded in humans such that it can establish within the infant brain a range of parameters which enable the child to acquire the syntax of its native language by setting each parameter simply by hearing a few sentences to determine which value of the parameter is consistent with them (Chomsky and Lasnik, 1993; Lightfoot, 2006). Rather, I agree with the construction grammarians (Croft, 2001; Goldberg, 2003) who see the grammar of each language as a more or less language-specific set of constructions which combine *form* (how to aggregate words) with *meaning* (how the meaning of the words constrains the meaning of the whole). This is to be contrasted with a grammar in which autonomous syntactic rules put words together in very general ways and without regard for the meaning of the result. Construction grammar seems more hospitable to accounts (historical linguistics/cultural evolution) of how languages emerge and change over time (see, e.g., Croft, 2000).

Various authors (Arbib and Hill, 1988; Tomasello, 2003) have explained how modern children acquire words and constructions without invoking a universal grammar. Hill (1983) showed that the child may first acquire what the adult perceives as two-word utterances as holophrases (e.g., "want-milk") whose parts initially have no distinct meanings for the child. Subsequently, the child develops a more general construction (e.g., "want x") in which "x" can be replaced by the name of any "wantable thing." Further experience will yield more subtle constructions and the development of word classes like "noun" defined by their syntactic roles in a range of constructions rather than their semantics.

Ontogeny does not in this case recapitulate phylogeny. Adult hunters and gatherers had to communicate about situations outside the range of a modern 2-year old, and protohumans were not communicating with adults who already used a large lexicon and set of constructions to generate complex sentences. Nonetheless, I argue that protolanguage and language emerged through the invention of an increasingly subtle interweaving of (proto)words and (proto) constructions, and that the same basic mechanisms may have served both protohumans inventing language and modern children acquiring the existing language of their community (Arbib, 2008):

(1) The ability to create a novel gesture or vocalization and associate it with a communicative goal.

(2) The ability both to perform and perceive such a gesture or vocalization. This would improve with experience as its use spread within the

community, as would sharpening of the perception of occasions of use by members of the community.

(3) Commonalities between two structures could yield to "fractionation," the isolation of that commonality as a gesture or vocalization came to be treated as if betokening some shared "semantic component" of the event, object, or action denoted by each of the two structures (see Wray, 2000 for how this might have operated in protohumans; and Kirby, 2000 for a related computer model). This could in time lead to the emergence of a construction for "putting the pieces back together," not only allowing recapture of the meanings of the original structures, but also with the original pieces becoming instances of an ever wider class of slot fillers (Arbib, 2005a). We may compare and contrast this "semantic fractionation" which defines new meaningful elements with the "motor fractionation" (whether manual or vocal) which, as we shall see in the next section, defines new meaningless elements as the basis for phonology.

It is complex imitation that makes these processes possible. In the case of protohumans, this could lead to the invention of new (proto)words and constructions. In the case of the modern child, it provides the basis for understanding that strings of sounds can be dissected into strings of words and that these words can be grouped by constructions. The constructions become of greater or more focused applicability both on a historical timescale as new words and constructions are invented over the course of many generations, and on a developmental timescale as the child has more experience of using fragments of the ambient language to understand and be understood.

Genotypes, brains, and social schemas

We now address, briefly, the very different levels of analysis involved in this enterprise. The first, which is outside the scope of this chapter is the EvoDevo view – that the genotype of a creature is not a specification of the adult creature, but rather the specification of the mechanisms whereby that creature will develop into its adult form. The subtlety is that this process is recursive. The genotype does not act directly. Rather, each cell of the body only expresses a few genes at any time. Thus the genotype determines which genes are available, and includes regulatory genes that can set constraints on how genes are turned on or off. In particular, then, particular cells will be fated to become parts of the brain, and we hold that the human genotype is unique in creating a language-ready brain. However, we now know that learning changes patterns of gene expression in neurons, as other aspects of the (internal and external) environment can change gene expression in cells more generally. In particular, then, the cellular architecture of the adult brain reflects not only the underlying genotype but also the social milieu as refracted through individual experience, and this architecture includes not only the shape and connections of the individual cells and the larger structures they form, but also the very chemistry of specific cells.

Leaving EvoDevo aside, I want here to address the difference between social reality as something we experience around us and our own interiorization of those structures. Much of my work has sought to analyze "schemas" as the "distributed programs" of the brain, at a level above, but reducible to, the functioning of neural networks in the brain. For example, we have *perceptual schemas* recognizing apples and doors, and *motor schemas* for peeling apples and opening doors. Each of these schemas constitutes a psychological reality and we can combine them into schema assemblages and coordinated control programs (Arbib, 1981; Arbib *et al.*, 1998) to define complex courses of action. In *The Construction of Reality* (Arbib and Hesse, 1986), Mary Hesse and I sought to integrate and reconcile an epistemology based on mental schemas and brain mechanisms "in the head" (Arbib) and an epistemology addressing the creation of social schemas by a community (Hesse). The upshot was to extend my approach to schema theory to embrace three levels, of which the third reflected my collaboration with Mary Hesse:

(1) **Basic Schema Theory**: Schema theory *simpliciter* has its basic definition at a functional level which associates schemas with specific perceptual, motor, and cognitive abilities and then stresses how our mental life results from the dynamic interaction – the competition and cooperation – of many schema instances. It refines and extends an overly phenomenological account of the "mental level."

(2) **Neural Schema Theory**: The "downward" extension of schema theory seeks to understand how schemas and their interactions may indeed be played out over neural circuitry – a basic move from psychology and cognitive science as classically conceived (viewing the mind "from the outside") to cognitive neuroscience.

(3) **Social Schema Theory**: The "upward" extension of schema theory seeks to understand how "social schemas" constituted by collective patterns of behavior in a society may provide an external reality for a person's acquisition of schemas "in the head" in the sense of basic schema theory. Conversely, it is the collective effect of behaviors which express schemas within the heads of many individuals that constitutes, and changes, this social reality.

Returning to language acquisition, the child is not exposed to a language as unified external reality, but rather as part of interactions with other people which may be associated with pragmatic or emotional consequences, and thus comes to interiorize that language as a set of schemas for words and constructions and the pragmatics of use that allow the child to become a member of the community. In doing so, however, the child does so with schemas that may lead to dissonance as well as consonance with currently dominant patterns of behavior, and so has the potential to change the social schemas that shaped its development. I will not make explicit the search for a rapprochement between social schemas (patterns in the behavior of a community) and neural schemas (brain mechanisms in the head of each individual), but it provides the implicit structuring for what follows: society shapes the individual, but individuals not only constitute but also change society.

Being deaf

A central claim of MSH is that the brain evolved to support language as a multimodal system of production and performance that involves voice, hands, and face. This makes us receptive to the lessons that can be learned when voice is ineffective. Most humans are born with adequate hearing and acquire speech as their primary mode of communication. Deaf people (as distinct from those just hard of hearing) can detect only the loudest of sounds, if any, so that hearing aids provide little if any help in making auditory input interpretable. For them the auditory signal cannot be the primary input. Hearing babies can recognize their mothers' voices within the first few days of life and seeing babies pay attention to the movements of caregivers' faces and their eye gaze (DeCasper and Fifer, 1980; DeCasper and Spence, 1991; see Polich 2005 for more such data), but 95% of children born deaf have hearing parents and soon become communicative outsiders in their families (Karchmer and Mitchell, 2003).

The newborn hearing infant exhibits effects of some months of auditory exposure while in the womb, and by six months after being born will exhibit language-specific responsiveness to auditory input (e.g., Japanese infants can initially respond to the distinction between /l/ and /r/ sounds but eventually lose this ability) and by nine months will respond best to the syllabic structure of the ambient language (so that an English infant will become attuned to CVC as well as CV syllables [C = consonant; V = vowel], whereas Japanese infants become attuned to a restricted range of "moras," syllables of the CV form, or /-n/). By one year of age, the hearing child will increasingly use vocal production to express herself, increasingly using something like words, complementing innate vocalizations like crying and laughing. However, it is worth stressing that even the hearing child makes extensive use of gesture. Iverson, Capirci, and Caselli (1994) found that gestures were more prevalent than (vocal) words in the children they observed as 16 month olds, whereas the majority of children had more words than gestures by 20 months of age. Moreover, Capirci *et al.* (1996) observed that, at both ages, the most frequent two-element utterances were gesture-word combinations; and production of these combinations increased significantly from 16 to 20 months even as the use of two-word utterances increased sharply.

Home sign

People for whom profound hearing loss occurs after adolescence will, in general, consider oral language their primary form of communication. However, children exposed to a sign language from birth acquire that language as readily as hearing children acquire the spoken language to which they are exposed, achieving major milestones at approximately the same ages (Lillo-Martin, 1999; Meier, 1991; Newport and Meier, 1985), and become members of a Deaf community for whom a signed language is the primary form of communication. (The capital D in Deaf indicates membership of such a community, as distinct from the loss of hearing.) This strengthens the argument that the brain mechanisms that support language are multimodal, rather than evolving to primarily support the vocal-auditory modality.

However, deaf children with only auditory exposure to language often reach six years of age with less than a 10 word receptive or expressive oral vocabulary. Even with intensive training, a deaf child's ability to understand and produce spoken language is greatly delayed compared with the ability of normally hearing children. Nonetheless, deaf children raised by non-signing parents do develop *home sign*, a rudimentary form of communication with family members (Goldin-Meadow, 1982).

Typically, such a child will have a small "vocabulary" of home signs together with just a few strategies for combining signs into longer messages Since this development does not rest on "direct input" from either a spoken language or a sign language, home sign will differ from child to child. I put quotes around "direct input" since it bears directly on the issues we will consider in distinguishing the evolution of the first languages in (proto)human prehistory from the emergence of new languages in the present day. First, there is no direct input from *sign language* because we are looking at children of speaking parents who do not know sign language, but there is the input from seeing gestures – both deictic gestures and more descriptive gestures – used as part of speech acts. Such gestures do not themselves constitute a language, but they do teach the child that pointing and pantomime can be used to communicate just as they do in the development of a hearing child (see the earlier discussion of the use of gesture by 16- and 20-month olds). The "indirect input" from *speech* is even less direct. But the fact that family members can be seen to take turns to speak and gesture, sometimes to no apparent end, but in other cases with clear links to emotional impact or achieving instrumental goals, creates an understanding of the general notion of dialogue conducted by a blend of gesture and facial expression. Moreover, a child's caregiver will provide a structured environment such as pointing at specific objects or actions as well as pictures in picture books which – even though the child cannot hear the spoken names of what is in the picture – encourages the understanding that objects and actions, etc., do have names. In some cases, the child can adapt a caregiver's gesture to provide such a name, in other cases a more or less ritualized pantomime will serve – but this process is far slower and more limited than for children to whom the names are supplied in speech (if the child can hear) or signed language (if not).

Home signers can combine a few signs to form what Goldin-Meadow calls a "sentence," though one must note that these are very simple in structure compared to the range of sentences seen in full human languages. However, these "sentences" do exhibit some basic "grammatical properties." Goldin-Meadow and Mylander (1998) find consistent word order among home signers (even those in different cultures) – they regularly produce two-gesture strings in which actions appear in final position (O-V, object-verb; or S-V, subject-verb), with intransitive actors and patients more likely to appear in such strings than transitive actors. Indeed, even when hearing speakers who know no sign language are asked to use their hands and not their mouths to communicate, the same O-V order arises despite the fact that their natural spoken language uses the S-V-O order (Goldin-Meadow *et al.*, 2000).

Two new sign languages

Nicaraguan Sign Language (NSL) is a new sign language that developed in just 25 years in tandem with the formation of a community of deaf Nicaraguans; while Al-Sayyid Bedouin Sign Language (ABSL) has arisen in the last 70 years in a community of deaf and speaking Bedouin. Both these sign languages are still developing – and researchers use the study of different "cohorts" (NSL) or generations (ABSL) of signers to gather insights into processes of language change. I will sample a few findings on NSL and ABSL to focus an analysis of the roles of invention and community in the emergence of language. I will emphasize that the first "signers" of these languages (when in fact there were no such languages, just a host of diverse, limited precursors) had the "language is all around, I just can't hear it" cues that are exploited by all home signers; and that the key to the transition from home sign to language was the creation of a community in which children could learn the creations of others and begin to build an expanding vocabulary and shared set of constructions.

A brief history of Nicaraguan Sign Language (NSL)

Before the 1970s, deaf Nicaraguans had little contact with each other (Polich, 2005; Senghas, 1997). Most deaf individuals stayed at home, and the few schools to which they had access treated them as mentally retarded. During this period, no sign language emerged. Different children developed home sign within their individual families, but the home sign systems thus developed varied widely in form and complexity (Coppola, 2002). Yet NSL was in common use in Managua's school for the deaf in 1986, when Judy Kegl initiated the academic study of NSL (Kegl, 1994; Kegl *et al.*, 1999).

An expanded elementary school for special education of the deaf was opened in Managua, Nicaragua in 1977, followed by a vocational school in 1981, also in Managua, and by the mid 1980s deaf adolescents were meeting regularly on the weekends (Polich, 2005). It is important to note that instruction was conducted in Spanish, though with minimal success. From the start, the children began to develop a new, gestural system for communicating with each other – in part by consolidating the different home signs each had developed. The gestures soon expanded to form a rudimentary sign language. It has been claimed that no one actually taught them to sign, but the section "The emergence of the Nicaraguan Deaf community" suggests that the situation is more subtle.

As the years passed, the early collection of gestures developed into an expressive sign language, Nicaraguan Sign Language (NSL). NSL continues to develop with successful innovations being learned naturally as new children enter the community each year. Senghas (2003) found that changes in its grammar first appear among pre-adolescent signers, soon spreading to subsequent, younger learners, but not to adults. This statement seems a little strong – a successful innovation would presumably spread to most children currently in school, whether or not they were younger than the innovators. Nonetheless, the fact remains that most adults fail to master innovations made by a cohort 10 years younger – just as many hearing adults around the world fail to develop a taste for the music currently popular with teenagers. Note that while NSL is the first language for these children it is not quite a native language, since they start learning NSL when they enter school at age six or younger.

A brief history of Al-Sayyid Bedouin Sign Language (ABSL)

The Al-Sayyid Bedouin group, in the Negev region of Israel, comprises descendants of a single founder, who arrived 200 years ago from Egypt and married a local woman. The group, now in its seventh generation, contains

about 3500 members, residing in a single community, with frequent consangui-
neous marriages. There are now about 125 congenitally deaf individuals distributed throughout the community, all descended from two of the founders'
five sons (Scott et al., 1995). All deaf individuals show profound neurosensory
hearing loss and are of normal intelligence. Unlike the deaf in Nicaragua, the
deaf members of this community are fully integrated into its social structure
and marry hearing individuals. Moreover, siblings and children of deaf individuals and other hearing members of the large extended family often become
fluent signers (Kisch, 2004). In other words, ABSL is a second language of the
village with each deaf infant born into an environment with adult models of the
language available to them (Sandler et al., 2005).

Emerging patterns of motion description in NSL

To exemplify what has been learned about the development of NSL, I
will focus on one study which exploits the difference between older signers,
who retain much of NSL's early nature, and younger signers who produce the
language in its most developed form. Senghas et al. (2004) studied 30 deaf
Nicaraguans who had been signing NSL since the age of six or younger: 10
from a first cohort (who started signing before 1984), 10 from a second cohort
(1984 to 1993), and 10 from a third cohort (after 1993). Their signed expressions
during description of motion were compared to the gestures produced by 10
hearing Nicaraguans while speaking Spanish.

Senghas et al. (2004) recorded hand movements made while describing a clip
from a Tweety and Sylvester cartoon (see McNeill, 1992 for more on this methodology for the study of hand gesture). In this clip, the cat, Sylvester, having
swallowed a bowling ball, proceeds rapidly down a steep street in a "rolling"
manner. (A ball would roll down the hill, the cartoon cat with a ball inside
wobbles down the hill but English speakers tend to say that the cat rolls down
the hill.) This event includes a *manner* (in this case, rolling) and a *path* of movement (here, descending) which are experienced as a unity. The most direct way
to iconically represent such an event is to represent manner and path simultaneously. However, languages will often encode manner and path in separate
elements. English, for example, uses the sequence "rolling down" to represent
manner (rolling) and path (down).

Senghas et al. (2004) found that all of the Spanish speakers' gestures and 73%
of the first-cohort NSL signers expressed manner and path simultaneously. By
contrast, almost 70% of second- and third-cohort signers expressed manner (by a
circling motion) and path (by a trajectory down to the signer's right) in two
separate signs in sequence.[2] This, then, provides dramatic evidence of an emergent feature of NSL: the speakers that signers could observe, and most of the

related signing by first-cohort signers, did not separate path and manner in describing such an event. Yet as second and third cohorts learned the language in the mid 1980s and 1990s, they rapidly made this segmented, sequenced construction their preferred (but not exclusive) means of expressing motion events. Thus NSL is not a copying of Spanish cospeech gestures but here exhibits a novel conventionalization. (It should also be noted that many sign languages do express manner and path simultaneously.)

Before going on, it should be stressed that the later cohort's preference for separating manner and path is not the only aspect of the above data worthy of comment. As Slobin, 2005 observes, we should also note (i) that 73% of the first-cohort NSL signers and more than 30% of second- and third-cohort signers used the strategy employed by Spanish speakers, and that (ii) 27% of the first-cohort NSL signers did separate path and manner. Thus, at least some of the original signs were strongly influenced by the cospeech gestures of the surrounding community, while the innovation of the separation of path and manner was achieved by individuals in the first cohort. What we see in the later cohorts is its increasingly wide adoption.

The drawback to expressing manner and path separately is that it may be unclear whether the two aspects of movement occurred within a single event. *Roll* followed by *downward* might mean "rolling, then descending." However, a key finding of Senghas *et al.* (2004) is that not only did NSL signers come to fractionate path and manner, they also developed a way to put the pieces back together again. NSL now has the X-Y-X construction, such as *roll-descend-roll*, to express simultaneity. This string can serve as a structural unit within a larger expression like *cat [roll descend roll]*, or it can even be nested, as in *waddle [roll descend roll] waddle*. These X-Y-X constructions appeared in about one-third of the recorded second- and third-cohort expressions. This construction never appeared in the gestures of the Spanish speakers and is also quite unlike any construction of spoken Spanish.

This is an important point – but one must distinguish the specific construction from the need to find a form to express a certain semantics. This need catalyzes the invention of new constructions, but a sign language can seek forms different from that of spoken languages. Which of the possible forms takes hold is a social matter, rather than a consequence of general learning principles. It is interesting that we see here in NSL a process earlier postulated as contributing to the development of human protolanguages (Kirby, 2000; Wray, 2000) wherein commonalities between two structures could yield to the isolation of that commonality as a gesture or vocalization, possibly leading to the emergence of a construction for "putting the pieces back together," with the original pieces becoming instances of an ever wider class of slot fillers.

Segmentation and sequencing of motion events has also been observed in home signers exposed only to unsegmented cospeech gestures. One home signer produced the sequence *flutter descend* to describe snowing (see Figure 3 in Goldin-Meadow, 2003). But what else could he do? He retrieves a sign "flutter" that does not exhaust what he perceives about the situation, and then produces another, "descend." This is a weak form of compositionality – one may encounter a new situation which resembles a situation for which a sign already exists, then be dissatisfied with the "gaps" left by that sign. If another sign is available to cover the gap, at least in part, then that may be uttered, too. This is much weaker than being able to marshal constructions to put together words that express the cognized relations in a situation.

Word order in Al-Sayyid Bedouin Sign Language

Sandler *et al.* (2005) found that the grammatical relation between subject (S), object (O), and verb (V) was fixed at a very early stage in the development of ABSL, providing a convention for expressing the relation between elements in a sentence without relying on external context. However, the particular word orders in ABSL differ from those found both in the ambient spoken languages in the community and in Israeli Sign Language (ISL, Meir and Sandler, 2004). (ABSL developed independently of ISL.) Therefore, the emerging grammatical structures should be regarded as an independent development within the language. Moreover, Sandler *et al.* (2005) further claim that these grammatical structures are "a reflection of a basic property of language in general," a claim which we must scrutinize.

Signers readily use ABSL to relate complex information such as descriptions of folk remedies, cultural traditions, and personal histories. Sandler *et al.* (2005) focused on eight signers of the second generation, seven deaf and one hearing, all currently in their 30s and 40s, except one in her 20s. (Preliminary results from the third generation, ranging from teenagers to young children, reveal interesting differences between the systems of the two generations.) They generated their corpus by presenting two tasks to the second generation of signers: (i) spontaneous recounting of a personal experience and (ii) descriptions of single events portrayed by actors in a series of short video clips. All responses were videotaped, translated by a hearing signer from the same generation, and transcribed with glosses for each individually identifiable sign production. Signs for actions or events were classified as the predicate nucleus of a sentence while subjects, objects, and indirect objects (IO) were identified depending on their semantic roles in a clause and the standard mapping of these roles onto syntactic positions (Jackendoff, 1987).

Most strings could be parsed unambiguously using semantic criteria, but in some cases prosodic criteria played a crucial role. Manual criteria at the intonational phrase boundary included holding the hands in place, pause and relaxation of the hands, or repeating the final sign in the constituent; non-manual cues included both a clear change in head or body position, and a concomitant change in facial expression (Nespor and Sandler, 1999). For example, one signer, in describing his personal history, produced the following string: MONEY COLLECT BUILD WALLS DOORS. The first prosodic constituent, MONEY COLLECT, means "I saved money," an O–V sentence. BUILD WALLS DOORS was parsed using a prosodic break between BUILD and WALLS. This break involved holding the hands in position at the end of BUILD, and then moving the body first forward, then up, then enumerating the things being built, WALLS and DOORS. The spontaneous translation of the string by a consultant was: "I saved some money. I started to build a house. Walls, doors."

The parsing of most utterances was more straightforward. Sandler *et al.* (2005) found the vast majority of sentences to be of the form S–O–V, although either subject or object could be unexpressed. For example, one description of a video clip showing a woman giving an apple to a man was WOMAN APPLE GIVE; MAN GIVE ["The woman gave an apple; (she) gave (it) to the man"], the first clause is S–O–V, and the second clause is IO–V. Another signer responded to the same clip with WOMAN GIVE MAN TAKE, i.e., two S–V sentences.

However, the basic word order in the spoken Arabic dialect of the hearing members of the community, as well as in Hebrew, is S–V–O. Nonetheless, the only hearing subject in their study – bilingual in Arabic and ABSL – uses the ABSL S–O–V word order in his signing. This generation of signers had little or no contact with ISL, whose word order appears to vary more widely in any case (Meir and Sandler, 2004). Hence, the S–O–V pattern is an independent development within ABSL. Sandler *et al.* (2005) speak of "a pattern rooted in the basic syntactic notions of subject, object, and verb or predicate" but it is not clear from their data that ABSL signers are relying on these syntactic relations rather than the semantic relations between action, agent, and theme, etc. Once languages have had time to accrue such mechanisms as case marking on nouns to indicate their relation to the verb, the roles of participants can be made clear, even without consistent word order. In the absence of such mechanisms, word order is the only way to disambiguate a message linguistically. Sandler *et al.* (2005) view the appearance of this conventionalization "at such an early stage in the emergence of a language [as] rare empirical verification of the unique proclivity of the human mind for structuring a communication system along grammatical lines." However, the "grammar" demonstrated in the above examples is very simple, and should not be over-interpreted. What is remarkable is that the order of constituents was not taken over from that used by the Arabic-speaking members of the community. How did that occur? The earlier discussion of why the X-Y-X construction of NSL differs from Spanish constructions offers some clues. My hypothesis is that ABSL and NSL differ from home sign because:

- The existence of a community provides more opportunities to use signs and choose signs, so that some get lost to the community while others gain power by being widely shared. "Natural selection by learning."
- Since knowledge of another language is possessed by some members of the community, they seek to translate this knowledge into the new medium (as is proven for the lexicon), but few attempts to capture a given property will become widespread in the community.

The emergence of the Nicaraguan Deaf community

It has been claimed that NSL arose "from scratch" (Pearson, 2004) in that the community of deaf Nicaraguans who developed it "lacked exposure to a developed language" (Senghas *et al.*, 2004). But did deaf Nicaraguans "reinvent language" – as the claim that NSL arose out of nothing might suggest – or did they "develop *a* language"? In the latter case we must understand how the presence of other languages may have complemented the language-readiness of the brain in the development of NSL. In this section, I want to give some sense of the social matrix that supported the emergence of NSL, summarizing material from the book, *The Emergence of the Nicaraguan Deaf Community in Nicaragua: "With Sign Language You Can Learn So Much"* (Polich, 2005). Laura Polich spent the year of 1997 in Managua, and during that time interviewed many people in and associated with the Deaf community. The result is an invaluable complement to the cohort-by-cohort analysis of specific linguistic features of NSL, showing how adolescents and young adults played important roles in the formation of the Deaf community and its sign language.

There is no evidence of sign language in use in Nicaragua in 1975. Until the late 1970s, deaf students were placed in special education classes where they were outnumbered by mentally retarded students and were unable to form a community. But then a vocational school was established that kept adolescents and young adults together "at a time when they were carving out their identities and craving a peer group in which to try out and enact their abilities to be social actors" (Polich, p. 146). Note here the crucial notions of *social actor*, *peer group*, and *creating one's identity*. The process that Polich charts is the transition from a deaf person in Nicaragua having no peer group and thus having the passive social role of an outcast, to persons with a language which empowered them to be true social actors within the Deaf community created by the enriched communication that came with the expanding capabilities of NSL. This process, as Polich shows, was catalyzed by a number of individuals, some deaf and others hearing people intent on opening up to the deaf the social opportunities which most hearing people could take for granted.

Teachers played an important role in developing a community which provided social opportunities for the deaf children, going beyond the classroom. Ruthy Doran, a hearing person who not only taught the deaf children at the vocational school but also did much to create a social environment for them, told Polich:

> There wasn't a sign language [around 1980] … But we were able to understand one another. We would … use a lot of the gestures that everyone around here (in Nicaragua) uses and we had a set of some signs that the students made up. (They aren't used now.) We had special signs like for the days of the week that we had used with each other for years, and they had learned new signs … which they taught me. And when everything else failed, we would write words down, or else act it out. (Polich, pp. 77–78)

Another teacher, Gloria Minero, remembers great diversity in the signs used before 1987:

> There was a lot of rudimentary gestures and ASL signs and mimicry, which are not "signs" but more "iconic." There wasn't much structure – that came later. (Polich, p.89)

Over a period of time they developed a system integrating home sign and gesture and a stronger grammar. The work of Annie Senghas and others shows that the grammaticization of NSL still continues and can be expected to continue.

Thus, in its early stages the community being formed was influenced by the gestures of the surrounding community and included hearing people who spoke Spanish. Even those who could not speak had at least a small vocabulary of written Spanish and the group had access to some signs of American Sign Language (ASL). Of course, using a few signs of ASL is very different from knowing ASL as such – just as a tourist in Paris may be able to say "bonjour" and "merci" but not know French. However, note the difference between the true statement "In the early 1980s, many deaf Nicaraguans knew no grammar" and the false statement "In the early 1980s, no deaf Nicaraguans knew grammar." The impressive achievement of creating this new language, NSL, did not have to rest solely on innate capabilities of the human brain (which distinguish us from other primates, for example) but could indeed exploit the cultural innovations of existing language communities.

In Nicaragua in the 1970s and beyond, most language teaching for deaf children was oral training based on Spanish, which was successful for relatively few students. It thus was a revelation when, in 1983, Ruthy Duran and two other teachers visited Costa Rica and saw how sign language was used there to augment an oral program (Polich, Chapter 7) and that signs could constitute a fully expressive language. However, they were unable to get approval for the use of Costa Rican sign language for instruction in Managua. Instead, the full use of sign language had to await the development of a sign language within Nicaragua. The point here, however, is that the *idea* of sign language was available to some members of the nascent community, even though the full use of a such language was not.

Gloria Minero encouraged the students to develop an association of deaf persons to work for more education and increased jobs for its members, assisting work on a constitution and bylaws. The official founding of the Association (APRIAS) came in 1986. Thus, while many of the deaf Nicaraguans could not speak Spanish, there were enough who did and could work with their hearing mentors to help develop a document written in Spanish. Most older deaf adults claim that it was at APRIAS meetings that they learned sign language. Communicative outsiders in their own homes, they became part of a developing community with APRIAS. The crucial point that Polich establishes is the virtuous circle of developing a language and a community which uses that language. The joy of conversation provides powerful social bonds. Through such conversation, one has the chance to gain fluency in available signs and to share experiences which drive the invention and spread of new signs and constructions to tell others about those experiences.

However, the talk of a community must not blind us to the fact that each aspect of the language has to meet two conditions: (i) a specific individual or dyad used it for the first time (or the first time that they and others knew about) and (ii) others, understanding its meaning, came to adopt it for their own use. Of course, as more people came to use it, the sign or construction may have shifted its "pronunciation" as well as its meaning. It is thus worth noting what Polich has to say about Javier Gómez López, whom many deaf adults who attended early APRIAS meetings credit with teaching sign language to all the others. Javier's interest in sign language began when he was given a sign language dictionary during a trip to Costa Rica in the late 1970s. He would seek out anyone who knew sign language or had access to a dictionary of any kind in order to improve his vocabulary, and would simultaneously teach what he learned to other deaf Nicaraguans.

In 1990, the Royal Swedish Deaf Association sent representatives to visit APRIAS. This was apparently one of the earliest major contacts between APRIAS and individuals who not only advocated the use of sign language and expected deaf individuals to enter the world of employment, but who also had a cultural conception of deafness as a difference rather than a defect. They urged the deaf members to attach more value to the use of sign language.

Javier was active in the workshops in the years around 1990 in which groups of members of the association discussed which signs should be adopted as the "standard" versions which members should use. A mimeographed dictionary of such signs was produced in 1992. In 1991, the Royal Swedish Deaf Association began to finance the collection of entries for a professionally published sign language dictionary. This makes clear that, at least from 1990 onwards, the Nicaraguan Deaf community was in no way isolated. Note, however, that the Swedes did not teach Swedish Sign Language. Rather, while helping the Nicaraguan systematize what they had achieved in the early stages of creating NSL, they also provided models of expressiveness of sign language which spurred Association members to extend NSL. Indeed, Annie Senghas (personal communication) observes that the second cohort studied both Spanish diction-aries and ASL videos as a basis for devising new signs to expand NSL. But, although NSL exhibits some lexical influences from other sign languages, it shows enough distinctness of syntax and vocabulary to be classified as a sepa-rate sign language.

Thus the communal use of sign language increased just when adolescents and young adults began to remain longer in the educational system and began to increase their after-school contact. Polich argues that (i) being at an age when participation as an independent social actor is important interacts with (ii) the formation of a group whose identity is based upon deafness, and both of these interact with (iii) the need for a communal sign language. All three elements seem to be needed, and do not arise one at a time but as a system that develops together.

Since most deaf children in Nicaragua have hearing parents, and almost none of these have any knowledge of NSL, it is true that families do not play for NSL the role they play in transmission of most human languages – including ABSL. However, we have seen that APRIAS played a vital role in building the Nicaraguan Deaf community as well as the language which made it possible.

The influences of culture and community

Is the implication of the rapid rise of ABSL and NSL that once the brain of *Homo sapiens* achieved its present form, a mere two or three generations sufficed for emergence of a full human language? On the contrary, it has been argued (Noble and Davidson, 1996) that the brain of *Homo sapiens* was biologically ready for language perhaps 200 000 years ago but, if increased complexity of artifacts like art and burial customs correlate with language of some subtlety, then human languages as we know them arose at most 50 000 to 90 000 years ago. If one accepts the idea that it took humans with brains based on a modern-like genotype 100 000 years or more to invent language-as-we-know-it, one must ask what advantage the NSL and ABSL communities had that early humans lacked. Recall the earlier hypothesis that ABSL and NSL differ from home sign because

(i)   The existence of a community provides more opportunities to use signs and choose signs, so that some get lost while increasingly many gain power by being widely shared.

(ii) Those members of the community with knowledge of another language seek to translate this knowledge into the new medium, but few attempts to capture a given property will become widespread in the community.

Polich (2005) has shown us how NSL developed as the medium of community building even as the growing community supported the development of NSL. But I claim that what catalyzed this development to take place in 20 years, more or less, was the overlap with a surrounding community in which language was already established, and the changed awareness that the deaf could aspire to the formation of a community of their own. By contrast, ABSL developed within an existing community as people – deaf and hearing – developed new forms of communication which enabled the deaf to become active members of that community. Even the relatively isolated home signer learns from his family that things can be freely named, and recognizes the success of speech acts of others even if he cannot understand what is being said. (Note, however, that the home signers studied by Goldin-Meadow do not remain isolated. Within a few years almost all are instructed within an oral or signed language. We shall shortly examine observations of a different scenario in Brazil.) Nicaraguan children (like home signers, and the first generation of deaf Al-Sayyid Bedouin) lived in a world of many distinctive objects, both natural and artificial, and could see that something more subtle than pointing could be used to show which object was required. Moreover, some of the first NSL cohort had at least basic knowledge of Spanish while the Al-Sayyid Bedouin community always integrated deaf and hearing people in the same extended family – and thus would be motivated to try to convey something of their needs, or share their interest in the current scene, by pantomime and the development of increasingly conventionalized gestures.

Early humans shared a community, but had no models of successful language use. For us, as modern humans, it seems almost inconceivable that the very *idea* of language is something that has to be invented. However, to take a related example, we know that writing was only invented some 5000 years ago. Yet, we have every reason to believe that no changes in brain genotype were required to support literacy (though the syndromes of dyslexia show that not all human brains are equally well prepared to match speech to writing; and the experience of literacy does indeed change the organization of the brain; Petersson *et al.*, 2000). Moreover, many societies have lasted till modern times with no written form for their spoken language. Yet, once one has the *idea* of phonetic writing, it is relatively straightforward to invent a writing system – as has been demonstrated by many Christian missionaries who wanted to bring literacy and the Bible to a people who had language but no writing. Even more pertinently, around 1820, Sequoyah, a Cherokee who knew very little English and could not read it, invented – inspired solely by the *idea* of writing – a syllabary with 86 characters to represent the sounds of the Cherokee language (Walker and Sarbaugh, 1993).

Design features vs. innate rules

But perhaps we would not need to discover the idea of language were the brains of *Homo sapiens* genetically endowed with a universal grammar which "pre-wired" all possible syntactic rules in the infant human brain. While researchers studying NSL and ABSL have been relatively circumspect in making claims for the implications of their research, science journalists discussing the work have not been so restrained. For example, Juliana Kettlewell (2004) claims that the work of Senghas *et al.* (2004) proved that:

- Some language rules may be innate.
- NSL follows many basic rules common to all languages, even though the children were not taught them.
- Some language traits are not passed on by culture, but instead arise due to the innate way human beings process language.

However, the above claims are misleading if (as seems natural) we understand a "language rule" as the sort of rule of syntax that (some suggest) would be defined by setting parameters in universal grammar. On the other hand, if we take a "language rule" to be a design feature in the sense of Hockett (1987), then the claim seems reasonable. The breaking out of symbols is a basic skill. We have already discussed how, on the path to the first human languages, fractionation might have replaced protowords by words denoting "semantic components" for those words and then, as protowords fractionated, constructions emerged to allow recapture of the meanings of protowords. The advantage of this development was that these constructions and the increased stock of more focused words allowed for recombinations that expressed many situations that were not captured by the original stock of protowords, and provided the space for the creation of new words to fill the slots in constructions in new ways. Exercising these skills lies in the domain of "design features" rather than parameters of a putative universal grammar. What is striking here is the ability of a community not only to add to its own stock of signs but also to develop new means to deploy them appropriately, as in the scenario observed by Senghas *et al.* (2004) in the decomposition of path and manner, and the development of the X-Y-X construction to retrieve the simultaneity of the original gesture.

Kettlewell (2004) quotes Annie Senghas as saying that the NSL study "does prove the fundamentals of language are part of the innate endowment. You don't have language or grammar in your head when you are born, but you do have certain learning abilities." I agree with "you do have certain learning abilities," but disagree with "it does prove the fundamentals of language are part of the innate endowment." I would see discreteness as a property of protolanguage rather than language (and I have noted its precursor in motor schemas) while *combinatorial patterning* rests on the learning abilities captured by complex imitation. The above section on "The emergence of the Nicaraguan Deaf community" (summarizing, and commenting upon, the observations of Polich, 2005) suggests that these capabilities, combined with a cumulative process of individual innovation and social acceptance forming an upward spiral, can explain what is going on. A counter claim, in the spirit of, e.g., Lightfoot (2006), might be that there is an innate language acquisition device that sets parameters in Universal Grammar, but can only do this when there are data to set them. But then this would not explain how NSL developed unless one were to characterize first-cohort NSL as a full language defined by default or random parameter settings, which it manifestly is not.

Pearson (2004) argues that the results of Senghas *et al.* (2004) show that children are born with a natural ability to break down language into, e.g., manner vs. path, and asserts that "hard wired rules like this help explain how language is acquired so easily," and quotes Annie Senghas as saying "You think it takes years and years of evolution, and then boom, one [language] emerges in a generation." I have already noted that the "hard-wired" rule is a "design feature" not a rule of grammar, and that the key feature here may be complex imitation, which is a design feature which is not specific to language. What needs to be critically examined here is

(i)   whether the term "easily" is justified, and
(ii) whether "emergence in one generation" is a product of such "language rules" at work in an isolated community.

To (i), note that if developing NSL innovations like the separation of signs for path and manner were the easy result of innate rules, then it should have been achieved by children in home sign and the first NSL cohort. This leads me to answer (ii) by suggesting that special cultural factors were at play, and that these go beyond the mere ending of isolation of deaf children that began in the late 1970s.

As demonstrated by Polich (2005), the sign language in Nicaragua did not develop in a vacuum, but owes a debt to multiple influences. The language and the community appear to have grown in tandem, and they grew most rapidly among a group that was not composed of children, but of those looking toward adulthood. Let us then re-examine a number of claims made in the following extract from Senghas *et al.* (2004, p.1781):

> The difference today between first- and second-cohort signers therefore indicates what children could do that adolescents and adults could not ... Using their early learning skills, those who were still children in the mid-1980s developed NSL into the more discrete and combinatorial system that they, and the children who followed in the 1990s, still exhibit today.

We have already noted (with Slobin 2005) that the innovations of concern to us were already present, if not widespread, in the first NSL cohort. New signs and constructions were devised by individuals, some of them children, some adolescents or older. However, the majority of children may have done nothing to increase the language other than to augment the community which could increase the probability that a useful new sign would spread widely rather than being part of an idiolect of just a few signers before being lost (as is the case with most home signs).

One must be careful to distinguish mechanisms which generate innovations from those which determine the spread or demise of each innovation. One is reminded here of the processes of cumulative cultural evolution which Tomasello (1999) attributes to a "ratchet effect" whereby "individual and group inventions are mastered relatively faithfully by conspecifics, including youngsters, which enables them to remain in their new and improved form within the group until something better comes along." The notion is that this is possible because human beings are biologically adapted for culture in ways that other primates are not. Tomasello argues that the key adaptation is one that enables individuals to understand other individuals as intentional agents like the self, but I think that *complex imitation* would suffice without invoking any "Theory of Mind" – which is not to deny that understanding the intentions of others does indeed play a vital role in the development of human social networks.

Continuing, Senghas *et al.* (2004, p. 1781) assert:

> Our observations highlight two of the learning mechanisms available during childhood.

(a)   a dissecting, segmental approach to bundles of information; *this analytical approach appears to override other patterns of organization in the input,* to the point of breaking apart previously unanalyzed wholes.

(b)   *a predisposition for linear sequencing; sequential combinations appear even when it is physically possible to combine elements simultaneously,* and despite the availability of a simultaneous model. [My italics.]

For me, complex imitation is the generic skill which underlies these phenomena. However, as a caveat to (a), note that languages do resist decomposition when the compound is in sufficiently frequent use: thus in English we say *kick* instead of *hit with the foot* and *punch* for *hit with the fist* but still have the decomposition *hit with the X* for use where X is a less common instrument or where the foot or fist require special emphasis. As a caveat to (b), we noted earlier that some signed languages do not segregate path and manner, while others do (or may employ either strategy on different occasions). To support (b), Senghas *et al.* (2004) note that children acquiring American Sign Language (ASL) do initially break complex verb expressions down into sequential morphemes (Meier, 1987; Newport, 1981), rather than producing the simultaneous expression found in adults. However, I suggest that this is a matter of attention and skill. Some compounds are easy to imitate, others are hard. Speaking children first progress towards speech by mastering sounds which involve differential control of one articulator and only later master differential control of multiple articulators simultaneously (Studdert-Kennedy, 2002 offers data consistent with this view). Complex imitation is cumulative. Moreover, deaf children within a Deaf community (as distinct from those creating home sign or in the first cohort or generation of NSL or ABSL) do not acquire signs by ritualizing pantomime, but rather emulate the signs themselves as entities within a communicative system. If a child sees a complicated sign, it will successfully mimic one or two features at first. I would thus suggest that what might look like breaking complex verb expressions down into sequential morphemes may be a matter of motor simplification rather than linguistic re-analysis. Breaking complex skills into pieces and then learning how to gracefully reconstitute them is a general property of motor learning, and should not be counted as a design feature specific to language.

Senghas *et al.* (2004) suggest that the elements chosen for segmentation may reveal the primitives that children are predisposed to seek out as basic, grammatical units. However, one must be careful with the notion of "primitives" here. When a speaking child simplifies a word, the result is clearly just a poor pronunciation of a word, since omitting parts of the phonological structure has no semantic correlate. However, if a child "mispronounces" a sign by better approximating the hand shape rather than the trajectory, say, one might interpret this as extracting a grammatical (or, perhaps better, semantic) primitive, but I think this would be a misinterpretation of the data. Nonetheless, I am happy to agree – once we switch to (a) and (b) as being available rather than universally applied – that:

> such learning processes leave an imprint on languages – observable in mature languages in their core, universal properties – including discrete elements (such as words and morphemes) combined into hierarchically organized constructions (such as phrases and sentences) (Senghas *et al.*, 2004, p. 1781)

with the caveat that we must distinguish the perhaps relatively rare discovery of ways to add expressive power by application of (a) and (b) from the ability to readily learn such innovations once they have been made.

In MSH, complex imitation – an analytical, combinatorial learning mechanism – is argued to evolve within the domain of praxis. Byrne's "feeding programs" (Byrne, 2003) show that gorillas can indeed learn complex hierarchical and conditional structures, but this requires a long drawn out process of "imitation by behavior parsing." My suggestion is that the ability to more rapidly acquire novel behaviors was a crucial evolutionary step that preceded the emergence of protolanguage, let alone language. MSH posits that the next crucial turning point came with pantomime – the transition from praxis to communication – but that the ability for conventionalization that yielded protosign as embedded within a "cultural system" required neurological innovations (witness the signers who lose signing but not the ability to pantomime; Corina *et al.*, 1992; Marshall *et al.*, 2004).

Emerging (dyadic) sign languages

The existence of Spanish *and its cospeech gestures* in the NSL environment creates, I suggest "communicative needs" which children then seek to reach in the new medium. Indeed, Russo and Volterra (2005) note that Senghas *et al.* (2004) provided no information about the extent of the influence of gestures of hearing people during the early stages of acquisition of the deaf learners and about the influence of spoken and written languages such as Spanish or English (see Capirci and Volterra, 2008 for further development of these ideas). They note that Fusellier-Souza (2001, 2006), studying the "emerging sign languages" (ESL) spontaneously developed by isolated deaf individuals in Brazil, shows the strong continuity between the gestures used by the hearing population and the lexicon of the emerging sign languages. However, one must be careful with the word "isolated." Each of the three deaf people Fusellier-Souza studied was isolated from any Deaf community, but each had a speaking person with whom they developed their own sign language, unique to this dyad. Moreover, each person developed a role within the broader Brazilian society and developed strategies for communication with other people. In some sense, then, an "emerging sign language" is better thought of as a "dyadic sign language" (DSL) to reflect the fact that it is the product of a community of at least two, but not necessarily more than two, people within their own lifetime. A DSL thus exhibits what can happen to home sign when it remains isolated from an existing sign language, but also shares the crucial property that it is shaped by input from speaking members of the surrounding community (in this case, the other member of the dyad). Where a DSL differs from NSL and ABSL is that it rests on the inventions of two people who can adapt to each other's idiosyncrasies, though perhaps within the context of the larger speaking community. Fusellier-Souza (personal communication, December 2007) reports that:

> Two of my subjects (Ivaldo and Jo) have always worked in contact with hearing Brazilian people of their settings. When they are not in communication with their privileged hearing interlocutor, the communication with other hearing people is characterized by a kind of "exolingue gestural communication" based on face to face interactions, shared knowledge, use of the iconisation process activating the intent of the speaker to "say by showing" (using highly iconic structures, gestures of the hearing culture and loads of pointing for referential constructions). None of my deaf informants mastered written Portuguese. However, I've observed that Ivaldo uses his arm as a kind of board on which to use specific written forms of Portuguese (city name abbreviations, numbers, short names) in order to communicate with his hearing interlocutor. It's a clever strategy showing the use of functional writing despite extremely limited knowledge of written language. [Slightly edited]

A DSL thus lacks the systematization that results when a larger Deaf community converges on a shared set of signs but nonetheless reflects active engagement with speakers, akin to what I have suggested was operative in the pre-systematization stages of ABSL and NSL. Fusellier-Souza, who adopts the theoretical framework of the French linguist Christian Cuxac (see, e.g., Sallandre and Cuxac, 2002), stresses the role of iconicity in the autonomous development of signs, seeing it as playing an important role in different linguistic levels (phonetic, morphemic, lexical, syntactic, semantic, discourse). Here we may recall the crucial role of pantomime in MSH, while also recalling that many processes serve to "erode" iconicity. Indeed, many signs in ASL make explicit the effects of bilingualism. For example, the ASL sign for BLUE is a reduced form of the finger spelling of B-L (Padden, 1996). Russo and Volterra (2005) stress that the way in which young signers are exposed to gestural, vocal, or written language in the first years of acquisition may strongly affect their language competence (Bates and Volterra, 1984; Volterra and Erting, 1994), so that differences between generations of signers may be attributable to the different communicative inputs to which they were exposed. ABSL and NSL each reflect the merging of many people's contributions over multiple cohorts or generations and this process continues. As already noted, some ABSL signs tend to vary from one extended family to another, with a resultant lack of convergence to a well-defined phonology for ABSL (Aronoff *et al.*, 2008).

Diffusion of communicative goals, not specific constructions

Senghas *et al.* (2005) note that "The vocal and written Spanish exposure afforded to young deaf children in Nicaragua appears not to have changed over the past 25 years. Both are minimally available. ... Spanish is taught in school, but by graduation at the completion of sixth grade, none of the students have an easy command of written or spoken Spanish." But this is to confuse two quite separate claims:

- All deaf children build on a knowledge of Spanish to contribute to the development of NSL,

which is false and

- The development of NSL had two catalysts: (i) the development of novel signs and constructions by perhaps only a minority of individuals, some of whom were influenced by their knowledge of Spanish or existing sign languages; and (ii) the development of a Deaf community so that such inventions could become widespread, passed on to younger members [at least] of the community, and to some extent regularized in the process.

Fluency is not required for (i) – just that a key word or construction is understood well enough by one child for him/her to invent a signing strategy that achieves a similar communicative goal.

Signed languages use "signing space" to make spatial relations clear in a way that is denied to speech, which is temporal rather than spatial. Indeed, unlike speech, the manual modality makes it relatively easy to invent forms that can be understood by naïve observers (e.g., indexical pointing gestures or iconic miming gestures). As a result, communication systems can be invented "on the spot" in the manual modality. ABSL developed in a community in which the deaf were integrated with Arabic speakers, and the latter already had the use of a language. Similarly, some members of the early NSL community knew a moderate amount of Spanish. The challenge was to find low-energy ways to express these thoughts in the new medium of sign. The result was that ABSL had many novel features not present in Arabic, and similarly for NSL in relation to Spanish, but this is very different from asserting there is *no* influence. Let me illustrate this with an example from English. The French expression "respondez s'il vous plait" – "reply, if it pleases you" – has passed into English as the abbreviation RSVP, spoken according to the English pronunciation of these four letters. This form is now used as both a noun and verb, and most people who use it do not know that it contains "please" as part of its meaning – thus the expression "Please RSVP." It would be mistaken to deny that RSVP derives from French influence, but it does demonstrate that once a sign is introduced into a language by those who do know its etymology it can take on a life of its own once adopted by those unaware of, or choosing to ignore, this etymology, and who thus can be quite free in the way they assimilate it to the structures of their own language. Returning to NSL and ABSL, there is little in the speech environment that can be adopted directly. But the issue is whether the children would have got as far if they had been isolated from all contact with other humans. I say "No."

Challenges for future research

All this opens up manifest directions for future research. In studies of home sign, I would like to see much more analysis of the role of the caregiver in the child's construction of home sign – e.g., by repeatedly pointing to pictures in picture books, thus creating categories which require names. I would also like to see more work on the interplay of mechanisms for action and sign. For ABSL and NSL, one pressing, and immensely hard, empirical issue is to go beyond "snapshots" of the capabilities of a cohort to an "epidemiology" of where novel signs and constructions arise and how they spread through the population and become transformed as they do so.

Notes

1. I use the terms "speaker" and "hearer" even when the use of language involves the production and visual observation of hand and face movements.

2. See www.sciencemag.org/cgi/content/full/305/5691/1779/DC1 for a video clip of (S1) the cospeech gestures of a Spanish speaker, and (S2) the signing of a third-cohort NSL signer.

References

Arbib, M. A. (1981). Perceptual structures and distributed motor control. In
    V. B. Brooks (Ed.), *Handbook of Physiology – The Nervous System II. Motor Control*,
    (pp. 1449–1480) Bethesda, MD: American Physiological Society.

Arbib, M. A. (2002). The mirror system, imitation, and the evolution of language. In
    K. Dautenhahn and C. L. Nehaniv (Eds.), *Imitation in Animals and Artifacts. Complex
    Adaptive Systems* (pp. 229–280). Cambridge, MA: MIT Press.

Arbib, M. A. (2005a). From monkey-like action recognition to human language: An
    evolutionary framework for neurolinguistics (with commentaries and author's
    response). *Behavioral and Brain Sciences*, **28**, 105–167.

Arbib, M. A. (2005b). Interweaving protosign and protospeech: Further developments
    beyond the mirror. *Interaction Studies: Social Behavior and Communication in Biological
    and Artificial Systems*, **6**, 145–171.

Arbib, M. A. (2007). How new languages emerge (Review of D. Lightfoot, 2006, *How
    New Languages Emerge*, Cambridge University Press). *Linguist List 18-432, Thu Feb 08
    2007*, http://linguistlist.org/issues/17/17-1250.html.

Arbib, M. A. (2008). Holophrasis and the protolanguage spectrum. *Interaction
    Studies: Social Behavior and Communication in Biological and Artificial Systems*, **9**(1),
    151–165.

Arbib, M. A., Érdi, P., and Szentágothai, J. (1998). *Neural Organization: Structure, Function,
    and Dynamics*. Cambridge, MA: The MIT Press.

Arbib, M. A. and Hesse, M. B. (1986). *The Construction of Reality*. Cambridge: Cambridge
    University Press.

Arbib, M. A. and Hill, J. C. (1988). Language acquisition: Schemas replace universal
    grammar. In J. A. Hawkins (Ed.), *Explaining Language Universals*, (pp. 56–72). Oxford:
    Basil Blackwell.

Arbib, M. A., Liebal, K., and Pika, S. (in press). Primate vocalization, ape gesture, and
    human language: an evolutionary framework. *Current Anthropology*.

Arbib, M. A. and Rizzolatti, G. (1997). Neural expectations: A possible evolutionary
    path from manual skills to language. *Communication and Cognition*, **29**, 393–424.

Arbib, M. A., Liebal, K., and Pika, S. (in press). Primate vocalization, age gesture, and
    human language: an evolutionary framework. *Current Anthropology*.

Armstrong, D. F., Stokoe, W. C., and Wilcox, S. E. (1995). *Gesture and the Nature of
    Language*. Cambridge: Cambridge University Press.

Armstrong, D. F. and Wilcox, S. E. (2007). *The Gestural Origin of Language*. Oxford: Oxford
    University Press.

Aronoff, M., Meir, I., Padden, C., and Sandler, W. (2008). The roots of linguistic
    organization in a new language. *Interaction Studies: Social Behavior and
    Communication in Biological and Artificial Systems*, **9**(1), 133–153

Baker, M. (2001). *The Atoms of Language: The Mind's Hidden Rules of Grammar*. New York:
    Basic Books.

Bates, E. and Volterra, V. (1984). On the invention of language: An alternative view.
    Monographs of the Society for Research in Child Development, **49**(3–4), 130–142.

Bickerton, D. (1995). *Language and Human Behavior*. Seattle: University of Washington Press.

Burgess, N. and O'Keefe, J. (2003). Neural representations in human spatial memory. *Trends in Cognative Science* **7**(12), 517–519.

Byrne, R. W. (2003). Imitation as behavior parsing. *Philosophical Transactions of the Royal Society of London (B)*, **358**, 529–536.

Byrne, R. W. and Byrne, J. M. E. (1993). Complex leaf-gathering skills of mountain gorillas (*Gorilla g. beringei*): Variability and standardization. *American Journal of Primatology*, **31**, 241–261.

Capirci, O., Iverson, J. M., Pizzuto, E., and Volterra, V. (1996). Gestures and words during the transition to two-word speech. *Journal of Child Language*, **23**, 645–673.

Capirci, O. and Volterra, V. (2008). Gesture and speech. The emergence and development of a strong and changing partnership. *Gesture*, **8**(1), 22–44.

Caro, T. M. and Hauser, M. D. (1992). Is there teaching in nonhuman animals? *The Quarterly Review of Biology*, **67**, 151–174.

Chomsky, N. and Lasnik, H. (1993). Principles and parameters theory. In J. Jacobs *et al.* (Eds.) *Syntax: An International Handbook of Contemporary Research*, vol. 1 (pp. 506–569). New York: Walter de Gruyter. (Reprinted in N. Chomsky, *The Minimalist Program*. Cambridge, MA: MIT Press.)

Coppola, M. (2002). The emergence of grammatical categories in home sign: Evidence from family-based gesture systems in Nicaragua. Unpublished Ph.D. thesis, University of Rochester.

Corballis, M. C. (2002). *From Hand to Mouth, the Origins of Language*. Princeton, NJ: Princeton University Press.

Corina, D. P., Poizner, H., Bellugi, U., Feinberg, T., Dowd, D., and O'Grady-Batch, L. (1992). Dissociation between linguistic and nonlinguistic gestural systems: A case for compositionality. *Brain and Language*, **43**(3), 414–447.

Croft, W. (2000). *Explaining Language Change: An Evolutionary Approach*. Harlow: Longman.

Croft, W. (2001). *Radical Construction Grammar: Syntactic Theory in Typological Perspective*. Oxford: Oxford University Press.

Deacon, T. W. (1997). *The Symbolic Species: The Co-Evolution of Language and the Brain*. WW Norton.

Deacon, T. W. (2007). The evolution of language systems in the human brain. In J. H. Kaas and T. M. Preuss (Eds.), *Evolution of Nervous Systems: A Comprehensive Reference. Volume 4 – Primates* (pp. 529–547). Elsevier.

DeCasper, A. J. and Fifer, W. P. (1980). Of human bonding: Newborns prefer their mothers' voices. *Science*, **208**(44–48), 1174–1176.

DeCasper, A. J. and Spence, M. J. (1991). Auditorily mediated behavior during the perinatal period: A cognitive view. In M. J. S. W. a. P. R. Zelazo (Ed.), *Newborn Attention: Biological Constraints and the Influence of Experience*. New York: Ablex Publishing Corp.

Fusellier-Souza, I. (2001). La création gestuelle des individus sourds isolés: de l'édification conceptuelle et linguistique à la sémiogenèse des langues des signes. *Acquisition et Interaction en Langue Étrangère (AILE)*, **15**, 61–95.

Fusellier-Souza, I. (2006). Emergence and development of signed languages: from a semiogenetic point of view. *Sign Language Studies*, **7**(1), 30–56.

Fuster, J. M. (2000). Prefrontal neurons in networks of executive memory. *Brain Research Bulletin*, **52**(5), 331–336.

Goldberg, A. E. (2003). Constructions: A new theoretical approach to language. *Trends in Cognitive Science*, **7**(5), 219–224.

Goldin-Meadow, S. (1982). The resilience of recursion: A study of a communication system developed without a conventional language model. In E. Wanner and L. R. Gleitman (Eds.), *Language Acquisition: The State of the Art* (pp. 51–77). Cambridge: Cambridge University Press.

Goldin-Meadow, S. (2003). *The Resilience of Language: What Gesture Creation in Deaf Children Can Tell Us About How All Children Learn Language*. New York: Psychology Press.

Goldin-Meadow, S. and Mylander, C. (1998). Spontaneous sign systems created by deaf children in two cultures. *Nature*, **391**(15), 279–281.

Goldin-Meadow, S., Yalabik, E., and Gershkoff-Stowe, L. (2000). *The resilience of ergative structure in language created by children and by adults*. Proceedings of the 24th Annual Boston University Conference on Language Development, Vol. 1, Somerville, MA, pp. 343–353.

Hauser, M. D., Chomsky, N., and Fitch, T. W. (2002). The language faculty: What is it, who has it, and how did it evolve? *Science*, **298**, 1568–1579.

Hewes, G. W. (1973). Primate communication and the gestural origin of language. *Current Anthropology*, **12**(1–2), 5–24.

Hill, J. C. (1983). A computational model of language acquisition in the two-year-old. *Cognition and Brain Theory*, **6**, 287–317.

Hockett, C. F. (1987). *Refurbishing Our Foundations: Elementary Linguistics from an Advanced Point of View*. Philadelphia, PA: John Benjamins.

Iverson, J. M., Capirci, O., and Caselli, M. C. (1994). From communication to language in two modalities. *Cognitive Development*, **9**, 23–43.

Jackendoff, R. J. (1987). The status of thematic relations in linguistic theory. *Linguistic Inquiry*, **18**, 369–411.

Karchmer, M. A. and Mitchell, R. E. (2003). Demographic and achievement characteristics of deaf and hard of hearing students. In M. M. a. P. E. Spencer (Ed.), *Oxford Handbook of Deaf Studies, Language, and Education* (pp. 21–37). Oxford: Oxford University Press.

Kegl, J. (1994). The Nicaraguan Sign Language project: An overview. *Signpost*, **7**(1), 40–46.

Kegl, J., Senghas, A., and Coppola, M. (1999). Creation through contact: Sign language emergence and sign language change in Nicaragua. In M. DeGraff (Ed.), *Comparative Grammatical Change: The Intersection of Language Acquisition, Creole Genesis, and Diachronic Syntax*, (pp. 179–237) Cambridge, MA: MIT Press.

Kendon, A. (2002). Historical observations on the relationship between research on sign languages and language origins theory. In D. Armstrong, M. Karchmer and J. V. V. Cleeve (Eds.), *The Study of Sign Languages – Essays in Honor of William C. Stokoe*, (pp. 35–52). Washington DC: Gallaudet University Press.

Kendon, A. (2004). *Gesture: Visible Action as Utterance*, Cambridge: Cambridge University Press.

Kettlewell, J. (2004). *Children create new sign language*, BBC News, http://news.bbc.co.uk/2/hi/science/nature/3662928.stm

Kirby, S. (2000). Syntax without natural selection: How compositionality emerges from vocabulary in a population of learners. In C. Knight, M. Studdert-Kennedy, and J. R. Hurford (Eds.), *The Evolutionary Emergence of Language*. Cambridge: Cambridge University Press.

Kisch, S. (2004). Negotiating (genetic) deafness in a Bedouin community. In J. V. V. Cleve (Ed.), *Genetics, Disability and Deafness*. Washington DC: Gallaudet University Press.

Lightfoot, D. (2006). *How New Languages Emerge*, Cambridge: Cambridge University Press.

Lillo-Martin, D. (1999). Modality effects and modularity in language acquisition: The acquisition of American Sign Language. In T. Bhatia and W. Ritchie (Eds.), *Handbook of Language Acquisition* (pp. 531–567). New York: Academic Press.

MacNeilage, P. F. and Davis, B. L. (2005). The frame/content theory of evolution of speech: Comparison with a gestural origins theory. *Interaction Studies: Social Behavior and Communication in Biological and Artificial Systems*, **6**, 173–199.

Marshall, J., Atkinson, J., Smulovitch, E., Thacker, A., and Woll, B. (2004). Aphasia in a user of British Sign Language: Dissociation between sign and gesture. *Cognitive Neuropsychology*, **21**, 537–554.

McNeill, D. (1992). *Hand and Mind*. Chicago, IL: University of Chicago Press.

McNeill, D. (2005). *Gesture and Thought*. Chicago, IL: University of Chicago Press.

Meier, R. P. (1987). Elicited imitation of verb agreement in American Sign Language: Iconically or morphologically determined? *Journal of Memory and Language*, **26**, 362–376.

Meier, R. P. (1991). Language acquisition by deaf children. *American Scientist*, **79**, 60–70.

Meir, I. and Sandler, W. (2004). *safa bamerxav: eshnav lesfat hasimanim hayisraelit (Language in Space: A Window on Israeli Sign Language)*. Haifa, Israel: University Haifa Press.

Meltzoff, A. N. and Moore, M. K. (1977). Imitation of facial and manual gestures by human neonates. *Science*, **198**, 75–78.

Nespor, M. and Sandler, W. (1999). Prosody in Israeli Sign Language. *Language and Speech*, **42**, 143–176.

Newport, E. L. (1981). Constraints on structure: Evidence from American Sign Language and language learning. In W. A. Collins (Ed.), *Aspects of the Development of Competence* (pp. 93–124). New York: Erlbaum.

Newport, E. L. and Meier, R. P. (1985). The acquisition of American Sign Language. In D. I. Slobin (Ed.), *The Cross-Linguistic Study of Language Acquisition. Vol. 1, The Data*, (pp. 881–938). New York: Erlbaum.

Noble, W. and Davidson, I. (1996). *Human Evolution, Language and Mind: A Psychological and Archaeological Inquiry*. Cambridge: Cambridge University Press.

Padden, C. A. (1996). Early bilingual lives of Deaf children. In I. Parasnis (Ed.), *Cultural and Language Diversity and the Deaf Experience* (pp. 99–116). Cambridge: Cambridge University Press.

Pearson, H. (2004). *The birth of a language*, news@nature.com, http://www.nature.com/news/2004/040913/full/040913-19.html

Petersson, K. M., Reis, A., Askelof, S., Castro-Caldas, A., and Ingvar, M. (2000). Language processing modulated by literacy: A network analysis of verbal repetition in literate and illiterate subjects. *Journal of Cognitive Neuroscience*, **12**(3), 364–382.

Pinker, S. and Bloom, P. (1990). Natural language and natural selection. *Behavioral and Brain Sciences*, **13**, 707–784.

Polich, L. (2005). *The Emergence of the Deaf Community in Nicaragua: "With Sign Language You Can Learn So Much"*. Washington DC: Gallaudet University Press.

Rizzolatti, G. and Arbib, M. A. (1998). Language within our grasp. *Trends in Neuroscience*, **21**(5), 188–194.

Roy, A. C. and Arbib, M. A. (2005). The syntactic motor system. *Gesture*, **5**, 7–37.

Russo, T. and Volterra, V. (2005). Comment on "Children creating core properties of language: Evidence from an emerging sign language in Nicaragua". *Science*, **309**, 56.

Sallandre, M. A. and Cuxac, C. (2002). Iconicity in sign language: A theoretical and methodological point of view. In *Gesture and Sign Language in Human-Computer Interaction, Lecture Notes in Computer Science 2298* (pp. 13–35). New York: Springer-Verlag.

Sandler, W., Meir, I., Padden, C. and Aronoff, M. (2005). The emergence of grammar: Systematic structure in a new language. *Proceedings of the National Academy of Science USA*, **102**(7), 2661–2665.

Scott, D., Carmi, R., Eldebour, K., Duyk, G., Stone, E., and Sheffield, V. (1995). Nonsyndromic autosomal recessive deafness is linked to the DFNB1 locus in a large inbred Bedouin family from Israel. *American Journal of Human Genetics*, **57**, 965–968.

Senghas, A. (2003). Intergenerational influence and ontogenetic development in the emergence of spatial grammar in Nicaraguan Sign Language. *Cognitive Development*, **18**, 511–531.

Senghas, A., Kita, S., and Özyürek, A. (2004). Children creating core properties of language: Evidence from an emerging sign language in Nicaragua. *Science*, **305**, 1779–1782.

Senghas, A., Özyürek, A., and Kita, K. (2005). Response to comment on "Children creating core properties of language: evidence from an emerging sign language in Nicaragua". *Science*, **309**, 56c.

Senghas, R. J. (1997). An 'unspeakable, unwriteable' language: Deaf identity, language & personhood among the first cohorts of Nicaraguan signers. Unpublished Ph.D. thesis, University of Rochester, NY.

Seyfarth, R. M., Cheney, D. L., and Bergman, T. J. (2005). Primate social cognition and the origins of language. *Trends in Cognitive Sciences*, **9**(6), 264–266.

Slobin, D. I. (2005). From ontogenesis to phylogenesis: What can child language tell us about language evolution? In J. Langer, S. T. Parker, and C. Milbrath (Eds.), *Biology and Knowledge Revisited: From Neurogenesis to Psychogenesis*, New York: Lawrence Erlbaum Associates.

Stokoe, W. C. (1960). *Sign Language Structure: An Outline of the Visual Communication Systems of the American Deaf.* Buffalo, Co: University of Buffalo.

Stokoe, W. C. (2001). *Language in Hand: Why Sign Came Before Speech.* Washington, DC: Gallaudet University Press.

Studdert-Kennedy, M. (2002). Mirror neurons, vocal imitation and the evolution of particulate speech. In M. Stamenov and V. Gallese (Eds.), *Mirror Neurons and the Evolution of Brain and Language* (pp. 207–227). Philadelphia, PA: John Benjamins.

Suddendorf, T. and Corballis, M. C. (1997). Mental time travel and the evolution of the human mind. *Genetic Social and General Psychology Monographs,* **123**(2), 133–167.

Tomasello, M. (1999). The human adaptation for culture. *Annual Review of Anthropology,* **28**, 509–529.

Tomasello, M. (2003). *Constructing a Language: A Usage-Based Theory of Language Acquisition.* Cambridge, MA: Harvard University Press.

Tomasello, M., Call, J., Warren, J., Frost, T., Carpenter, M., and Nagell, K. (1997). The ontogeny of chimpanzee gestural signals. In S. Wilcox, King, B., and Steels, L. (Eds.), *Evolution of Communication* (pp. 224–259). Philadelphia, PA: John Benjamins Publishing Company.

Visalberghi, E. and Fragaszy, D. (1990). Do monkeys ape? In S. Parker and K. Gibson (Eds.), *Language and Intelligence in Monkeys and Apes: Comparative Developmental Perspectives* (pp. 247–273). Cambridge: Cambridge University Press.

Visalberghi, E. and Fragaszy, D. (2001). Do monkeys ape? Ten years after. In K. Dautenhahn and C. Nehaniv (Eds.), *Imitation in Animals and Artifacts* (pp. 471–500). Cambridge, MA: The MIT Press.

Volterra, V. and Erting, C. J. (Eds.) (1994). *From Gesture to Language in Hearing and Deaf Children.* Washington, DC: Gallaudet University Press.

Walker, W. and Sarbaugh, J. (1993). The early history of the Cherokee syllabary. *Ethnohistory,* **40**(1), 70–94.

Wohlschläger, A., Gattis, M., and Bekkering, H. (2003). Action generation and action perception in imitation: An instance of the ideomotor principle. *Philosophical Transactions of the Royal Society London,* **358**, 501–515.

Wray, A. (2000). Holistic utterances in protolanguage: The link from primates to humans. In C. Knight, M. Studdert-Kennedy, and J. Hurford (Eds.), *The Evolutionary Emergence of Language: Social Function and the Origins of Linguistic Form* (pp. 285–302). Cambridge: Cambridge University Press.

6

Origins of the language: Correlation between brain evolution and language development

ALFREDO ARDILA

Introduction

The question about when and how language emerged in human evolution has been a major and intriguing question since at least the classical Egyptian times. It is reported that the Pharaoh Psamtik took two children to be raised by deaf-mutes, in order to find out what was the first and natural language. When these children were later observed, one of them said something that sounded like *bekos*, the Phrygian word for *bread*. From this, Psamtik concluded that Phrygian was the first and original language. During the following centuries, the origin of language continued as a most intriguing and polemic question. Different approaches and interpretations were proposed throughout history. At a certain point the debate became so complex and hot that in 1866 the Linguistic Society of Paris banned discussion of the origin of language, arguing that it is an unanswerable problem.

Contemporary research on linguistics, archeology, comparative psychology and genetics has significantly advanced understanding of the origins of human language (e.g., Bickerton, 1990; Corballis, 2002, 2006; Enard *et al.*, 2002; Mallory, 1989; Nowak and Krakauer, 1999; Ruhlen, 1994; Swadesh, 1967; Tallerman, 2005). Different disciplines have contributed from their own perspective to make the human communication system more comprehensible.

The purpose of this paper is not to further review and discuss the historical origins of language, but to relate what is known (or supposed) on the origins of language, with contemporary neurology and neuropsychology data, particularly with the area of aphasia. Aphasia knowledge can potentially also make a significant contribution to understanding about the origin and evolution of human language.

Foundations in Evolutionary Cognitive Neuroscience, ed. Steven M. Platek and Todd K. Shackelford.
Published by Cambridge University Press. © Cambridge University Press 2009.

Initially, some basic neuropsychological data about language impairments in cases of brain pathology will be presented. It will be emphasized that there are two basic linguistic operations (selecting and sequencing; i.e., language as a paradigm and syntagm) (Jakobson and Halle, 1956; Jakobson, 1971). There are also two basic types of aphasia syndromes, named in different ways (e.g., motor/sensory; anterior/posterior; nonfluent/fluent; Broca-type/Wernicke-type; encoding/decoding disorder; expressive/impressive disorder, etc.), each one related to the disturbance of one of these two basic language elements (lexical/semantic and grammatical). Hence, in considering language evolution these two different dimensions of language have to be recognized. Each one may have emerged at a different historical moment. Analyzing this basic distinction and including it in an interpretation about language evolution can potentially further language evolution understanding.

There are only two fundamental aphasia syndromes

Since the nineteenth century it has been well known that there are two major aphasic syndromes, named in different ways, but roughly corresponding to Wernicke-type aphasia and Broca-type aphasia (e.g., Albert *et al.*, 1981; Bastian, 1898; Benson and Ardila, 1996; Freud, 1891/1973; Goldstein, 1948; Head, 1926; Hécaen, 1972; Kertesz, 1979; Lichtheim, 1885; Luria, 1976; Pick, 1931; Schuell *et al.*, 1964; Taylor-Sarno, 1998; Wilson, 1926). These two major aphasic syndromes have been related with the two basic linguistic operations: selecting (language as paradigm) and sequencing (language as syntagm) (Jakobson and Halle, 1956; Jakobson, 1971; Luria, 1972/1983). Jakobson (1964) proposed that aphasia tends to involve one of two types of linguistic deficiency. A patient may lose the ability to use language in two rather different ways: the language impairment can be situated on the paradigmatic axis (similarity disorder) or the syntagmatic axis (contiguity disorder).

The similarity disorder restricts the patient's ability to select words from the paradigmatic axis. These patients (Wernicke-type aphasia) cannot find words that exist as parts of the system (vocabulary). These aphasics have severely limited access to this language repertoire system. Specific nouns tend to be inaccessible and more general ones (*cat* becomes *animal*) take their place. These patients cannot select among alternative names (*dog, cat, fox*, etc). These patients may instead fill out their discourse with circumlocutions (the clock is referred as "*to know the time*"). Words no longer have a generic (paradigmatic) meaning for these patients, so verbal expressions tend to be strongly contextualized, and speech becomes empty. A "*dog*" can be referred to as "*animal*," "*it barks*," "*fox*," etc.

Luria (1972/1983) emphasized that the selection disorder can be observed at different levels of the language, corresponding to different aphasia subtypes: phoneme selection (acoustic agnosic aphasia), word selection (acoustic amnesic aphasia), and meaning selection (amnesic aphasia). By the same token, the contiguity disorder can be observed at different levels: sequencing words (kinetic motor aphasia – Broca aphasia) or sequencing sentences (dynamic aphasia – transcortical motor aphasia). Noteworthily, different subtypes of Wernicke aphasia are frequently distinguished (e.g., Ardila, 2006). Luria's acoustic agnosic, acoustic amnesic, and amnesic aphasia are indeed subtypes of the language impairment syndrome referred to as a whole as Wernicke aphasia.

The selection disorder

The Wernicke-type of aphasia represents the clinical syndrome characterized by impairments in the selection process (paradigmatic axis defect). In Wernicke aphasia, the lexical repertoire tends to decrease and language understanding difficulties are evident. Wernicke aphasia patients do not fully discriminate the acoustic information contained in speech. Lexical (word) and semantic (meaning) association become deficient. Patients have problems in recalling the words (memory of the words) and also in associating the words with specific meanings. It means that at least three different deficits underlie Wernicke-type aphasia: (1) phoneme discrimination defects, (2) verbal memory defects, and finally (3) lexical/semantic association deficits (Ardila, 1993).

In the Wernicke-type of aphasia obviously the language defect is situated at the level of the meaningful words (nouns). Phoneme and word selection are deficient, but language syntax (contiguity: sequencing elements) is well preserved and even overused (paragrammatism in Wernicke aphasia).

Nouns seem to depend on an organized pattern of brain activity. Contemporary clinical and neuroimaging studies have corroborated that different semantic categories are differentially impaired in cases of brain pathology. For instance, in anomia it has been traditionally recognized that naming body-parts, external objects, and colors depend (and are altered) upon the activity of different brain areas (Hécaen and Albert, 1978). It has also been found that finer distinctions can be made with regard to naming defects, which can be limited to a rather specific semantic category (e.g., people's names, living things, tools, geographical names, etc) (e.g., Harris and Kay, 1995; Goodglass *et al.*, 1986; Lyons *et al.*, 2002; Warrington and Shallice, 1984) and even as specific as "medical terms" (Crosson *et al.*, 1997). A brain "mapping" of the memory organization of different semantic categories could be supposed.

The sequencing disorder

The Broca-type of aphasia represents the clinical syndrome character-ized by impairments in the sequencing process (syntagmatic axis defect). It is usually cognized that Broca aphasia has two different distinguishing character-istics: (a) a motor component (lack of fluency, disintegration of the speech kinetic melodies, verbal–articulatory defects, etc., that is usually referred to as *apraxia of speech*); and (b) agrammatism (e.g., Benson and Ardila, 1996; Luria, 1976; Goodglass, 1993; Kertesz, 1985). If both defects are simultaneously observed (i.e., they are very highly correlated), it simply means they are both just two different manifestations of a single underlying defect. It is not easy to understand what could be the single factor responsible for these two clinical manifestations; but it may be a kind of "*inability to sequence expressive elements*" (Ardila and Bernal, 2007). A single common factor underlying both defects should be assumed. Broca's area, most likely, is not specialized in producing language, but in certain neural activities that can support not only skilled movements required for speech, but also morphosyntax. It is interesting to note that deaf-mute subjects (who, in consequence have never produced verbal articulatory movements) present a virtually total impossibility to learn, understand, and use language grammar (Poizner *et al.*, 1987). It is probable that the lack of normal verbal articulatory development is necessarily asso-ciated with a lack of normal grammatical development.

Other aphasia syndromes

Some aphasic syndromes can eventually be considered as variants of the Broca and Wernicke aphasia. For instance, amnesic (anomic or nominal) aphasia (usually due to damage in the vicinity of Brodmann's area 37) (Hécaen and Albert, 1978; Head, 1926; Luria, 1976) can be interpreted as a subtype of Wernicke aphasia in which the semantic associations of the words are signifi-cantly impaired.

Some other aphasic syndromes can be interpreted as language distur-bances due to a more general underlying disorder. For instance, extrasylvian (transcortical) motor aphasia associated with left convexital prefrontal damage could be interpreted as an executive function defect specifically affecting language use. The ability to actively and appropriately use language appears impaired, while the phonology, lexicon, semantics, and grammar are preserved. It does not seem difficult to argue that the ability to correctly use language can be interpreted as an executive function and as a metacog-nitive ability rather than a purely linguistic ability. Some rationales to support this interpretation are: (1) in extrasylvian (transcortical) motor aphasia there is a defect in verbal initiative rather than in language knowledge (Kleist, 1934); (2) this type of aphasia shares the general characteristics of the prefrontal (i.e., dysexecutive) syndrome but specifically with regard to the verbal processes so that it is the prefrontal (dysexecutive) syndrome affecting the verbal processes (Luria, 1976, 1980); (3) further, the language defect in extrasylvian (transcortical) motor aphasia does not affect the language understanding, and the fundamental linguistic processes are preserved (Berthier, 1999); and finally, (4) it could be argued that the prefrontal cortex does not participate in basic cognition but in metacognition (e.g., Ardila and Surloff, 2006). Extrasylvian (transcortical) motor aphasia could indeed be referred to as "dysexecutive aphasia." Some authors have interpreted extrasylvian motor aphasia in a similar way (e.g., Alexander, 2006; Luria, 1976, 1980).

Conduction aphasia, on the other hand, has usually been interpreted as a disconnection syndrome (e.g., Damasio and Damasio, 1980; Geschwind, 1965; Wernicke, 1874) usually due to an impairment in the arcuate fasciculus and sporadically in an indirect pathway passing through inferior parietal cortex (Catani et al., 2005). Alternatively, conduction aphasia has also been interpreted as a segmentary ideomotor apraxia (e.g., Ardila and Rosselli, 1990; Brown, 1972, 1975; Luria, 1976, 1980).

Usually it is recognized that conduction aphasia has three fundamental (fluent conversational language; comprehension almost normal; and significant impairments in repetition) and five secondary characteristics (defects in naming; reading defects; variable writing difficulties; ideomotor apraxia; and neurological abnormalities); so-called secondary characteristics are frequently but not necessarily found in conduction aphasia (Benson et al., 1973; Benson and Ardila, 1996).

This description of conduction aphasia clearly recognizes that spontaneous language production and language understanding are significantly preserved. In consequence, some mechanism required for correct language repetition is abnormal, but the knowledge of the language itself (phonology, lexicon, semantics, and grammar) is not impaired. Should conduction aphasia be interpreted as a primary aphasic syndrome? Obviously, if parrots can repeat, that means that language repetition cannot be considered as a primary linguistic ability.

Conduction aphasia is not really a primary form of aphasia but rather a secondary (or "peripheral") defect in language affecting a specific language ability (i.e., the ability to repeat). The language itself is not impaired, but rather the ability to reproduce aloud the auditory information that is heard.

Linguistic and anthropological data: three stages in language development

The question "*When did language begin?*" could be rephrased as the question "*How did language begin?*" Different steps in language development can be proposed, at least:

(1) Initial communication systems using sounds and other types of information – such as gestures, etc., similar to the communication systems observed in other animals, including nonhuman primates.

(2) Primitive language systems using combined sounds (words) but without a grammar (*language as paradigm*). This type of language could be likened to the holophrasic period in language development, observed in children around 1 to 1.5 years of age (Hoff, 2003).

(3) Communication systems using grammar (*language as syntagm*). During a child's language development, it is observed that the use of grammar is found after the holophrasic period. It simply means that it is a more advanced and complex stage. By the end of their second year, children begin to combine words into simple sentences. Initially, sentences represent a telegraphic speech (around 24–30 months of age), including two-word utterances in which connecting elements are omitted (e.g., "*other dog*," "*child eat*") (Hoff, 2003). It means language initially emerges as a system of words (language as a paradigm: lexical/semantic system), and only later as a system of relations among the words (language as a syntagm: grammatical system).

Initial communication systems

It is easy to assume that at the beginning of the human language, communication systems were like the communication systems found in non-human primates. It is known that chimpanzees and other nonhuman primates in their natural environment can use some communication strategies.

Chimpanzees employ a variety of gestures and facial expressions to communicate and keep in touch with each other. They possess a simple repertoire of noises and postures (body language) that can be used in different contexts with specific communication purposes. Observations have been collected in different environments, including natural environments and captive groups in human-controlled environments (McCrone, 1991). Chimpanzees make use of simple gestures, make facial expressions, and produce a limited amount of vocalizations. Unlike humans, chimps only produce about 12 different vocalizations. In captive conditions and under human training, chimpanzees can learn some artificial languages and close to about 200 "words" (Cheney and Seyfarth, 1997; McCrone, 1991).

Different attempts have been made to teach nonhuman primates to use a more complex communication system. Initially, Hayes and Hayes (1952) trained the chimp Vicki. She became able to produce only four different sounds in six years ("mom," "pa," "cup," and "up")! Other chimps and gorillas have also participated in communication training programs: Nim and Koko used signs; Sara used plastic chips; Lana, Sherman, and Austion manipulated combinations of buttons to communicate (Gardner and Gardner, 1979; Limber 1982; Patterson and Linden, 1981).

Regardless of the relatively large amount of meaningful elements that chimpanzees can learn, they fail in developing sequencing of elements (grammar). Kanzi learned to use around 200 symbols on a portable electronic symbol board. While chimpanzees can learn to order their symbols to get what they want, it is not clear that they have mastered syntax (Mitani, 1995; Savage-Rumbaugh and Lewin, 1994). The reason is that when they initiate communication, they often abandon the order they have learned and word order becomes random.

There have been occasional reports of chimpanzees signing new combinations of words in response to new situations. Washoe, for example, was in a boat on a pond when she encountered her first duck. She signed "*water bird*" (Terrace *et al.*, 1979). This could be a new compound noun or it could be two separate responses to the water and a bird. But between two nouns, there is not a grammatical relationship and hence no grammar is involved in "*water bird*."

In conclusion, there is not convincing evidence that chimpanzees and other nonhuman primates can learn language syntax (language as syntagm) even after intensive and controlled training.

The question becomes how this type of simple communication system found in subhuman primates in natural conditions (i.e., to use a few vocalizations, gestures, and facial expressions) further developed into contemporary human language. Certain mechanisms potentially could be used, e.g., words can be created departing from onomatopoeias, emotional expressions, etc. Indeed, a diversity of mechanisms has been proposed throughout history to account for how human words emerged. It means that different strategies could potentially be useful to create words. This is an ability that is not found in nonhuman primates. Using these strategies certainly requires a brain notoriously more advanced than the chimpanzee's brain.

During the nineteenth century different hypotheses were presented in an attempt to explain the origin of language from the lexical point of view. Jespersen (1922) referred to such hypotheses using some unusual names, as a way of deriding the hypotheses as simplistic speculation. However, these names became popular and they have continued to be used even in contemporary literature. Some hypotheses are (Yule, 1996):

(1) Language began as imitations of natural sounds. It means that words are created departing from onomatopoeias.

(2) Language began with interjections, emotive cries, and emotional expressions.

(3) Gestures are at the origin of language, and body movement preceded language. Oral language represents the use of oral gestures that began in imitation of hand gestures that were already in use for communication. Contemporarily, several authors (e.g., Arbib, 2005; Corballis, 2002) have argued that gestures represent the most important element in creating human language.

(4) Language arose in rhythmic chants and vocalisms uttered by people engaged in communal labor. Language began as rhythmic chants, perhaps ultimately from the grunts of heavy work, or related to assistance or cooperation accompanied by appropriate gestures.

(5) Language began with the easiest syllables attached to the most significant objects.

(6) It has been pointed out that there is a certain correspondence between sounds and meanings. Small, sharp, high things tend to have words with high front vowels in many languages, while big, round, low things tend to have round back vowels! This is often referred to as phonetic symbolism.

(7) It has also been suggested that language comes out of play, laughter, cooing, courtship, emotional mutterings, and the like.

(8) Considering that there is a need for interpersonal contact, language may have begun as sounds to signal both identity (here I am!) and belonging (I'm with you!).

All these hypotheses may be partially true, and all these factors may have contributed to the creation of new words. As a matter of fact, these hypotheses attempt to explain how the initial communication systems (observed in non-human primates) evolved to the second stage in language: the development of a lexical system, which potentially can be transmitted to the offspring. But they do not account for the development of grammar. These mechanisms for creating new words continue being useful in the contemporary world. For instance, onomatopoeias continue to represent a mechanism in the creation of new words (e.g., the game of ping-pong). The phonetic symbolism is particularly useful in the creation of adjectives (qualities of the objects).

The function of noises (grunts) in human communication

No mention about the function of noises (grunts) in human everyday communication is readily available. As noted above, noises represent a basic communication strategy in chimpanzees, and noises have continued to play a communication function throughout human history. It is evident that people in everyday life use a diversity of noises to say "yes," "no," to express different emotions, to communicate with animals (e.g., "come here," "go away"), etc. These noises are close to interjections, and sometimes become real interjections (e.g., "ooph!"). Even though there is not a "dictionary" of noises, the author of this paper has been able to identify over 30 different noises commonly used in contemporary Spanish language. Some of these noises seem understandable by speakers of other languages, but others seem idiosyncratic of Spanish-speaking people. It can be speculated that these utterances/noises are only partially cross-linguistic.

Second stage: lexical/semantic

Bickerton (1990) developed the idea that a protolanguage must have preceded the full-fledged syntax of today's discourse. Echoes of this protolanguage can be seen, he argued, (1) in pidgin languages, (2) in the first words of infants, (3) in the symbols used by trained chimpanzees, and (4) in the syntax-free utterances of children who do not learn to speak at the normal age.

It is not easy to imagine what these original words were like. But the analogy with the child's initial vocabulary can be taken: (1) They were articulatory easiest to produce, most likely using those phonemes regarded as "universal" (e.g., /p/, /a/). (2) They contained a simple syllable (consonant-vowel) that may have been repeated (e.g., *papapa*). In this regard, they were alike to the infantile words. (3) They were mostly "nouns" (real objects) even though they obviously did not have a grammatical category.

To move from grunts, onomatopoeias, and emotional expression to words, requires the progressive development of a series of oppositions. According to Jakobson (1968) the most basic one is the opposition between vowels and consonants. The second most important one is between oral and nasal articulations. But the production of these oppositions requires some anatomical adaptations.

Human articulatory ability has been related to the specific position and configuration of the larynx. The human larynx descends during infancy and the early juvenile periods, and this greatly contributes to the morphological foundations of speech development. This developmental phenomenon is frequently believed to be unique to humans. However, Nishimura (2005; Nishimura *et al.*, 2003) demonstrated that chimpanzees' larynxes also descend during infancy, as in human infants. This descent is completed primarily through the rapid descent of the laryngeal skeleton relative to the hyoid, but it is not accompanied by the descent of the hyoid itself. The descent is possibly associated with developmental changes in the swallowing mechanism. Moreover, it contributes physically to an increased independence between the processes of phonation and articulation for vocalization. Thus, the descent of the larynx and the morphological foundations for speech production must have evolved in part during hominoid evolution and not in a single shift during human evolution.

Several authors have attempted to find universal language characteristics, and even to reconstruct extinct languages (e.g., Greenberg, 1978; Hagége, 1982; Van den Berghe 1979) such as the Indo-European language (Anderson, 1973; Lehmann, 1974; Martinet, 1975; Shevoroshkin, 1990), whose last speaker passed away over 10 000 years ago. Furthermore, examples of which words could have been the initial ones in human language have been proposed. Swadesh (1971) refers to the communality existing in some words across the world. If we cannot be sure what the initial words used by humans were, there are clues about the initial meaning sounds and approximately how the initial words may have been formed.

Third stage: grammar

What was the crucial leap for the development of grammar? (i.e., syntagmatic dimension of the language). Obviously grammar was initially simple, and "sentences" contained only two words. How to link two words to create a new higher-level unit (syntagm)? Further, how to mark the relationship between the two words? The mechanism has to be the simplest one, and it is not unlikely that it may be similar to the mechanism observed in children during language development.

Suppose that we have two lexical units:

   -animal – fruit

Different relations between these two words can exist; but the relationship requires an action (verb); it means that there is an interaction between both elements: *animal eats fruit; animal has fruit; animal receives fruit; animal likes fruit*, etc.

In consequence, before creating a syntagmatic relationship between the words, different word categories have to be separated (e.g., objects and actions). According to the *Swadesh word list* (1952, 1967), the following categories are found across different languages, and may represent the initial word categories: (1) grammatical words (e.g., I/me), (2) quantifiers (e.g., all), (3) adjectives (e.g., big), (4) human distinctions (e.g., person), (5) animals (e.g., fish), (6) highly frequent elements (e.g., tree), (7) body parts (e.g., hair), (8) actions (e.g., drink), (9) natural phenomena (e.g., sun), and (10) colors (e.g., red).

Indeed, for creating a phrase only two types of elements are really required: nouns (nominal phrase) and verbs (verbal phrase). If putting together two words corresponding to two different classes (e.g., *animal sleep*), a syntagm and grammar have already appeared. In childhood language it is observed that words corresponding to two different classes are combined such as "*big dog*," "*food good*," "*dad gone*." They contain a grammar, because the words belong to two different classes. In the first two examples, there is an existence verb (to be) that is omitted (as currently observed in some contemporary languages, such as Russian). "*Mom dad*" is not a phrase, but "*mom big*" is a primitive sentence.

Brown (1973) found that the majority of the utterances at the beginning of the child's grammar could be described by a small set of functional relationships between words:

(1)   "agent + action" *baby kiss*
(2)   "action + object" *pull car*
(3)   "agent + object" *daddy ball*
(4)   "action + location" *sit chair*
(5)   "object + location" *cup table*
(6)   "possessor + possession" *mommy sock*
(7)   "object + attribute" *car red*
(8)   "demonstrative + object" *there car*

So, the crucial point in emerging grammar is not the extension of the vocabulary. What is really crucial is to have words corresponding to different classes that can be combined to form a higher-level unit (syntagm). One of the words has to be a noun; the other is usually a verb.

Hence, the problem becomes, how verbs appeared. To create nouns does not seem so complicated using the hypothesis mentioned above (e.g., nouns can be created departing from onomatopoeias, etc). Verbs, on the other hand, can be created departing from the nouns, but with the meaning of an action (e.g., *baby kiss*). Action usually means moving, doing, executing, not simply perceiving and associating with some visual (or auditory or tactile) information. "*Kiss*" can be associated with some sensory information, and obviously the temporal, parietal, and occipital brain areas have to participate (*kiss* as a noun). "*Kiss*" can also be associated with an action, and obviously the frontal areas have to be involved in this second type of association (*kiss* as a verb).

Brain organization of nouns and verbs

It has been observed that verbs and nouns clearly depend on different brain area activity, and naming objects and actions are disrupted in cases of different types of brain pathology. While speaking or thinking in nouns increased activity is observed in the temporal lobe, whereas speaking or thinking verbs activates the Broca frontal area (Raichle, 1994). By the same token, impairments in finding nouns are associated with temporal lobe pathology, whereas impairments in finding verbs are associated with left frontal damage and Broca aphasia (Ardila and Rosselli, 1994; Damasio and Tranel, 1993). Naming actions activates the left frontal operculum roughly corresponding to Broca's area (Damasio *et al.*, 2001). The neural correlates of naming concrete entities such as tools (with nouns) and naming actions (with verbs) are partially distinct: the former are linked to the left inferotemporal region, whereas the latter are linked to the left frontal opercular and left posterior middle temporal regions (Tranel *et al.*, 2005).

The recent discovery of mirror neurons could significantly contribute to the understanding of the brain organization of verbs. A mirror neuron is a neuron which fires both when an animal performs an action and also when the animal observes the same action performed by another animal. In humans, brain activity consistent with mirror neurons has been found in the premotor cortex and the inferior parietal cortex (Rizzolatti, Fadiga, Gallese, and Fogassi, 1996; Rizzolatti and Craighero, 2004). These neurons (mirror neurons) appear to represent a system that matches observed events to similar, internally generated actions. Transcranial magnetic stimulation and positron emission tomography (PET) experiments suggest that a mirror system for gesture recognition also exists in humans and includes Broca's area (Rizzolati and Arbib, 1998). The discovery of mirror neurons in the Broca's area might have important consequences for understanding brain language organization and language evolution (Arbib, 2006; Craighero, Metta, Sandini, and Fadiga, 2007). An obvious implication of mirror neurons is that they can participate in the internal representation of actions.

Two memory systems in language

Two major memory systems are frequently distinguished in contemporary memory literature: declarative memory (divided into semantic and episodic or experiential) and procedural memory (Tulving *et al.*, 2004). It has been suggested that the lexical/semantic and grammar aspects of the language are subserved by different neuroanatomic brain circuitries and depend upon these two different memory systems (Fabbro, 1999, 2001; Paradis, 2004; Ullman, 2001;

2004). Whereas lexical/semantic aspects of the language depend on a declarative semantic memory (knowledge about the meaning of the words), grammar depends on a procedural memory. Lexical/semantic aspects of the language (language as a paradigm) is explicitly learned, and represent a type of knowledge we are aware of (declarative memory). It depends on retro-rolandic cortical structures and the hippocampus. Grammar (language sequences, contiguity) is acquired incidentally. Procedural memory for grammar supposes implicit language knowledge. Procedural grammatical learning is related to the execution of sequences of elements (skilled articulatory acts and grammar) used for speaking but also for syntax. Procedural memory is related with frontal/subcortical circuitries (Tulving *et al.*, 2004).

Broca's area damage results in a defect in grammar and also in an inability to find verbs. In consequence, brain representation of actions and brain representation of grammar is coincidental. *Using verbs and using grammar depends upon the very same type of brain activity* and both are simultaneously disrupted in cases of Broca aphasia. It can be conjectured that verbs and grammar appeared almost simultaneously in human language; or rather, they are the two sides of the same coin. Furthermore, grammar is associated with oral praxis skills (i.e., agrammatism and apraxia of speech appear simultaneously in Broca aphasia), and hence, all three have to have appeared simultaneously in the evolution of human language: using verbs, using grammar, and rapidly sequencing movements with the articulatory organs.

Integrating aphasia, anthropology, and genetics

As emphasized above, language activity depends on two discrete brain areas (so-called Wernicke's and Broca's areas). Damage in these two brain regions results in disturbances in language as a paradigm (similarity: selection; lexical/semantic system) and syntagm (contiguity: combination; grammatical system).

At what moment in human history did the first and the second aspects of language emerge? There is not a simple answer, but obviously language as a lexical/semantic system appeared before language as a grammatical system.

Prehuman communication systems continue to play a role in contemporary human communication. Onomatopoeias continue to represent a source for the creation of new words. Noises and gesture are actively used nowadays in everyday communication.

The lexical/semantic system

Paleoneurology (the study and analysis of fossil endocasts) can also significantly contribute to the understanding of the origins of the language. How did the brain areas participating in human lexical/semantic knowledge (i.e., temporal lobes) evolve? In monkeys, the temporal lobes are involved in recognizing the sounds and calls of their own species (Rauschecker *et al.*, 1995; Wang *et al.*, 1995; Wollberg and Newman, 1972), and obviously the temporal lobe was a crucial area in developing a complex lexical/semantic system.

Gannon *et al.* (1998) observed that the anatomic pattern and left hemisphere size predominance of the planum temporale, a language area of the human brain, are also present in chimpanzees. They found that the left planum temporale was significantly larger in 94% of chimpanzee brains examined. Hence, the crucial lexical/semantic difference between humans and chimpanzees cannot be related to the planum temporale. By the same token, it has been observed that anatomical temporal-lobe asymmetries favoring the left hemisphere are found in several Old and New World monkey species (Heilbroner and Holloway, 1988). Development of a human lexical/semantic communication system cannot be related to temporal lobe asymmetry, because this asymmetry is observed long before the beginning of the human language.

Nonetheless, differences can be related to the temporal lobe volume. Rilling and Seligman (2002) analyzed the volume of the temporal lobe in different primates. Whole brain, T1-weighted MRI scans were collected from 44 living anthropoid primates spanning 11 species. The surface areas of both the entire temporal lobe and the superior temporal gyrus were measured, as was temporal cortical gyrification. Allometric regressions of temporal lobe structures on brain volume consistently showed apes and monkeys to scale along different trajectories, with the monkeys typically lying at a higher elevation than the apes. Within the temporal lobe, overall volume, surface area, and white matter volume were significantly larger in humans than predicted by the ape regression lines. The largest departure from allometry in humans was for the temporal lobe white matter volume which, in addition to being significantly larger than predicted for brain size, was also significantly larger than predicted for temporal lobe volume. Among the nonhuman primate sample, *Cebus* have small temporal lobes for their brain size, and *Macaca* and *Papio* have large superior temporal gyri for their brain size. The observed departures from allometry might reflect neurobiological adaptations supporting species-specific communication in both humans and Old World monkeys. The authors concluded that the entire human temporal lobe and some of its component structures are significantly larger than predicted for a primate brain of human size. The most dramatic allometric departure is in the volume of the human temporal lobe white matter, which, in addition to being large relative to brain size, is also large relative to temporal lobe size. These allometric departures in humans could reflect a reorganization of the temporal lobes driven by expansion of language cortex and its associated connections. It is interesting to note that in primates the superior temporal gyrus contains neurons tuned to species-specific calls and the magnitude of different species relate to the repertoire of vocal communicative signals as reflections of the complexity of their respective social environments.

It has been calculated that this enlargement of the temporal lobe occurred some 200–300 000 years ago (Kochetkova, 1973). It can thus be conjectured that hominids existing before the contemporary Cro-Magnon *Homo sapiens* could have developed certain complex lexical/semantic communication systems. For instance, it could be speculated that Neanderthal man could have had a relatively complex language as a lexical/semantic system.

Brain organization of the lexicon seems to be related to the type of association between words and perceptions. When the word is associated with own-body information, brain representation of the lexicon seems associated with a parietal extension (e.g., body-part names); when the word has visual associations, an occipital extension is found (Roux *et al.*, 2006).

Origins of the language

Departing from the above observations, it can be speculated that grammar, speech praxis movements, and using verbs appeared roughly simultaneously in human history. Rather, they are strongly interrelated and depend upon a common neural activity.

Recently, a milestone observation was made that significantly enlightened our understanding about the origin of language in general and grammar in particular. In England a family, usually referred to as the KE family, was found. Over three generations of this family, about half the family members had presented a significant disturbance in language development. Speech was largely unintelligible, and as children they were taught sign language as a supplement to speech. Affected members presented severe disturbances in articulation and other linguistic skills, and broader intellectual and physical problems. From the genetic point of view the disorder was associated with a mutation in a single autosomal-dominant gene, FOXP2, located in chromosome 7 (Vargha-Khadem *et al.*, 1995). The disorder was not restricted to speech and also included the following characteristics: defects in processing words according to grammatical rules; poor understanding of more complex sentence structure such as sentences with embedded relative clauses; inability to form intelligible speech; defects in the ability to move the mouth and face not associated with speaking (relative immobility of the lower face and mouth, particularly the upper lip); and significantly reduced IQ in the affected members compared with the unaffected members in both the verbal and the nonverbal domain.

Furthermore, affected family members presented a pronounced developmental verbal dyspraxia. The authors refer to the core deficit as one involving sequential articulation and orofacial praxis (Vernes *et al.*, 2006; Vargha-Khadem *et al.*, 1998). A PET study revealed functional abnormalities in both cortical and subcortical motor-related areas of the frontal lobe, while quantitative analyses of MRI revealed structural abnormalities in several of these same areas, particularly the caudate nucleus, which was found to be abnormally small bilaterally. An abnormal gene (SPCH1) in the chromosomal band 7q31 was localized. The genetic mutation or deletion in this region was proposed to result in marked disruption of speech and expressive language, including grammar (Fisher *et al.*, 1998).

Enard *et al.* (2002) analyzed the evolution of the gene FOXP2. They noted the extremely conservative nature of FOXP2. The mouse FOXP2 differs in just one amino acid from chimpanzee, gorilla, and rhesus monkey. However, human FOXP2 differs from gorilla, chimp, and rhesus macaque in two further amino acids (and thus differs from mouse in three amino acids out of 715). So, in the 75 million years since the divergence of mouse and chimpanzee lineages, only one change occurred in FOXP2, while in the six million years since the divergence of man and chimpanzee lineages, two changes have occurred in the human lineage. The authors estimated that the last two mutations occurred between 10 000 and 100 000 years ago and speculate that the mutations have been critical for the development of contemporary human speech.

This genetic approach to the origins of language seems particularly provocative. Replication of the KE family genetic findings is expected in the near future.

Conclusions

Aphasia can contribute to the understanding of human language evolution. According to contemporary aphasia knowledge, in cases of brain pathology language can be disturbed in two rather different ways: as a lexical/semantic system (Wernicke-type aphasia) and as a grammatical system (Broca-type aphasia). Both language systems not only depend upon different brain areas (temporal and frontal) but also upon different types of learning (declarative and procedural) supported by different neuroanatomical circuitries. Observations of children's language development and experiments with nonhuman primates demonstrate that language initially appears a lexical/semantic system. Grammar is correlated with the ability to represent and use actions. This is an ability that depends on the so-called Broca's area and related brain circuits, but also depends, is correlated, and likely appeared simultaneously in human history with the ability to rapidly sequence articulatory movements (speech praxis).

Language as a lexical/semantic system may have appeared long before language as a syntactic system. The first may have appeared some 200–300 000 years ago, and may have existed in other hominids. Language as a grammatical system may have appeared relatively recently, maybe some 10–100 000 years ago and seems to be exclusive to *Homo sapiens*.

Acknowledgments

My gratitude to Dr. S. M. Platek and Dr. T. K. Shackelford for their support and valuable suggestions for this paper.

References

Albert., M. L., Goodglass, H., Helm, N. A., Rubers, A. B., and Alexander, M. P. (1981). *Clinical Aspects of Dysphasia*. New York: Springer-Verlag.

Alexander, M. P. (2006). Impairments of procedures for implementing complex language are due to disruption of frontal attention processes. *Journal of the International Neuropsychological Society*, **12**, 236–247.

Anderson, J. M. (1973). *Structural Aspects of Language Change*. Harlow: Longman.

Arbib, M. A. (2005). From monkey-like action recognition to human language: An evolutionary framework for neurolinguistics. *Behavioral and Brain Sciences*, **28**, 105–124.

Arbib, M. A. (2006). Aphasia, apraxia and the evolution of the language-ready brain. *Aphasiology*, **20**, 1125–1155.

Ardila, A. (1993). Toward a model of phoneme perception. *International Journal of Neuroscience*, **70**, 1–12.

Ardila, A. (2006). Las aphasias [The aphasias]. http://www.aphasia.org/libroespanol.php

Ardila, A. and Bernal, B. (2007). What can be localized in the brain? Towards a "factor" theory on brain organization of cognition. *International Journal of Neurosciences*, **117**, 935–969.

Ardila, A. and Rosselli, M. (1990). Conduction aphasia and verbal apraxia. *Journal of Neurolinguistics*, **5**, 1–14.

Ardila, A. and Rosselli, M. (1994). Averbia as a selective naming disorder: A single case report. *Journal of Psycholinguist Research*, **23**, 139–148.

Ardila, A. and Surloff, C. (2006).Executive dysfunction. *Medlink Neurology*.

Bastian, D. C. (1898).*Aphasia and Other Speech Defects*. London: H. K. Lewis.

Benson, D. F. and Ardila, A. (1994). Conduction aphasia: A syndrome of language network disruption. In H. Kirshner (Ed.), *Handbook of Speech and Language Disorders*. New York: Mercel Dekker Inc.

Benson, D. F. and Ardila, A. (1996). *Aphasia: A Clinical Perspective*. Oxford: Oxford University Press.

Benson, D. F. and Geschwind, N. (1971). Aphasia and related cortical disturbances. In A. B. Baker and L. H. Baker (Eds.), *Clinical Neurology*. New York: Harper and Row.

Benson, D. F., Sheretaman, W. A., Bouchard, R., Segarra, J. M., Price, D., and Geschwind, N. (1973). Conduction aphasia: A clinicopathological study. *Archives of Neurology*, **28**, 339–346.

Berthier, M. (1999). *Transcortical Aphasias*. New York: Psychology Press.

Bickerton, D. (1990). *Language and Species*. Chicago: The University of Chicago Press.

Brown, R. (1973). *A First Language: The Early Stages*. Cambridge, MA: Harvard University Press.

Brown, J. W. (1972). *Aphasia, Agnosia and Apraxia*. New York: Thomas.

Brown, J. M. (1975). The problem of repetition: A case study of conduction aphasia and the 'isolation' syndrome. *Cortex*, **11**, 37–52.

Caramazza, A., Micelli, G., Silveri, M. C., and Laudanna, A. (1985). Reading mechanisms and the organization of the lexicon: Evidence from acquired dyslexia. *Cognitive Neuropsychology*, **2**, 81–114.

Catani, M., Jones, D. K., and ffytche, D. H. (2005). Perisylvian language networks of the human brain. *Annals of Neurology*, **57**, 8–16.

Cheney, D. L. and R. M. Seyfarth (1997). Why animals don't have language. *The Tanner Lectures on Human Values*, **19**, 173–210.

Coltheart, M. (1978). Lexical access in simple reading tasks. In G. Underwood (Ed.), *Strategies of Information Processing*. New York: Academic Press.

Corballis, M. C. (2002). *From Hand to Mouth: The Origins of Language*. Princeton: Princeton University Press.

Corballis, M. C. (2006). The evolution of language: From hand to mouth. In S. M. Platek, J. P. Keenan, and T. K. Shackelford (Eds.), *Evolutionary Cognitive Neuroscience* (pp. 403–430). Boston: The MIT Press.

Craighero, L., Metta, G., Sandini, G., and Fadiga, L. (2007). The mirror-neurons system: Data and models. *Progress in Brain Research*, **164**, 39–59.

Crosson, B., Moberg, P. J., Boone, J. R., Rothi, L. J., and Raymer, A. (1997). Category-specific naming deficit for medical terms after dominant thalamic/capsular hemorrhage. *Brain and Language*, **60**, 407–442.

Damasio, H. and Damasio, A. (1980). The anatomical basis of conduction aphasia. *Brain*, **103**, 337–350.

Damasio, A. R. and Tranel, D. (1993). Nouns and verbs are retrieved with differently distributed neural systems. *Proceedings of the National Academy of Sciences*, **90**, 4957–4960

Damasio, H., Grabowski, T. J., Tranel, D., Ponto, L. L., Hichwa, R. D., and Damasio, A, R. (2001). Neural correlates of naming actions and of naming spatial relations. *Neuroimage*, **13**, 1053–1064.

Dejerine, J. (1892). Contribution a l'étude anatomo-pathologique et clinique des différèrent variétés de cécité verbale. *Comptes Rendus Société de Biologie*, **4**, 61–90.

Dejerine, J. (1914). *Sémiologie des affections du système nerveux*. Paris: Masson.

Enard, W., Przeworski, M., Fisher, S. E., Lai, C. S., Wiebe, V., Kitano, T., Monaco, A. P., and Paabo, S. (2002). Molecular evolution of FOXP2, a gene involved in speech and language. *Nature*, **418**, 869–872.

Fabbro, F. (1999). *The Neurolinguistics of Bilingualism: An Introduction*. New York: Psychology Press.

Fabbro, F. (2001). The bilingual brain, cerebral representation of languages. *Brain and Language*, **79**, 211–222.

Fisher, S. E., Vargha-Khadem, F., Watkins, K. E., Monaco, A. P., and Pembrey, M, E. (1998). Localisation of a gene implicated in a severe speech and language disorder. *Nature Genetics*, **18**, 168–170.

Freud, S. (1891/1973). *Las Afasias*. Buenos Aires: Ediciones Nueva Visión.

Friedman, R. B. (1988). Acquired alexia. In F. Boller, J. Grafman, G. Rizzolatti, and H. Goodglass (Eds.), *Handbook of Neuropsychology*. New York: Elsevier.

Gannon, P. J., Holloway, R. L., Broadfield, D. C., and Braun, A. R. (1988). Asymmetry of chimpanzee planum temporale: Humanlike pattern of Wernicke's brain language area homolog. *Science*, **279**, 220–222.

Gardner, R. A. and Gardner, B. T. (1979). Teaching sign language to a chimpanzee. *Science*, **165**, 664–672.

Geschwind, N. (1965). Disconnection syndromes in animals and man. *Brain*, **88**, 237–294.

Goldstein, K. (1948). *Language and Language Disturbances*. New York: Grune and Stratton.

Goodglass, H., Wingfield, A., Hyde, M. R., and Theurkauf, J. C. (1986). Category specific dissociations in naming and recognition by aphasic patients. *Cortex*, **22**, 87–102.

Goodglass, H. (1993). *Understanding Aphasia*. New York: Academic Press.

Greenberg, J. H. (1978). *Universals of Human Language*. Palo Alto, CA: Stanford University Press.

Hagége, C. (1982). *La Structure des Langues*. Paris: Presses Universitaires de France.

Harris, D. M. and Kay, J. (1995). Selective impairment of the retrieval of people's names: A case of category specificity. *Cortex*, **31**, 575–582.

Hayes, K. J. and Hayes, C. (1952). Imitation in a home-raised chimpanzee. *Journal of Comparative and Physiological Psychology*, **45**, 450–459.

Head, H. (1926). *Aphasia and Kindred Disorders of Speech*. Cambridge: Cambridge University Press.

Hécaen, H. (1972). *Introduction a la Neuropsychologie*. Paris: Larousse.

Hécaen, H., and Albert, M. L. (1978). *Human Neuropsychology*. Chichester: John Wiley & Sons, Ltd..

Heilbroner, P. L. and Holloway, R. L. (1988). Anatomical brain asymmetries in New World and Old World monkeys: Stages of temporal lobe development in primate evolution. *American Journal of Physical Anthropology*, **76**, 39–48.

Hoff, E. (2003). *Language Development*, 3rd edn. Belmont, CA: Wadsworth.

Jakobson R. (1964).Toward a linguistic typology of aphasic impairments. In A. V. S. DeReuck and M. O'Connor (Eds.), *Disorders of Language*. London: Little and Brown.

Jakobson, R. (1968). *Child Language, Aphasia, and Phonological Universals*. The Hague: Mouton.

Jakobson, R. (1971). *Studies on Child Language and Aphasia*. The Hague: Mouton.

Jakobson, R. and Halle, M. (1956). *Two Aspects of Language and Two Types of Aphasic Disturbances*. The Hague: Mouton.

Jespersen, O. (1922). *Language: Its Nature, Development and Origin*. Sydney: Allen and Unwin.

Kertesz, A. (1979). *Aphasia and Associated Disorders*. New York: Grune and Stratton.

Kertesz, A. (1985). Aphasia. In J. A. M. Frederiks (Ed.), *Handbook of Clinical Neurology, vol 45: Clinical Neuropsychology*. New York: Elsevier.

Kleist, K. (1934). *Gehirnpathologie*. Leipzig: Barth.

Kochetkova, V. I. (1973). *Paleoneurology*. Moscow: Moscow State University Press.

Lecours, A. R., Lhermitte, F., and Bryans, B. (1983). *Aphasiology*. London: Baillere-Tindall.

Lehmann, W. P. (1974). *Proto Indoeuropean Syntax*. Austin: University of Texas Press.

Lichtheim, L. (1885). On aphasia. *Brain*, **7**, 433–484.

Limber, J. (1982). What can chimps tell us about the origins of language? In S. Kuczaj (Ed.), *Language Development*. Mahwah, NJ: Erlbaum.

Luria, A. R. (1966). *Human Brain and Psychological Processes*. New York: Harper and Row.

Luria, A. R. (1970). *Traumatic Aphasia: Its Syndromes, Psychology, and Treatment*. The Hague: Mouton.

Luria, A. R. (1972/1983). Sobre las dos formas básicas del alteraciones afásicas en el lenguaje [*On the two basic forms of aphasic disturbances*] In A. Ardila (Ed.), *Psicobiología del Lenguaje*. Mexico: Trillas.

Luria, A. R. (1976). *Basic Problems of Neurolinguistics*. The Hague: Mouton.

Luria, A. R. (1980). *Higher Cortical Functions in Man*. 2nd edn. New York: Harper and Row.

Lyons, F., Hanley, J. R., and Kay, J. (2002). Anomia for common names and geographical names with preserved retrieval of names of people: A semantic memory disorder. *Cortex*, **38**, 23–35.

Mallory, J. P. (1989). *In Search of the Indo-Europeans*. New York: Thames and Hudson.

Martinet, A. (1975). *Evolution of Langues et Reconstruction*. Paris: Presses Universitaires de France.

McCrone, J. (1991). *The Ape That Spoke: Language and the Evolution of the Human Mind*. New York: Avon Books.

Mitani, J. (1995). Review of Savage-Rumbaugh and Lewin's "Kanzi: The ape at the brink of the human mind. *Scientific American*, **272**, 43–54.

Nishimura, T. (2005). Developmental changes in the shape of the supralaryngeal vocal tract in chimpanzees. *American Journal of Physical Anthropology*, **126**, 193–204.

Nishimura, T., Mikami, A., Suzuki, J., and Matsuzawa, T. (2003). Descent of the larynx in chimpanzee infants. *Proceedings of the National Academy of Sciences*, **100**, 6930–6933.

Nowak, M. A. and Krakauer, D. C. (1999). The evolution of language. *Proceedings of the National Academy of Sciences*, **96**, 8028–8033.

Paradis, M. (2004). *A Neurolinguistic Theory of Bilingualism*. Philadelphia, PA: John Benjamins.

Patterson, F. and Linden, E. (1981). *The Education of Koko*. Austin, TX: Holt, Rinehart and Winston.

Patterson, K. and Kay, J. (1982). Letter-by-letter reading: Psychological descriptions of a neurological syndrome. *Quarterly Journal of Experimental Psychology*, **34**, 411–441.

Pick, A. (1931). *Aphasia*. Springfield, IL: Charles C. Thomas.

Poizner, H., Klima, E. S., and Bellugi, U. (1987). *What the Hands Reveal About the Brain*. Cambridge, MA: MIT Press.

Raichle, M. E. (1994). Visualizing the mind. *Scientific American*, **270**, 58–65.

Rauschecker, J. P., Tian, B., and Hauser, M. (1995). Processing of complex sounds in the macaque nonprimary auditory cortex. *Science*, **268**, 111–114.

Rilling, J. K. and Seligman, R. A. (2002). A quantitative morphometric comparative analysis of the primate temporal lobe. *Journal of Human Evolution*, **42**, 505–533.

Rizzolatti, G. and Arbib, M. A. (1998). Language within our grasp. *Trends in Neurosciences*, **21**, 188–194.

Rizzolatti G., Fadiga L., Gallese V., and Fogassi L. (1996). Premotor cortex and the recognition of motor actions. *Cognitive Brain Research*, **3**, 131–141

Rizzolatti, G. and Craighero, L. (2004). The mirror-neuron system. *Annual Review of Neuroscience*, **27**, 169–192

Roeltgen, D. P. (1993). Agraphia. In Heilman, K. M. and Valenstein, E. (Eds.), *Clinical Neuropsychology*. Oxford: Oxford University Press.

Roux, F. E., Lubrano, V., Lauwers-Cances, V., Mascott, C. R., and Demonet, J. F. (2006). Category-specific cortical mapping: Color-naming areas. *Journal of Neurosurgery*, **104**, 27–37.

Ruhlen, M. (1994). *The Origin of Language*. Chichester: John Wiley & Sons, Ltd.

Savage-Rumbaugh, S. and Lewin, R. (1994). *Kanzi: The Ape at the Brink of the Human Mind*. Chichester: John Wiley & Sons Ltd.

Savage-Rumbaugh, S., Rumbaugh, D. M., and Boysen, S. (1980). Do apes use language? *American Scientist*, **68**, 49–61.

Schuell, H., Jenkins, J. J., and Jimenez-Pabon, E. (1964). *Aphasia in Adults*. New York: Harper and Row.

Shevoroshkin, V. (1990). The mother tongue: how linguistics have reconstructed the ancestor of all living languages. *The Sciences*, **199**, 20–27.

Swadesh, M. (1951). Lexicostatistic dating of prehistoric ethnic contacts. *Proceedings of the American Philosophical Society*, **96**, 152–163.

Swadesh, M. (1952). Lexicostatistic dating of prehistoric ethnic contacts. *Proceedings of the American Philosophical Society*, **96**, 152–163.

Swadesh, M. (1967). El Lenguaje y la Vida Humana. *Fondo de Cultural Económica*.

Swadesh, M. (1971). *The Origin and Diversification of Language*. Venice: Aldine.

Tallerman, M. (2005). *Language Origins: Perspectives on Evolution*. Oxford: Oxford University Press.

Taylor-Sarno, M. (1998). *Acquired Aphasia*. New York: Academic Press.

Terrace, H. S., Petitto, L. A., Sanders, R. J., and Bever, T. G. (1979). Can an ape create a sentence? *Science*, **206**, 891–902.

Tranel, D., Martin, C., Damasio, H., Grabowski, T. J., and Hichwa, R. (2005). Effects of noun-verb homonymy on the neural correlates of naming concrete entities and actions. *Brain and Language*, **92**, 288–299.

Tulving, E., Fergus, I., and Craik, M. (2004). *The Oxford Handbook of Memory*. Oxford: Oxford University Press.

Ullman, M. T. (2001). The declarative/procedural model of lexicon and grammar. *Journal of Psycholinguistic Research*, **30**, 37–69.

Ullman, M.T (2004). Contributions of memory circuits to language: The declarative/procedural model. *Cognition*, **92**, 231–270.

Van den Berghe, P. L. (1979). *Human Family Systems*. New York: Elsevier.

Vargha-Khadem, F., Watkins, K., Alcock, K., Fletcher, P., and Passingham, R. (1995). Praxic and nonverbal cognitive deficits in a large family with a genetically transmitted speech and language disorder. *Proceedings of the National Academy of Sciences*, **92**, 930–933.

Vargha-Khadem, F., Watkins, K. E., Price, C. J., Ashburner, J., Alcock, K. J., Connelly, A., Frackowiak, R. S., Friston, K. J., Pembrey, M. E., Mishkin, M., Gadian, D. G., and Passingham, R. E. (1998). Neural basis of an inherited speech and language disorder. *Proceedings of the National Academy of Sciences*, **95**, 12695–12700.

Vernes, S. C., Nicod, J., Elahi, F. M., Coventry, J. A., Kenny, N., Coupe, A. M., Bird, L. E., Davies, K. E., and Fisher, S. E. (2006). Functional genetic analysis of mutations implicated in a human speech and language disorder. *Human Molecular Genetics*, **15**, 3154–3167.

Wang, X., Merzenich, M. M., Beitel, R., and Schreiner, C. E. (1995). Representation of a species-specific vocalization in the primary auditory cortex of the common marmoset: Temporal and spectral characteristics. *Journal of Neurophysiology*, **74**, 2685–2706.

Warrington, E. K. and Shallice, T. (1984). Category specific semantic impairments. *Brain*, **107**, 829–854.

Wernicke, C. (1874). *Der Aphasiche Symptomencomplex*. Breslau: Cohn and Weigert.

Wilson, S. A. K. (1926). *Aphasia*. London: Kegan Paul.

Wollberg, Z. and Newman, J. D. (1972). Auditory cortex of squirrel monkey: response patterns of single cells to species-specific vocalizations. *Science*, **175**, 212–214.

Yule, G. (1996). *The Study of Language*, 2nd edn. Cambridge: Cambridge University Press.

7

The evolutionary cognitive neuropsychology of face preferences

ANTHONY C. LITTLE AND BENEDICT C. JONES

Introduction

The human face has been a source of great interest to psychologists and other scientists in recent years because of the extraordinarily well-developed ability of humans to process, recognize, and extract information from others' faces. Our magazines and television screens are not just filled with any faces – they are filled with attractive faces, and both women and men are highly concerned with good looks in a potential partner (Buss and Barnes, 1986). Physical appearance is important to humans and there appear to be certain features that are found attractive across individuals and cultures (Langlois *et al.*, 2000). The same holds true across the animal kingdom: most nonhuman species rely on external factors, such as the size, shape, and color of adornments (e.g., feathers, fur, and fins) to attract mates (Andersson, 1994). Research on animals has focused on individual traits that are attractive across individuals, and even species, such as symmetry (e.g., Møller and Thornhill, 1998).

An evolutionary view assumes that perception and preferences serve an adaptive function: the external world provides information to guide biologically and socially functional behaviors (Zebrowitz-McArthur and Baron, 1983). If in our evolutionary past, information was present about a person's value (e.g., genetic quality) in any way, then an advantage would accrue to those who utilized these signs and those individuals would leave more genes behind in the next generation. Theoretically then, preferences guide us to choose mates that will provide the best chance of our genes surviving. In many studies this evolutionary view of attractiveness has been used to predict the specific characteristics of attractive faces (Thornhill and Gangestad, 1999 for review).

Foundations in Evolutionary Cognitive Neuroscience, Steven M. Platek and Todd K. Shackelford. Published by Cambridge University Press. © Cambridge University Press 2009.

Although we can say whether a face is attractive or unattractive it is extremely difficult to articulate the specific features that determine this attraction. Evolutionary theorists have long posited special brain mechanisms that are focused on particular adaptive problems (Cosmides and Tooby, 1994; Pinker, 1997). Mate choice is a complicated problem faced by our ancestors and assessment of different aspects of quality in a partner may involve specialized mechanisms. Fodor (1983) famously described the human brain as modular and has also argued that there is no continuity from perception to cognition (i.e., low level visual processes do not interact with higher cognitive processes). Potentially a modular nature is why it is so difficult to articulate the specific features that make faces attractive.

The Fusiform Face Area is the area of the brain proposed to be relatively specialized for face perception (but see Gauthier and Tarr, 1997; Kanwisher *et al.*, 1997), and is perhaps an excellent example of neural substrates dedicated to a specific task. As the detection of beauty represents an important selection pressure we then might expect specialized "beauty detectors" in the brain (Senior, 2003). Much research has been conducted on reward mechanisms and face processing but as yet neuroimaging studies addressing the perception of attractiveness are few. In recent years several important papers have been published on facial attractiveness and in this chapter we review these studies as well as discussing the more well known reward and face processing brain mechanisms. We also review behavioral cognitive work which links to how beauty is processed in the brain in the second part.

Part A: Brain mechanisms of reward and face perception

Reward in the brain

While how the brain processes facial attractiveness is currently poorly understood, general reward processes have received much attention (see Berridge, 2003 for a more detailed review). The brain areas implicated in reward function that underpin appetitive behavior are likely to also be involved in determining our attraction to others (Aharon *et al.*, 2001; O'Doherty *et al.*, 2003). In this section we briefly outline this reward system. The major components associated with positive affect covered here fall into cortical and subcortical regions and are summarized in Figure 7.1.

Cortical areas involved in reward

The prefrontal cortex, in particular the orbitofrontal cortex, has long been associated with a diverse range of positive and negative emotional

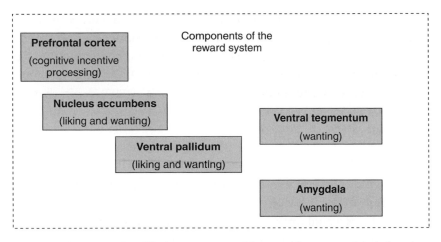

Figure 7.1 Simplified components of the reward system and their function. Adapted from Berridge and Robinson (2003).

responses (for reviews see Bechara *et al.*, 2000; Rolls, 1999). The role of the prefrontal cortex in regulating emotions goes back to the classic example of Phineas Gage for whom prefrontal damage led to major changes in emotional behavior (Damasio *et al.*, 1994).

Animal studies suggest that orbitofrontal activity is involved in encoding the importance of rewarding stimuli. Neurons in the rat prefrontal cortex are active in direct response to cocaine or heroin (Chang *et al.*, 1998) and also respond to the reward value of food (Bassareo and DiChiara, 1997). Interestingly, the reaction of frontal cortex also comes to be associated with factors correlated with food reward via conditioning such that presentation of the food box leads to increased activity and with repeated exposure with no reward this stimulus loses its rewarding property (Bassareo and DiChiara, 1997). In monkeys, orbitofrontal neurons fire vigorously on tasting or seeing a favorite food and also when seeing a cue that predicts such reward (Rolls, 2000). It has been suggested, then, that the orbitofrontal cortex is involved in decoding and representing rewarding stimuli, in learning associations of other stimuli to reward, and in controlling reward-related behavior (Rolls, 2000).

Human brain imaging studies support the notion that this area is strongly tied to rewarding stimuli. Responses in the orbitofrontal cortex are found to be rewarding to drugs (Breiter *et al.*, 1997), pleasant tastes and odors (Zald *et al.*, 1998; Zald and Pardo, 1997), pleasant touch (Francis *et al.*, 1999), pleasant sounds (Blood and Zatorre, 2001), and monetary rewards (Thut *et al.*, 1997). As noted by Berridge (2003), however, the case that orbitofrontal cortex actually generates positive affective reactions is not clear, only that the cortex is activated by rewarding stimuli. Potentially, as suggested by Rolls (2000), orbitofrontal cortex serves to represent rewarding stimuli (and associated stimuli) and does not generate the feelings of reward. Cingulate cortex, especially anterior cingulate cortex, is also implicated in reward. It is activated by positive and negative affective stimuli similar to orbitofrontal or prefrontal cortex (Breiter *et al.*, 1997). Again there is little evidence available to suggest cingulate cortex causes positive affective reaction (Berridge, 2003).

Sub-cortical regions involved in reward

Sub-cortical regions have been associated with reward since research on direct stimulation of the pleasure centers by Olds (1956). Olds and Milner (1954) found that rats would work to deliver electrical stimulation to the lateral hypothalamus and suggested this was based on positive affect and pleasure. Areas which elicit self-stimulation sites include the ventral tegmentum, the ventral pallidum, ventral thalamus and the nucleus accumbens, and the prefrontal cortex (McBride, Murphy, and Ikemoto, 1999; Phillips, 1984; Shizgal, 1999; Yeomans, 1989). Such is power of the reward here that rats were found to self-stimulate to the point of exhaustion and in preference to all other activities. While these studies are powerful in demonstrating a link with reward, Berridge and colleagues have argued this may represent wanting and not liking, that self-stimulation may involve incentive salience rather than the feeling of liking (see Berridge and Robinson, 1998; Berridge and Valenstein, 1991; Robinson and Berridge, 2000).

Berridge and colleagues have identified two subcortical brain systems that are associated with "liking." The nucleus accumbens shell is proposed as a principal sufficient cause for enhanced sweetness "liking." In one study, positive affective reactions were increased by activation of opioid neurotransmitter receptors within the medial caudal portion of the nucleus accumbens shell (Pecina and Berridge, 2000, 2005). The ventral pallidum, which lies immediately adjacent to the lateral hypothalamus, has also been found to be a necessary cause for at least one form of positive affective reaction. Cromwell and Berridge and other colleagues (Cromwell and Berridge, 1993; Tindell *et al.*, 2006) have found that excitotoxin lesions that destroyed neurons in the ventral pallidum cause rats to respond to a sweet taste with aversion as though it were a bitter taste, which suggests the removal of a hedonic response directly coded by these neurons.

Two further components of the reward system that are linked to wanting rather than liking are the ventral tegmentum and the amygdala. The ventral tegmentum appears intimately tied to predicting reward value as there is evidence that subpopulations of nucleus accumbens neurons that respond to predictive cues require the dopaminergic projection from the ventral tegmental area to promote reward-seeking behavior (Yun *et al.*, 2004). The amygdala has been associated with a wide range of cognitive functions, including emotion, learning, and memory. The amygdala is best known for its role in negative emotions, such as fear, but recent evidence supports a role for the amygdala in processing positive emotions as well as negative ones (for review see Baxter and Murray, 2002).

General face processing by the brain

As noted by Senior (2003), most studies concerning the cognitive neuro-anatomy of face perception address recognition and not the processing of facial beauty. It is useful, however, to first consider this data before discussing studies that specifically relate to attraction and mate-choice as much work has been done to try and understand general face processing in the brain.

In an important model by Haxby, Hoffman, and Gobbini (2000) called "The distributed human neural system for face perception," the authors outline the brain systems that have been found to process specific aspects of faces and put these systems into a model. This model is redrawn in Figure 7.2, and

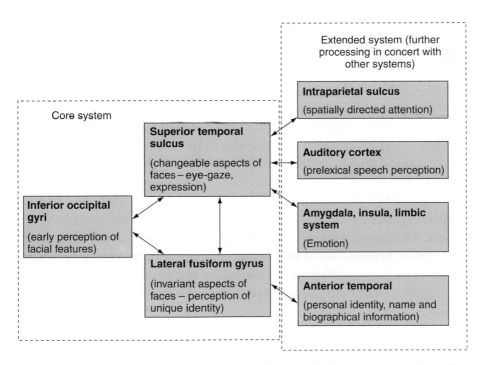

Figure 7.2 The distributed human neural system for face perception redrawn from Haxby *et al.* (2000). Function is presented in brackets.

as can be seen a neural substrate specific to each task in face processing is drawn. For a full description of the model and evidence for each components underlying brain region, interested readers are pointed to the original paper (Haxby *et al.*, 2000).

The distributed neural system for face processing broadly encompasses regions in the visual cortex, the limbic system, and the prefrontal cortex (Haxby *et al.*, 2000; Ishai *et al.*, 2005). In Haxby *et al.*'s model the processes involved in face perception are divided into two main systems: the core system which deals with initial structural analysis of faces, and the extended system which involves more subunits dealing with particular reactions to faces.

Core system

In the initial stages of face processing in the core system, following previous cognitive models of face perception (Bruce and Young, 1986), Haxby *et al.* highlight the separable and parallel processing of invariant and variant face traits, though the two systems may interact. There are theoretical reasons for such a distinction. Knowing a person's identity requires recognition of features that do not rapidly change, invariant features, aspects such as feature position and size. Other aspects of faces are more changeable, variant features, and are important for social interaction such as emotional expression, eye and head direction, and lip movements. The inferior occipital gyri is thought to process basic facial shape information before the split in processing as its location suggests it may provide input to both the superior temporal sulcus and inferior temporal cortex (Hoffman and Haxby, 2000). Evidence for the dissociation in processing routes comes from studies of monkeys where face-selective cells have been found to respond selectively either to identity or expression whereby cells that responded differentially to identity did so across expressions and cells that responded differentially to different expressions did so across different identities (Hasselmo *et al.*, 1989). Further, cells tuned for expression were found primarily in the superior temporal sulcus, whereas the cells that tuned for identity were found primarily in inferior temporal cortex (Hasselmo *et al.*, 1989). Data for the same dissociation in humans comes from an fMRI study in which participants were engaged in either attention to eye-gaze or attention to identity by asking participants to judge eye-direction or whether the face was the same or different to the previous identity (Hoffman and Haxby, 2000). Attention to eye gaze elicited a stronger response in the superior temporal sulcus than attention to identity did, and attention to identity elicited a stronger response in the lateral fusiform gyrus than attention to gaze did (Hoffman and Haxby, 2000). A similar pattern is also seen dissociating identity from expression such that identity changes a caudal segment of superior temporal sulcus and emotional expression changes a more rostral region (Winston *et al.*, 2004). This then supports the dissociation between processing variant and invariant aspects of faces in the brain.

Extended system

Functional brain imaging also suggests brain regions are recruited to process information gleaned from faces and these regions are placed but become part of the face perception system when they act with other face processing regions (Haxby *et al.*, 2000). Eye and head direction give important information about the orientation of the attention of others. Neuroimaging studies have demonstrated that in humans the intraparietal sulcus participates in spatial perception and covert shifts in spatial attention (Corbetta *et al.*, 1998, 1995). Reciprocal connections between the superior temporal sulcus and the intraparietal sulcus could facilitate an interaction (Harries and Perrett, 1991). Visual information from the lips contributes to understanding what we hear, and watching lips move while speaking, in the absence of sound, elicits activation of auditory areas in the superior temporal gyrus that are also known to be active when hearing words spoken (Calvert *et al.*, 1997). This suggests that auditory processing is tied into the extended face processing system to provide an integrated perception. The amygdala has long been associated with emotion and data suggests it is critical in the perception of fearful facial expressions (Morris *et al.*, 1996; Phillips *et al.*, 1998, 1997). Damage to the amygdala also disrupts fear expression processing (Adolphs *et al.*, 1994; Calder *et al.*, 1996). As the amygdala is involved in fear conditioning (LaBar *et al.*, 1998), this suggests perception of fear is tied to other fear processing mechanisms. Fear expression perception appears dissociated with disgust expression perception, with disgust expressions evoking responses in the anterior insula (Phillips *et al.*, 1998, 1997) a region which may more generally process disgust in rejecting foods based on appearance and smell. Both the amygdala and the insular cortex, then, appear specialized for processing facial emotions and inferring useful social information from them. Finally, as noted above, the perception of identity is associated with activity in the inferior occipital and lateral fusiform gyri (George, *et al.*, 1999). Further, recognition of the faces of personally known individuals and famous faces is associated with activity in anterior temporal regions (Leveroni *et al.*, 2000; Sergent *et al.*, 1992). Evidence for separation of processing comes from an fMRI study demonstrating that structural aspects of faces are processed in the inferior occipital gyri while recognition of identity is more associated with activity in the fusiform face area (Rotshtein *et al.*, 2005). These brain areas are thought to be specialized for face perception (Kanwisher *et al.*, 1997) though can be recruited for nonface stimuli for which expertise is acquired (Gauthier *et al.*, 1999).

Current data on face preferences and the human brain

As noted earlier there are only a limited number of neurobiological studies that deal with the perception of attractive faces. Here we briefly review these studies (see also Senior, 2003). We also review other relevant studies moving beyond facial attractiveness that have examined neural responses to the faces of loved ones and sex differences in response to sexual stimuli and same- and opposite-sex faces.

Attractive faces

One of the earliest studies addressing the processing of attractiveness in the brain measured regional cerebral blood flow using positron emission tomography (PET) while participants assessed facial attractiveness from photographs. Two left frontal regions showed a significant increase in activation while assessing facial attractiveness. Blood flow in the left anterior frontal cortex was correlated with the percentage of assessments of a face as unattractive, while blood flow in the left frontotemporal junction correlated with the percentage of assessments of faces as attractive (Nakamura *et al.*, 1998).

While this first study places the judgment of attractiveness in the frontal lobes, recent functional brain imaging studies have reported that facial beauty evokes activation in the reward circuitry. Aharon *et al.* (2001) have shown that while men rate male and female attractiveness at similar levels, men find attractive female faces more rewarding as they are only willing to "work" (assessed as button presses to maintain viewing a face) to view attractive female faces and not for attractive male faces. In subsequent fMRI block presentation the authors found that attractive female faces elicited activation in the right orbitofrontal gyrus and nuclueus accumbens and to a lesser extent activation in the ventral tegmentum and amygdala (and surrounding areas – the sublenticular extended amygdala). The authors also examined reaction to attractive male faces, which were not found to be rewarding, and also found activation in the ventral tegmentum but that activity was decreased in the extended amygdala and nucleus accumbens. The authors then postulated a difference in the processing of "liking" faces and "wanting" them based on reward value in a manner akin to Berridge's distinction in food preferences (Berridge, 2003). This study is suggestive that reward of faces is processed by the sublenticular extended amygdala and nucleus accumbens and that the general aesthetic properties of faces are governed by the ventral tegmentum (see also Senior, 2003).

Further fMRI studies have shown that brain responses are moderated by variant aspects of faces (gaze direction and expression). In one study the perceived attractiveness of an unfamiliar face was associated with increased brain activity in the ventral striatum, which prominently includes the nucleus accumbens, only when the eyes were pointed at the observer and in fact activity was decreased when eye-gaze was averted (Kampe *et al.*, 2001). The opposite pattern is seen for unattractive faces. These findings are in line with predictions that eye-gaze from attractive individuals might be rewarding as their attention is on the observer but averted gaze suggests their attention is directed elsewhere. A similar interaction has been observed with smiling and attractiveness. O'Doherty *et al.* (2003) found that attractive faces produced more activation of the medial orbitofrontal cortex, a region involved in processing rewards, than unattractive faces and that this difference in activation was greater when the faces had a smiling facial expression than when they were shown with relatively negative expressions. Again this may be predicted as positive (social interest by attractive individuals can be rewarding while a lack of positive response may be less so). Both of these studies suggest integration of brain mechanisms involved in processing eye-gaze and facial expression and the reward system, though no effects in subcortical regions of reward systems for attractive faces were seen in the second study. Interestingly, in behavioral studies, attractive faces are rated as most attractive when eye-gaze is directed towards the viewer and when the face is smiling, the two factors combined with attractiveness generate the strongest attractiveness judgments (Jones *et al.*, 2006).

Other relevant responses: love, sexual arousal, and sex differences

So far, studies of brain activation in processing have highlighted the role of involving frontal cortex and the classic component of reward, the nucleus accumbens. Some studies that have examined neural responses when looking at loved individuals highlight the importance of the amygdala. Using fMRI it has been shown that looking at people whom you love, compared to similarly aged friends, evokes deactivations in the posterior cingulate gyrus and in the amygdala (Bartels and Zeki, 2000). In a different study Bartels and Zeki, (2004) compared this activation with activation found when viewing one's children, specifically of mothers observing their children to examine the difference between maternal and romantic love. They found that both types of attachment activated regions specific to each, as well as overlapping regions in the brain's reward system that coincide with areas rich in oxytocin and vasopressin receptors, both neuropeptides involved in the formation and maintenance of attachment between individuals (e.g., Pedersen and Boccia, 2006). Both types of viewing also deactivate the amygdala and mesial prefrontal cortex which are associated with negative emotions (Calder *et al.*, 1996; Morris *et al.*, 1996) and social judgments (Frith and Frith, 2001) respectively. The authors suggest that human attachment might employ a push–pull mechanism that deactivates networks used for social assessment and negative emotions, while attracting individuals to each other through reward circuitry. Hypothalamic activation was found to be specific to romantic love and the authors suggest this might reflect a component of erotic arousal (Bartels and Zeki, 2004).

This brings us to some interesting data regarding sex differences in responses to sexual stimuli. In rats the medial amygdala moderates appetitive behavior to sexual signals from smell and vision in males but not females (Newman, 1999) and in humans a larger amygdala is related to higher sex drive (Baird et al., 2004). These studies are suggestive that the amygdala plays an important role in sexual attraction and moderates sex differences in motivation to pay attention to attractiveness. Recent fMRI studies have shown that the amygdala and hypothalamus are more strongly activated in men than in women when viewing sexual stimuli (Hamann et al., 2004). In other studies the thalamus and hypothalamus, a sexually dimorphic area of the brain known to play a pivotal role in physiological arousal and sexual behavior, has been shown to activate to sexual stimuli in a sexually dimorphic way, with men showing more activation than women (Karama et al., 2002).

A study has also used fMRI to examine how the brain responds to sexually preferred faces. Kranz and Ishai (2006) examined heterosexual and homosexual men and women who viewed photographs of male and female faces and assessed facial attractiveness. Multiple regions in the visual cortex limbic system, and prefrontal cortex, demonstrated similar patterns of activation across all participants to both male and female faces. A significant interaction was found between sex of face and the sexual preference of the participant in the thalamus and medial orbitofrontal cortex, whereby heterosexual men and homosexual women responded more to female faces and heterosexual women and homosexual men responded more to male faces. The authors suggest that the oribitofrontal cortex plays a general role in representing the reward value of faces of potential sexual partners, including same-sex mates.

Together then these studies suggest a strong role of the subcortical amygdala and thalamus/hypothalamus, and the orbitofrontal cortex in generating responses to individuals you may be attracted to. Interestingly the study by Kranz and Ishai suggests that the reward system codes sexually preferred faces and simple sex-specific responses to same and opposite-sex faces.

Additions to the distributed model of face perception to process attractiveness

The data reviewed above suggests several areas of overlap between the reward system and the distributed network for face recognition. Certain regions of the reward circuitry are associated with activation by attractive faces, including the nucleus accumbens and orbitofrontal cortex (Aharon et al., 2001; Kampe *et al.*, 2001; O'Doherty *et al.*, 2003). Data also suggests a distinction between the reward value and the general aesthetics of faces (Aharon *et al.*, 2001). Two of the studies examining facial attractiveness in the brain demonstrate the response is moderated by variant aspects of facial appearance (eye-gaze, smiling) which is suggestive that the response to attractiveness occurs after the processing of these features, or at least in parallel.

Senior (2003) has already proposed extensions to the distributed model for beauty evaluation (see Figure 7.3). Following the findings of Aharon (2001), Senior suggests that the extended amygdala system and the ventral tegmentum are involved in the initial processing of beautiful faces. The model already incorporates connections between the superior temporal sulcus and the amygdala (Haxby *et al.*, 2000) and Senior suggests that processing by the extended amygdala system and ventral tegmentum is distinct from emotion processing. Rewarding faces also generate activity in the orbitofrontal gyrus, ventromedial prefrontal cortex, and nucleus accumbens but nonrewarding (same-sex) beautiful faces are associated with a reduction in activity in the extended amygdala and the nucleus accumbens (Aharon *et al.*, 2001). The opposite directions of signal response suggest processing occurs separately so that projections from the module representing the extended amygdala system/ventral tegmentum diverge into separate pathways.

While these additions are important, there are other ways to think about how attractiveness is processed. Different studies, and different types of study, have generated a mixture of results highlighting the importance of various brain mechanisms. Below we briefly reiterate the main components of a system to process facial attractiveness.

Ventral tegmentum and nucleus accumbens

The ventral tegmentum is rich in dopamine and serotonin neurons and an important part of the reward system (Berridge and Robinson, 2003). Its role in the processing of attractive faces is supported by fMRI studies directly showing the reward value of opposite-sex faces (Aharon *et al.*, 2001). The nucleus accumbens has long been associated with reward and it also appears to play a crucial role in processing the attractiveness of faces being activated by viewing rewarding faces (Aharon *et al.*, 2001) and implicated in ventral striatum activation when the eyes of attractive individuals are pointed at the observer (Kampe *et al.*, 2001). The ventral tegmentum is closely tied to the nucleus accumbens as some nucleus accumbens neurons require dopaminergic projections from the ventral tegmental area to promote reward-seeking behavior (Yun *et al.*, 2004). These two structures may then form an associated component processing attractive faces.

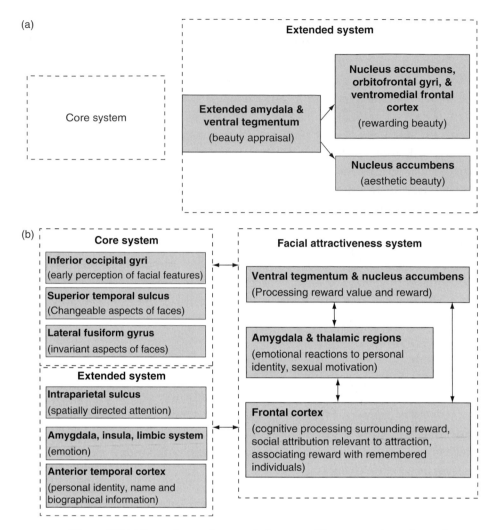

Figure 7.3 (a) Extension to the extended system of face processing redrawn from Senior (2003). (b) The distributed system of face processing extended with speculative further additions to process attractiveness of faces. We infer that attractiveness is processed subsequent (or in parallel) to the extended system because reward value is changed for faces based on variant traits processed in the extended system (Kampe *et al.*, 2001; O'Doherty *et al.*, 2003). We also connect the core system as invariant aspects of face not linked to identity are likely linked to attraction. It is currently unclear exactly how these subsystems are interconnected.

Extended amygdala and thalamus/hypothalamus

The amygdala is already present in the extended system for face processing. The amygdala has been strongly associated with the processing of threatening facial expressions and is also involved in social perception more generally (Adolphs *et al.*, 1998). Following the outlined studies showing activation (or deactivation) in response to loved faces we can further suggest that the amygdala is involved in the judgment of positive feelings felt towards particular valued individuals. The amygdala is activated in response to attractive faces (Aharon *et al.*, 2001) and interestingly in humans a larger amygdala is related to higher sex drive (Baird *et al.*, 2004). The amygdala is also implicated in sex differences in response to sexual stimuli (Hamann *et al.*, 2004; Karama *et al.*, 2002), with men showing more amygdala activation than women to such stimuli. Other fMRI studies have provided evidence for a similar role for the thalamic regions. The thalamus appears to play a role in the reward of sexually preferred faces, responding more in heterosexual men to female faces and more in heterosexual women to male faces (Kranz and Ishai, 2006). Hypothalamic activation is significantly greater in men when shown sexual stimuli and, for men, the magnitude of hypothalamic activation is positively correlated with reported levels of sexual arousal (Karama *et al.*, 2002). These studies further cement the role of the amygdala and thalamic regions in attaching salience to attractive stimuli. In terms of processing facial attractiveness the role of the amygdala is somewhat separable from its role in emotion processing as suggested by Senior (2003) and must be related to identity processing and sex processing, both invariant aspects of faces. Of course some emotion processing is also involved in determining the attractiveness of faces as beauty is more rewarding when the face smiles (O'Doherty *et al.*, 2003).

Frontal cortex

One of the first studies addressing where attractiveness is processed in the brain highlighted the role of frontal cortex (Nakamura *et al.*, 1998). This work is supported by many of the other studies discussed above. Orbitofrontal cortex is involved in attraction to sexually preferred faces (Kranz and Ishai, 2006) and attractive faces that are gazing at the observer also produce activation in the medial orbitofrontal cortex (O'Doherty *et al.*, 2003). Medial frontal cortex is relevant to many different aspects of social cognitive processing (Amodio and Frith, 2006). Strong ties to social cognitive processing are predicted based on studies that show personality attributions may be important in making attractiveness judgments (Little *et al.*, 2006; Perrett *et al.*, 1998). Frontal cortex is then possibly tied to attractiveness processing via processing associated behavioral or potential behavioral traits of the observed faces.

Fit with general reward structures

The results for attractiveness processing show that facial beauty fits very well into current understanding of general reward systems. The ventral tegmentum, nucleus accumbens, and amygdala are all core units in general reward (Berridge and Robinson, 2003) and the frontal cortex is involved in representing the reward value of various sensory stimuli (Rolls, 2004). These areas are the main components also associated with judgments of facial attractiveness. Generally, activity (or reduction of activity) in these areas is associated with a variety of responses important in the judgments of beauty including sexual arousal and reaction to rewarding opposite-sex faces. Two areas mentioned in the review of general reward above have not been highlighted but could be implicated in processing facial attractiveness. Cingulate cortex plays a role in general reward and looking at people whom you love does evoke deactivations in the posterior cingulate gyrus (Bartels and Zeki, 2000). Anterior cingulate is also activated to sexual stimuli in both men and women (Karama et al., 2002). Berridge has highlighted the ventral pallidum as an area associated with liking. Notably this structure lies immediately adjacent to the lateral hypothalamus which is linked to sexual arousal. Overall, the processing of facial beauty appears very closely tied to general reward mechanisms.

Part B: Examples integrating evolution, cognition, and neuropsychology

Currently we are only just beginning to understand the neural mechanisms underlying attraction to certain faces. While reward mechanisms may be implicated in viewing attractive faces this raises the crucial question of what makes a face attractive. Presumably the brain processes certain traits and the presence or absence of these traits generates the reward and attraction. The studies described above all begin with the notion that attractiveness is a quality of faces but the brain must compute which faces are and which are not attractive somewhere in the system. Here we focus on invariant aspects of faces in contrast to variant aspects such as eye-gaze or smiling. We might draw a distinction between invariant traits that are attractive based on their structure and attraction to traits perceived as normal or due to experience. In discussion of structure we can say that all faces share certain properties by which they can be described, factors such as whether a person's face looks more like a man or a woman. In comparison we can say that what appears normal or familiar in structure is likely to be closely linked to one's personal experience. Of course normality/familiarity is tied to structure and assumes structural differences. In the next part of this chapter we outline behavioral data addressing attraction to these two broad distinctions of trait using symmetry as structural trait detectable across different faces and the phenomenon of adaptation to highlight experience driven attraction. For each

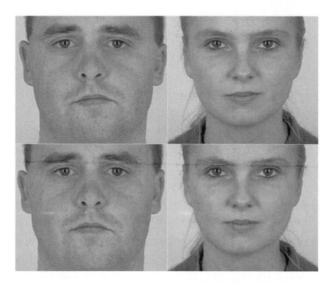

Figure 7.4 Asymmetric (top) versus symmetric faces (bottom). Symmetric images are usually found more attractive (e.g., Perrett *et al.* 1999).

we discuss evolutionary pressures, the cognitive processing of the face traits, and proposed links to brain mechanisms.

Attraction to specific physical traits: symmetry

Symmetry refers to how one half of a visual stimulus mirrors the other half and is a basic property of the visual world. Many studies of face preferences have focused on attraction to symmetry (for a review of these studies see Gangestad and Simpson, 2000; Thornhill and Gangestad, 1999). Symmetry is found attractive by many animals (see review by Møller and Thornhill, 1998) and studies of naturally occurring human facial asymmetries have shown that symmetry assessed by facialmetric and perceptual measures is positively correlated with attractiveness judgments (Grammer and Thornhill, 1994; Penton-Voak *et al.*, 2001; Scheib *et al.*, 1999). Consistent with preferences for naturally occurring symmetry in real faces, computer graphic studies (Little *et al.*, 2001; Perrett *et al.*, 1999; Rhodes *et al.*, 1998, 2001b) have shown preferences for faces that had been manipulated to increase symmetry (see Figure 7.4 for example stimuli). Cross-cultural agreement (Rhodes *et al.*, 2001b), and even cross-species agreement (Waitt and Little, 2006), on the attractiveness of symmetry may indicate a biological basis for symmetry preference. While symmetry is considered an attractive trait, individuals may not necessarily consciously look for it. Indeed, in a study manipulating only symmetry in faces, individuals preferred symmetry but none reported seeing symmetry as the manipulation made (Perrett *et al.*, 1999).

Evolution

One explanation for the preference for symmetric faces comes from a postulated link to an evolutionary adaptation to identify high-quality mates (Little and Jones, 2003; Thornhill and Gangestad, 1999, for review). Symmetry in human faces has been linked to potential heritable fitness because symmetry is a useful measure of the ability of an organism to cope with developmental stress, both genetic and environmental. In other words, symmetry may act as an indicator of both phenotypic and genotypic quality (e.g., the ability to resist disease, Møller and Thornhill, 1998, for reviews).

Cognition

Currently there is debate about whether symmetry preferences reflect an adaptation or are a functionless cognitive by-product. An alternative explanation for a preference for symmetrical faces is that symmetrical stimuli are more easily processed by the visual system. This can be referred to as the perceptual bias view, as it proposes symmetry preferences arise from biases based on properties of perceptual systems (e.g., Little and Jones, 2003, for brief review). Preferences for symmetry have been observed for stimuli not related to mate-choice, such as everyday objects (Rensch, 1963) and decorative art (Gombrich, 1984). "Simple" perceptual bias views posit that symmetry is preferred via simple stimulus properties such as redundancy of information in symmetric stimuli or that symmetric stimuli match the human visual system's own bilaterally symmetric organization (Attneave, 1955; Herbert and Humphrey, 1996; Mach, 1897).

A more complicated perceptual bias view for symmetry preference comes from cognitive theories about prototype formation. From this view, symmetry is attractive because when asymmetries in stimuli are randomly distributed the average stimuli are very symmetric. We therefore find symmetry attractive in faces and other stimuli as it represents something closer to our internal prototypes for these stimuli and may be attractive as it is perceived as familiar (see Jansson *et al.*, 2002; Little and Jones, 2003, for reviews). In this way symmetry preferences may arise as a by-product of experience of asymmetric stimuli which are on average symmetric (Enquist and Arak, 1994; Enquist and Ghirlanda, 1998; Enquist and Johnstone, 1997).

Little and Jones (2003) have shown that while symmetry is preferred in upright faces, it is preferred less in inverted faces. Inversion disrupts the perception of faces, particularly configural processing, to the extent that inverted faces are processed in a manner more similar to other objects (i.e., less like faces, Murray *et al.*, 2000). As bilateral symmetry remains constant in inverted images Little and Jones' findings for inversion effects on symmetry preferences are evidence against a simple perceptual bias view, but not a more complicated perceptual bias view as described above. Little and Jones also show that symmetry is preferred in familiar faces when the familiar version is the asymmetric version, suggesting symmetry is not preferred solely via an association with familiarity. Further, it has been shown that attraction to symmetry occurs for real faces controlling for rated distinctiveness (Rhodes *et al.*, 1999), suggesting attraction to symmetry is independent of prototypicality. Together these studies are problematic for perceptual bias views that posit that symmetry is attractive because symmetrical faces are closer to prototypes and that symmetry preferences are linked to familiarity with symmetric prototypes. Other studies have presented evidence that human symmetry preferences are focused on mate-choice relevant factors. For example, Jones *et al.* (2001) have shown that the attractiveness-symmetry relationships may be mediated by perceived health, and both Little *et al.* (2001) and Penton-Voak *et al.* (2001), using different methodologies, have shown that preferences for symmetry are strongest in opposite-sex faces. Findings that symmetry is preferred in mate-choice relevant stimuli are indeed suggestive that there may be special mechanisms involved in human symmetry preferences. Following Fodor (1983), it is possible that if symmetry preference is "modular" then preference may not influence higher cognitive functions. Certainly that symmetry can be preferred and yet judges not perceive symmetry manipulation explicitly (Perrett *et al.*, 1999) is consistent with symmetry preferences reflecting an unconscious response.

In other areas there are distinctions in brain mechanisms involved in processing and preference. For example in face judgments, neuroimaging studies have revealed that conscious social judgment recruits different neural responses to passive viewing, suggesting a dissociation between automatic and intentional processing (Winston *et al.*, 2002). Furthermore, in the taste domain patient data suggests that preference can be found without recognition of flavor (Adolphs *et al.*, 2005). We have recently shown that symmetry preferences appear dissociable from the ability to detect symmetry. Individuals who find symmetry attractive are not able to detect symmetry any better than those who have relatively low preferences for symmetry (Little and Jones, 2006).

Our findings also give some explanation as to why humans are quickly able to judge attractiveness and yet have difficulty in expressing exactly what physical traits are attractive. If attraction is partly or even wholly determined by mechanisms that are largely unconscious then an overall feeling of attraction may be all that reaches consciousness.

Overall the data reviewed here suggests that symmetry preference mechanisms are somewhat different to symmetry detection mechanisms, that symmetry preferences might not be a simple by-product of cognitive machinery, and that symmetry preferences may have dedicated neural processing.

Neuropsychology

There is limited information on how symmetry is processed in the brain. It has been shown using fMRI that symmetric versus random dot stimuli produces activity in higher-order regions of human visual cortex, especially areas V3, V4, and V7 (Sasaki *et al.*, 2005), but little activity elsewhere in the brain including no activity in the basic visual processing areas (V1 and V2). Interestingly, the authors found weaker responses to symmetry in analogous regions of macaque visual cortex and suggest that processing visual symmetry is specifically enhanced in the human brain.

There are limits to what can be concluded from this study. The stimuli were not socially relevant and perhaps the processing of facial symmetry occurs elsewhere. More importantly the authors found that the activation was closely tied to detection of symmetry in the stimuli. Since preference and detection appear somewhat dissociated when judging the attractiveness of faces (Little and Jones, 2006) we have to be cautious in interpreting how closely these regions might factor into preference for facial symmetry. That said, that there are neural substrates that detect symmetry is supportive that symmetry is an important general property of the world. Potentially, symmetry is a property processed early in the core part of the distributed face processing model (Haxby *et al.*, 2000) which feeds into the ventral tegmentum and nucleus accumbens of the reward system.

Changeable attraction: Neural tuning influencing the attractiveness of faces

Familiarity is a powerful determinant of attraction. For many types of stimuli, including faces, exposure increases attraction even when the exposure is unconscious (Bornstein, 1989; Zajonc, 2001; Zajonc and Rajecki, 1969). Structural features of the face must be stored and represented in order to determine familiarity. Tied to these findings, as well as symmetry, another face trait that has received much attention is averageness – how closely they resemble the majority of other faces within a population; nonaverage faces have more extreme characteristics than the average of a population. Francis Galton (1878) first noted that multiple faces blended together were more attractive than the constituent faces. Recent studies have improved upon these techniques using computers to create digitally blended composite faces and generally the more images in a composite the more attractive it is found (Langlois and Roggman, 1990; Little and Hancock, 2002).

Evolution

Familiarity, when not paired with aversive stimuli, is thought to be rewarding (Zajonc, 2001) and indeed there are obvious benefits to avoiding the unfamiliar. Imprinting-like effects are also an example of learning in mate choice. Average faces may be attractive because an alignment of features that is close to a population average is linked to genetic diversity (Thornhill and Gangestad, 1993). Thornhill and Gangestad have argued that average faces may be preferred to less average faces because owners of average faces possess a more diverse set of genes, which may result in less common proteins to which pathogens are poorly adapted. Parasites are generally best adapted to proteins that are common in the host population, hence parasites are adapted to the genes that code for the production of these proteins. A second evolutionary based theory for the attractiveness of averageness in faces is that extreme (nonaverage) genotypes are more likely to be homozygous for deleterious alleles, that is, to be more likely to possess genes that are detrimental to an individual than those with more average genotypes (Thornhill and Gangestad, 1993). Both of these theories propose evolutionary benefits to mating with those possessing average faces.

Imprinting, whereby individuals are attracted to parental traits, is well studied in nonhuman animals (Kendrick *et al.*, 1998; Lorenz, 1943) and there is increasing evidence for similar effects in humans. Following studies of facial similarity, judges have been shown to correctly match wives to their mother-in-law at a significantly higher rate than expected by chance and that wife–mother-in-law similarity is higher than similarity between the husbands and their wives (Bereczkei *et al.*, 2002). Such effects are also seen with adopted daughters, controlling for genetic effects, with significant facial resemblance between the daughter's husband and her adoptive father (Bereczkei *et al.*, 2004). Other studies have shown that for hair and eye color the best predictors of partner traits are the opposite-sex parent's color traits (Little *et al.*, 2003) and that individuals are attracted to age in faces consistent with the age of their parents when they were born (Perrett *et al.*, 2002). Imprinting-like effects may be adaptive as they increase the coefficient of relatedness between parent and offspring when male and female partners have genetic similarity. Potentially, then, a system that learns about known individuals and increases attraction to them or even their face traits could be adaptive.

Cognition

We are unlikely to have an inbuilt representation of an average face and what is average must be calculated from experience. For each class of stimuli the human visual system encounters it may develop an individual representation, or prototype, made up of an average of the characteristics of all the different stimuli of that type that have been seen (Enquist and Arak, 1994; Giese and Leopold, 2005; Johnstone, 1994; Loffler *et al.*, 2005; Valentine, 1991). Computer modeling has revealed that algorithms trained to discriminate different stimuli produce stronger responses to stimuli that represent the average of the training set, even though this average was not previously encountered (Enquist and Arak, 1994; Johnstone, 1994). These findings have been interpreted as evidence that prototype formation is a property of learning to recognize different stimuli as members of a class (Enquist and Arak, 1994; Johnstone, 1994).

Studies on category learning have a long history (e.g., Posner and Keele, 1968). Learning studies examine how categorical perception develops using abstract stimuli. In classic studies it has been shown that exposure to different dot patterns with particular configurations results in abstraction so that the average of each of the patterns, while never previously seen, is recognized as belonging to the set of patterns from which it was derived (Posner and Keele, 1968). These results were originally taken as evidence for prototype formation but there is much debate about whether it does represent abstraction of a prototype or whether individuals store individual exemplars and use these to determine category (Ashby and Maddox, 2005; Nosofsky and Zaki, 2002; Smith and Minda, 2002).

Faces have been the focus of much research regarding recognition and proto-type formation. While it has been proposed that faces may be coded as veridical representations of individuals or exemplars (Valentine, 1991), recent neuroimaging and single-cell recording studies have supported a prototype-referenced model of face coding (Giese and Leopold, 2005; Loffler *et al.*, 2005). Exposure to faces biases subsequent perceptions of novel faces by causing faces similar to those initially viewed to appear more prototypical than they would otherwise be perceived as, presumably, a prototype or population of exemplars becomes updated (Leopold *et al.*, 2001, 2005; Rhodes *et al.*, 2001a, 2003, 2004; Webster *et al.*, 2004). For example, adaptation to faces with contracted features causes novel faces with contracted features to be perceived as more normal than prior to this exposure (Rhodes *et al.*, 2003, 2004). Analogous visual after-effects have been observed following exposure to faces varying in identity (Leopold *et al.*, 2001; Rhodes *et al.*, 2001a), ethnicity (Webster *et al.*, 2004), sex (Rhodes *et al.*, 2004; Webster *et al.*, 2004), expression (Webster *et al.*, 2004), and sexual dimorph-ism (Buckingham *et al.*, 2006; Little *et al.*, 2005). Such after-effects are thought to reflect changes in the responses of neural mechanisms underlying face proces-sing (Leopold *et al.*, 2005; Moradi *et al.*, 2005; Rhodes *et al.*, 2003, 2004; Webster *et al.*, 2004).

These studies may then shed light on how the brain builds an average representation that other faces can be compared to. Importantly, exposure in the manner described above also influences attractiveness judgments. After exposure to faces possessing certain traits, these traits come to be preferred (Buckingham *et al.*, 2006; Little *et al.*, 2005; Rhodes *et al.*, 2003). For example if exposed to faces which look more like one identity, then new faces that resemble that identity are found more attractive than if exposed to the opposite set of face traits. A similar effect has also been observed for judgments of the trustworthiness of faces (Buckingham *et al.*, 2006).

Neuropsychology

Adaptation effects are thought to reflect neural responses giving a strong link to neuropsychology. The representation of individual identity involves the anterior temporal cortex and invariant aspects of faces the lateral fusiform gyrus (Haxby *et al.*, 2000) and these are likely the seat of where representations of faces are processed. These areas likely link to both the frontal cortex, which serves to draw cognitive information about the behavior of individuals, and to the amygdala, which represents emotional feelings towards known individuals. These same systems also potentially compare unknown individuals to known identities. In this way the brain may draw recognition as familiarity which is then attractive and also be able to compare novel faces to known identities, or prototypes of faces, a comparison to which can generate attraction.

Summary and conclusions

In Part A we reviewed work on both the general reward system and the distributed model of face perception alongside current evidence on the neurobiology of face preferences. We find much in common between the areas dedicated to reward and those found active in judging the attractiveness of faces. We also suggest that both the core and extended face processing mechanisms feed into the reward system to represent the attractiveness of faces both accounting for changeable (eye-gaze, smiling) and unchangeable (shape) aspects of faces that make them more or less attractive.

In Part B we discussed two examples of aspects of faces that might lead to them being considered as attractive and the mechanism by which this may occur. Symmetry is an invariant aspect of faces and is likely processed early in the model, possibly in the core system, and potentially linked directly to reward centers in the brain. Learning what an average face is and comparing other faces to this ideal requires computation and potentially this is done alongside processing and representation of new faces in the same way as identity is stored. Comparison to stored representations could account for the attractiveness of averageness and also ties these mechanisms to judging familiar individuals.

We have proposed a model of how attractiveness is processed in the brain, however there is still much work to be done to dissect the various aspects of this model and discover whether some of the assumptions we have made are justified. Future studies on the neurobiology of beauty processing are necessary to truly understand exactly what mechanisms are activated when the brain encounters attractive and unattractive faces and in what order.

Acknowledgments

We thank L. M. DeBruine, D. I. Perrett, D. M. Burt, and B. P. Tiddeman for useful discussion. Anthony Little is supported by a Royal Society University Research Fellowship.

References

Adolphs, R., Tranel, D., and Damasio, A. R. (1998). The human amygdala in social judgement. *Nature*, **393**, 470–474.

Adolphs, R., Tranel, D., Damasio, H., and Damasio, A. (1994). Impaired recognition of emotion in facial expressions following bilateral damage to the human amygdala. *Nature*, **372**, 669–672.

Adolphs, R., Tranel, D., Koenigs, M., and Damasio, A. R. (2005). Preferring one taste over another without recognizing either. *Nature Neuroscience*, **8**, 860–861.

Aharon, I., Etcoff, N., Ariely, D., Chabris, C. F., O'Connor, E., and Breiter, H. C. (2001). Beautiful faces have variable reward value: fMRI and behavioral evidence. *Neuron*, **32**, 537–551.

Amodio, D. M. and Frith, C. D. (2006). Meeting of minds: The medial frontal cortex and social cognition. *Nature Reviews Neuroscience*, **7**, 268–277.

Andersson, M. (1994). *Sexual Selection*. Princeton, NJ: Princeton University Press.

Ashby, E. G. and Maddox, W. T. (2005). Human category learning. *Annual Review of Psychology*, **56**, 149–178.

Attneave, F. (1955). Symmetry, information, and memory for patterns. *American Journal of Psychology*, **68**, 209–222.

Baird, A. D., Wilson, S. J., Bladin, P. F., Saling, M. M., and Reutens, D. C. (2004). The amygdala and sexual drive: Insights from temporal lobe epilepsy surgery. *Annals of Neurology*, **55**, 87–96.

Bartels, A. and Zeki, S. (2000). The neural basis of romantic love. *Neuroreport*, **11**, 3829–3834.

Bartels, A. and Zeki, S. (2004). The neural correlates of maternal and romantic love. *Neuroimage*, **21**, 1155–1166.

Bassareo, V. and DiChiara, G. (1997). Differential influence of associative and nonassociative learning mechanisms on the responsiveness of prefrontal and accumbal dopamine transmission to food stimuli in rats fed ad libitum. *Journal of Neuroscience*, **17**, 851–861.

Baxter, M. G. and Murray, E. A. (2002). The amygdala and reward. *Nature Reviews Neuroscience*, **3**, 563–573.

Bechara, A., Damasio, H., and Damasio, A. R. (2000). Emotion, decision making and the orbitofrontal cortex. *Cerebral Cortex*, **10**, 295–307.

Bereczkei, T., Gyuris, P., Koves, P., and Bernath, L. (2002). Homogamy, genetic similarity, and imprinting; parental influence on mate choice preferences. *Personality and Individual Differences*, **33**, 677–690.

Bereczkei, T., Gyuris, P., and Weisfeld, G. E. (2004). Sexual imprinting in human mate choice. *Proceedings of the Royal Society of London Series B-Biological Sciences*, **271**, 1129–1134.

Berridge, K. C. (2003). Pleasures of the brain. *Brain and Cognition*, **52**, 106–128.

Berridge, K. C. and Robinson, T. E. (1998). What is the role of dopamine in reward: Hedonic impact, reward learning, or incentive salience? *Brain Research Reviews*, **28**, 309–369.

Berridge, K. C. and Robinson, T. E. (2003). Parsing reward. *Trends in Neurosciences*, **26**, 507–513.

Berridge, K. C. and Valenstein, E. S. (1991). What psychological process mediates feeding evoked by electrical-stimulation of the lateral hypothalamus. *Behavioral Neuroscience*, **105**, 3–14.

Blood, A. J. and Zatorre, R. J. (2001). Intensely pleasurable responses to music correlate with activity in brain regions implicated in reward and emotion. *Proceedings of the National Academy of Sciences of the United States of America*, **98**, 11818–11823.

Bornstein, R. F. (1989). Exposure and effect: Overview and meta-analysis of research 1968–1987. *Psychological Bulletin*, **106**, 265–289.

Breiter, H. C., Gollub, R. L., Weisskoff, R. M., Kennedy, D. N., Makris, N., Berke, J. D., Goodman, J. M., Kantor, H. L., Gastfriend, D. R., Riorden, J. P., Mathew, R. T., Rosen, B. R., and Hyman, S. E. (1997). Acute effects of cocaine on human brain activity and emotion. *Neuron*, **19**, 591–611.

Bruce, V. and Young, A. W. (1986). Understanding face recognition. *British Journal of Psychology*, **77**, 307–327.

Buckingham, G., DeBruine, L. M., Little, A. C., Welling, L. L. M., Conway, C. A., Tiddeman, B. P., and Jones, B. C. (2006). Visual adaptation to masculine and feminine faces influences generalized preferences and perceptions of trustworthiness. *Evolution and Human Behavior*, **27**, 381–389.

Buss, D. M. and Barnes, M. (1986). Preferences in human mate selection. *Journal of Personality and Social Psychology*, **50**, 559–570.

Calder, A. J., Young, A. W., Rowland, D., Perrett, D. I., Hodges, J. R., and Etcoff, N. L. (1996). Facial emotion recognition after bilateral amygdala damage – differentially severe impairment of fear. *Cognitive Neuropsychology*, **13**, 699–745.

Calvert, G. A., Bullmore, E. T., Brammer, M. J., Campbell, R., Williams, S. C. R., McGuire, P. K., Woodruff, P. W. R., Iverson, S. D., and David, A. S. (1997). Activation of auditory cortex during silent lipreading. *Science*, **276**, 593–596.

Chang, J. Y., Janak, P. H., and Woodward, D. J. (1998). Comparison of mesocorticolimbic neuronal responses during cocaine and heroin self-administration in freely moving rats. *Journal of Neuroscience*, **18**, 3098–3115.

Corbetta, M., Akbudak, E., Conturo, T. E., Snyder, A. Z., Ollinger, J. M., Drury, H. A., Linenweber, M. R., Petersen, S. E., Raichle, M. E., Van Essen, D. C., and Shulman, G. L. (1998). A common network of functional areas for attention and eye movements. *Neuron*, **21**, 761–773.

Corbetta, M., Shulman, G. L., Miezin, F. M., and Petersen, S. E. (1995). Superior parietal cortex activation during spatial attention shifts and visual feature conjunction. *Science*, **270**, 802–805.

Cosmides, L. and Tooby, J. (1994). Origins of domain specificity: The evolution of functional organization. In L. A. Hirschfeld and S. A. Gelman (Eds.), *Mapping the Mind: Domain Specificity in Cognition and Culture*. Cambridge, UK: Cambridge University Press.

Cromwell, H. C. and Berridge, K. C. (1993). Where does damage lead to enhanced food aversion – the ventral pallidum substantia innominata or lateral hypothalamus. *Brain Research*, **624**, 1–10.

Damasio, H., Grabowski, T., Frank, R., Galaburda, A. M., and Damasio, A. R. (1994). The return of Gage, Phineas – clues about the brain from the skull of a famous patient. *Science*, **264**, 1102–1105.

Enquist, M. and Arak, A. (1994). Symmetry, beauty and evolution. *Nature*, **372**, 169–172.

Enquist, M. and Ghirlanda, S. (1998). The secrets of faces. *Nature*, **394**, 826–827.

Enquist, M. and Johnstone, R. A. (1997). Generalization and the evolution of symmetry preferences. *Proceedings of the Royal Society of London, B*, **264**, 1345–1348.

Fodor, J. (1983). *The Modularity of Mind*. Cambridge, MA: MIT Press.

Francis, S., Rolls, E. T., Bowtell, R., McGlone, F., O'Doherty, J., Browning, A., Clare, S., and Smith, E. (1999). The representation of pleasant touch in the brain and its relationship with taste and olfactory areas. *Neuroreport*, **10**, 453–459.

Frith, U. and Frith, C. (2001). The biological basis of social interaction. *Current Directions in Psychological Science*, **10**, 151–155.

Galton, F. J. (1878). Composite portraits. *Nature*, **18**, 97–100.

Gangestad, S. W. and Simpson, J. A. (2000). The evolution of human mating: trade-offs and strategic pluralism. *Behavioural and Brain Sciences*, **23**, 573–644.

Gauthier, I. and Tarr, M. J. (1997). Becoming a "greeble" expert: Exploring mechanisms for face recognition. *Vision Research*, **37**, 1673–1682.

Gauthier, I., Tarr, M. J., Anderson, A. W., Skudlarski, P., and Gore, J. C. (1999). Activation of the middle fusiform "face area" increases with expertise in recognizing novel objects. *Nature Neuroscience*, **2**, 568–573.

George, N., Dolan, R. J., Fink, G. R., Baylis, G. C., Russell, C., and Driver, J. (1999). Contrast polarity and face recognition in the human fusiform gyrus. *Nature Neuroscience*, **2**, 574–580.

Giese, M. A. and Leopold, D. A. (2005). Physiologically inspired neural model for the encoding of face spaces. *Neurocomputing*, **65**, 93–101.

Gombrich, E. H. (1984). *The Sense of Order: A Study in the Psychology of Decorative Art*. London: Phaidon.

Grammer, K. and Thornhill, R. (1994). Human (*Homo sapiens*) facial attractiveness and sexual selection: The role of symmetry and averageness. *Journal of Comparative Psychology*, **108**, 233–242.

Hamann, S., Herman, R. A., Nolan, C. L., and Wallen, K. (2004). Men and women differ in amygdala response to visual sexual stimuli. *Nature Neuroscience*, **7**, 411–416.

Harries, M. H. and Perrett, D. I. (1991). Visual processing of faces in temporal cortex – physiological evidence for a modular organization and possible anatomical correlates. *Journal of Cognitive Neuroscience*, **3**, 9–24.

Hasselmo, M. E., Rolls, E. T., and Baylis, G. C. (1989). The role of expression and identity in the face-selective responses of neurons in the temporal visual-cortex of the monkey. *Behavioural Brain Research*, **32**, 203–218.

Haxby, J. V., Hoffman, E. A., and Gobbini, M. I. (2000). The distributed human neural system for face perception. *Trends in Cognitive Sciences*, **4**, 223–233.

Herbert, A. M. and Humphrey, G. K. (1996). Bilateral symmetry detection: Testing a "callosal" hypothesis. *Perception*, **25**, 463–480.

Hoffman, E. A. and Haxby, J. V. (2000). Distinct representations of eye gaze and identity in the distributed human neural system for face perception. *Nature Neuroscience*, **3**, 80–84.

Ishai, A., Schmidt, C. F., and Boesiger, P. (2005). Face perception is mediated by a distributed cortical network. *Brain Research Bulletin*, **67**, 87–93.

Jansson, L., Forkman, B., and Enquist, M. (2002). Experimental evidence of receiver bias for symmetry. *Animal Behaviour*, **63**, 617–621.

Johnstone, R. A. (1994). Female preference for symmetrical males as a by-product of selection for mate recognition. *Nature*, **372**, 172–175.

Jones, B. C., DeBruine, L. M., Little, A. C., Conway, C. A., and Feinberg, D. R. (2006). Integrating gaze direction and expression in preferences for attractive faces. *Psychological Science*, **17**, 588–591.

Jones, B. C., Little, A. C., Penton-Voak, I. S., Tiddeman, B. P., Burt, D. M., and Perrett, D. I. (2001). Facial symmetry and judgements of apparent health – support for a "good genes" explanation of the attractiveness-symmetry relationship. *Evolution and Human Behavior*, **22**, 417–429.

Kampe, K. K. W., Frith, C. D., Dolan, R. J., and Frith, U. (2001). Reward value of attractiveness and gaze – making eye contact enhances the appeal of a pleasing face, irrespective of gender. *Nature*, **413**, 589–589.

Kanwisher, N., McDermott, J., and Chun, M. M. (1997). The fusiform face area: A module in human extrastriate cortex specialized for face perception. *Journal of Neuroscience*, **17**, 4302–4311.

Karama, S., Lecours, A. R., Leroux, J., Bourgouin, P., Beaudoin, G., Joubert, S., and Beauregard, M. (2002). Areas of brain activation in males and females. During viewing of erotic film excerpts. *Human Brain Mapping*, **16**, 1–13.

Kendrick, K. M., Hinton, M. R., and Atkins, K. (1998). Mothers determine male sexual preferences. *Nature*, **395**, 229–230.

Kranz, F. and Ishai, A. (2006). Face perception is modulated by sexual preference. *Current Biology*, **16**, 63–68.

LaBar, K. S., Gatenby, J. C., Gore, J. C., LeDoux, J. E., and Phelps, E. A. (1998). Human amygdala activation during conditioned fear acquisition and extinction: A mixed-trial fMRI study. *Neuron*, **20**, 937–945.

Langlois, J. H., Kalakanis, L., Rubenstein, A. J., Larson, A., Hallamm, M., and Smoot, M. (2000). Maxims or myths of beauty? A meta-analytic and theoretical review. *Psychological Bulletin*, **126**, 390–423.

Langlois, J. H. and Roggman, L. A. (1990). Attractive faces are only average. *Psychological Science*, **1**, 115–121.

Leopold, D. A., O'Toole, A. J., Vetter, T., and Blanz, V. (2001). Prototype-referenced shape encoding revealed by high-level aftereffects. *Nature Neuroscience*, **4**, 89–94.

Leopold, D. A., Rhodes, G., Muller, K. M., and Jeffery, L. (2005). The dynamics of visual adaptation to faces. *Proceedings of the Royal Society B-Biological Sciences*, **272**, 897–904.

Leveroni, C. L., Seidenberg, M., Mayer, A. R., Mead, L. A., Binder, J. R., and Rao, S. M. (2000). Neural systems underlying the recognition of familiar and newly learned faces. *Journal of Neuroscience*, **20**, 878–886.

Little, A. C., Burt, D. M., Penton-Voak, I. S., and Perrett, D. I. (2001). Self-perceived attractiveness influences human female preferences for sexual dimorphism and symmetry in male faces. *Proceedings of the Royal Society of London, B*, **268**, 39–44.

Little, A. C., Burt, D. M., and Perrett, D. I. (2006). What is good is beautiful: Face preference reflects desired personality. *Personality and Individual Differences*, **41**, 1107–1118.

Little, A. C., DeBruine, L. M., and Jones, B. C. (2005). Sex-contingent face after-effects suggest distinct neural populations code male and female faces. *Proceedings of the Royal Society B-Biological Sciences*, **272**, 2283–2287.

Little, A. C. and Hancock, P. J. B. (2002). The role of masculinity and distinctiveness in judgments of human male facial attractiveness. *British Journal of Psychology*, **93**, 451–464.

Little, A. C. and Jones, B. C. (2003). Evidence against perceptual bias views for symmetry preferences in human faces. *Proceedings of the Royal Society of London Series B-Biological Sciences*, **270**, 1759–1763.

Little, A. C. and Jones, B. C. (2006). Attraction independent of detection suggests special mechanisms for symmetry preferences in human face perception. *Proceedings of the Royal Society B-Biological Sciences*, **273**, 3093–3099.

Little, A. C., Penton-Voak, I. S., Burt, D. M., and Perrett, D. I. (2003). Investigating an imprinting-like phenomenon in humans: Partners and opposite-sex parents have similar hair and eye colour. *Evolution and Human Behaviour*, **24**, 43–51.

Loffler, G., Yourganov, G., Wilkinson, F., and Wilson, H. R. (2005). fMRI evidence for the neural representation of faces. *Nature Neuroscience*, **8**, 1386–1390.

Lorenz, K. (1943). The innate forms of potential experience. *Zietschrift fur Tierpsychologie*, **5**, 234–409.

Mach, E. (1897). *Contributions to the Analysis of the Sensations*. LaSalle, IL: Open Court.

McBride, W. J., Murphy, J. M., and Ikemoto, S. (1999). Localization of brain reinforcement mechanisms: Intracranial self-administration and intracranial place-conditioning studies. *Behavioural Brain Research*, **101**, 129–152.

Møller, A. P. and Thornhill, R. (1998). Bilateral symmetry and sexual selection: A meta-analysis. *American Naturalist*, **151**, 174–192.

Moradi, F., Koch, C., and Shimojo, S. (2005). Face adaptation depends on seeing the face. *Neuron*, **45**, 169–175.

Morris, J. S., Frith, C. D., Perrett, D. I., Rowland, D., Young, A. W., Calder, A. J., and Dolan, R. J. (1996). A differential neural response in the human amygdala to fearful and happy facial expressions. *Nature*, **383**, 812–815.

Murray, J. E., Yong, E., and Rhodes, G. (2000). Revisiting the perception of upside-down faces. *Psychological Science*, **11**, 492–496.

Nakamura, K., Kawashima, R., Nagumo, S., Ito, K., Sugiura, M., Kato, T., Nakamura, A., Hatano, K., Kubota, K., Fukuda, H., and Kojima, S. (1998). Neuroanatomical correlates of the assessment of facial attractiveness. *Neuroreport*, **9**, 753–757.

Newman, S. W. (1999). The medial extended amygdala in male reproductive behavior – a node in the mammalian social behavior network. In *Advancing from the Ventral Striatum to the Extended Amygdala*, Vol. **877**, pp. 242–257.

Nosofsky, R. A. and Zaki, S. R. (2002). Exemplar and prototype models revisited: Response strategies, selective attention, and stimulus generalization. *Journal of Experimental Psychology-Learning Memory and Cognition*, **28**, 924–940.

O'Doherty, J., Winston, J., Critchley, H., Perrett, D., Burt, D. M., and Dolan, R. J. (2003). Beauty in a smile: The role of medial orbitofrontal cortex in facial attractiveness. *Neuropsychologia*, **41**, 147–155.

Olds, J. (1956). A preliminary mapping of electrical reinforcing effects in the rat brain. *Journal of Comparative and Physiological Psychology*, **49**, 281–285.

Olds, J. and Milner, P. (1954). Positive reinforcement produced by electrical stimulation of septal area and other regions of rat brain. *Journal of Comparative and Physiological Psychology*, **47**, 419–427.

Pecina, S. and Berridge, K. C. (2000). Opioid site in nucleus accumbens shell mediates eating and hedonic 'liking' for food: map based on microinjection Fos plumes. *Brain Research*, **863**, 71–86.

Pecina, S. and Berridge, K. C. (2005). Hedonic hot spot in nucleus accumbens shell: Where do mu-opioids cause increased hedonic impact of sweetness? *Journal of Neuroscience*, **25**, 11777–11786.

Pedersen, C. A. and Boccia, M. L. (2006). Vasopressin interactions with oxytocin in the control of female sexual behavior. *Neuroscience*, **139**, 843–851.

Penton-Voak, I. S., Jones, B. C., Little, A. C., Baker, S., Tiddeman, B., Burt, D. M., and Perrett, D. I. (2001). Symmetry, sexual dimorphism in facial proportions, and male facial attractiveness. *Proceedings of the Royal Society of London, B*, **268**, 1617–1623.

Perrett, D. I., Burt, D. M., Penton-Voak, I. S., Lee, K. J., Rowland, D. A., and Edwards, R. (1999). Symmetry and human facial attractiveness. *Evolution and Human Behavior*, **20**, 295–307.

Perrett, D. I., Lee, K. J., Penton-Voak, I. S., Rowland, D. R., Yoshikawa, S., Burt, D. M., Henzi, S. P., Castles, D. L., and Akamatsu, S. (1998). Effects of sexual dimorphism on facial attractiveness. *Nature*, **394**, 884–887.

Perrett, D. I., Penton-Voak, I. S., Little, A. C., Tiddeman, B. P., Burt, D. M., Schmidt, N., Oxley, R., Kinloch, N., and Barrett, L. (2002). Facial attractiveness judgements reflect learning of parental age characteristics. *Proceedings of the Royal Society of London Series B-Biological Sciences*, **269**, 873–880.

Phillips, A. G. (1984). Brain reward circuitry – a case for separate systems. *Brain Research Bulletin*, **12**, 195–201.

Phillips, M. L., Young, A. W., Scott, S. K., Calder, A. J., Andrew, C., Giampietro, V., Williams, S. C. R., Bullmore, E. T., Brammer, M., and Gray, J. A. (1998). Neural responses to facial and vocal expressions of fear and disgust. *Proceedings of the Royal Society of London Series B-Biological Sciences*, **265**, 1809–1817.

Phillips, M. L., Young, A. W., Senior, C., Brammer, M., Andrew, C., Calder, A. J., Bullmore, E. T., Perrett, D. I., Rowland, D., Williams, S. C. R., Gray, J. A., and David, A. S. (1997). A specific neural substrate for perceiving facial expressions of disgust. *Nature*, **389**, 495–498.

Pinker, S. (1997). *How the Mind Works*. Harmondsworth, UK: The Penguin Press.

Posner, M. I. and Keele, S. W. (1968). On genesis of abstract ideas. *Journal of Experimental Psychology*, **77**, 353–363.

Rensch, B. (1963). Vesuche uber menschliche Auslosermerkmale beider Geschlecter. *Zeitschrift fur Morphologische Anthropologie*, **53**, 139–164.

Rhodes, G., Halberstadt, J., and Brajkovich, G. (2001a). Generalization of mere exposure effects in social stimuli. *Social Cognition*, **19**, 57–70.

Rhodes, G., Jeffery, L., Watson, T. L., Clifford, C. W. G., and Nakayama, K. (2003). Fitting the mind to the world: Face adaptation and attractiveness aftereffects. *Psychological Science*, **14**, 558–566.

Rhodes, G., Jeffery, L., Watson, T. L., Jaquet, E., Winkler, C., and Clifford, C. W. G. (2004). Orientation-contingent face aftereffects and implications for face-coding mechanisms. *Current Biology*, **14**, 2119–2123.

Rhodes, G., Proffitt, F., Grady, J. and Sumich, A. (1998). Facial symmetry and the perception of beauty. *Psychonomic Bulletin Review*, **5**, 659–669.

Rhodes, G., Sumich, A., and Byatt, G. (1999). Are average facial configurations attractive only because of their symmetry? *Psychological Science*, **10**, 52–58.

Rhodes, G., Yoshikawa, S., Clark, A., Lee, K., McKay, R., and Akamatsu, S. (2001b). Attractiveness of facial averageness and symmetry in non-Western populations: In search of biologically based standards of beauty. *Perception*, **30**, 611–625.

Robinson, T. E. and Berridge, K. C. (2000). The psychology and neurobiology of addiction: An incentive-sensitization view. *Addiction*, **95**, S91–S117.

Rolls, E. T. (1999). The functions of the orbitofrontal cortex. *Neurocase*, **5**, 301–312.

Rolls, E. T. (2000). The orbitofrontal cortex and reward. *Cerebral Cortex*, **10**, 284–294.

Rolls, E. T. (2004). The functions of the orbitofrontal cortex. *Brain and Cognition*, **55**, 11–29.

Rotshtein, P., Henson, R. N. A., Treves, A., Driver, J., and Dolan, R. J. (2005). Morphing Marilyn into Maggie dissociates physical and identity face representations in the brain. *Nature Neuroscience*, **8**, 107–113.

Sasaki, Y., Vanduffel, W., Knutsen, T., Tyler, C., and Tootell, R. (2005). Symmetry activates extrastriate visual cortex in human and nonhuman primates.

Proceedings of the National Academy of Sciences of the United States of America, **102**, 3159–3163.

Scheib, J. E., Gangestad, S. W., and Thornhill, R. (1999). Facial attractiveness, symmetry, and cues to good genes. *Proceedings of the Royal Society of London, B*, **266**, 1913–1917.

Senior, C. (2003). Beauty in the brain of the beholder. *Neuron*, **38**, 525–528.

Sergent, J., Ohta, S., and Macdonald, B. (1992). Functional neuroanatomy of face and object processing – a positron emission tomography study. *Brain*, **115**, 15–36.

Shizgal, P. (1999). On the neural computation of utility: Implications from studies of brain stimulation reward. In Kahneman, D., Diener, E., and Schwarz, N. (Eds.), *Well-being: The Foundations of Hedonic Psychology* (pp. 500–524). New York: Russell Sage Foundation.

Smith, J. D. and Minda, J. P. (2002). Distinguishing prototype-based and exemplar-based processes in dot-pattern category learning. *Journal of Experimental Psychology-Learning Memory and Cognition*, **28**, 800–811.

Thornhill, R. and Gangestad, S. W. (1993). Human facial beauty: Averageness, symmetry, and parasite resistance. *Human Nature*, **4**, 237–269.

Thornhill, R. and Gangestad, S. W. (1999). Facial attractiveness. *Trends in Cognitive Sciences*, **3**, 452–460.

Thut, G., Schultz, W., Roelcke, U., Nienhusmeier, M., Missimer, J., Maguire, R. P., and Leenders, K. L. (1997). Activation of the human brain by monetary reward. *Neuroreport*, **8**, 1225–1228.

Tindell, A. J., Smith, K. S., Pecina, S., Berridge, K. C., and Aldridge, J. W. (2006). Ventral pallidum firing codes hedonic reward: When a bad taste turns good. *Journal of Neurophysiology*, **96**, 2399–2409.

Valentine, T. (1991). A unified account of the effects of distinctiveness, inversion, and race in face recognition. *The Quarterly Journal of Experimental Psychology*, **43**, 161–204.

Waitt, C. and Little, A. C. (2006). Preferences for symmetry in conspecific facial shape among Macaca mulatta. *International Journal of Primatology*, **27**, 133–145.

Webster, M. A., Kaping, D., Mizokami, Y., and Duhamel, P. (2004). Adaptation to natural facial categories. *Nature*, **428**, 557–561.

Winston, J. S., Henson, R. N. A., Fine-Goulden, M. R., and Dolan, R. J. (2004). fMRI-adaptation reveals dissociable neural representations of identity and expression in face perception. *Journal of Neurophysiology*, **92**, 1830–1839.

Winston, J. S., Strange, B. A., O'Doherty, J., and Dolan, R. J. (2002). Automatic and intentional brain responses during evaluation of trustworthiness of faces. *Nature Neuroscience*, **5**, 277–283.

Yeomans, J. S. (1989). Two substrates for medial forebrain bundle self-stimulation: Myelinated axons and dopamine axons. *Neuroscience and Biobehavioral Review*, **13**, 91–98.

Yun, I. A., Wakabayashi, K. T., Fields, H. L., and Nicola, S. M. (2004). The ventral tegmental area is required for the behavioral and nucleus accumbens neuronal firing responses to incentive cues. *Journal of Neuroscience*, **24**, 2923–2933.

Zajonc, R. B. (2001). Mere exposure: a gateway to the subliminal. *Current Directions in Psychological Science*, **10**, 224–228.

Zajonc, R. B. and Rajecki, D. W. (1969). Exposure and affect – a field experiment. *Psychonomic Science*, **17**, 216.

Zald, D. H., Lee, J. T., Fluegel, K. W., and Pardo, J. V. (1998). Aversive gustatory stimulation activates limbic circuits in humans. *Brain*, **121**, 1143–1154.

Zald, D. H. and Pardo, J. V. (1997). Emotion, olfaction, and the human amygdala: Amygdala activation during aversive olfactory stimulation. *Proceedings of the National Academy of Sciences of the United States of America*, **94**, 4119–4124.

Zebrowitz-McArthur, L. and Baron, R. M. (1983). Toward an ecological approach to social perception. *Psychological Review*, **90**, 215–238.

8

Sex differences in the neural correlates of jealousy

HIDEHIKO TAKAHASHI AND YOSHIRO OKUBO

Sexual jealousy and mate retention behaviors

Jealousy is an emotional response generated by a threat to a valued relationship with another person, due to an actual or imagined rival (Dijkstra and Buunk, 2002). Jealousy, however, may become maladaptive when it causes distress in the jealous person or the target person and could be associated with behavioral problems observed not only in a psychiatric setting but also in a general social environment.

One of the most common forms of violence against women is that perpetrated by a husband or an intimate male partner (Wathen and MacMillan, 2003; Watts and Zimmerman, 2002). Research on intimate partner violence, often termed domestic violence, occurs in all countries, irrespective of social, economic, religious, or cultural group (WHO, 2002). Although women can be violent in relationships with men, the overwhelming majority of victims of partner violence are women (WHO, 2002). In 48 population-based surveys from around the world, between 10% and 69% of women were reported to be physically assaulted by an intimate male partner at some point in their lives (WHO, 2002). Although there are multiple risk factors for intimate partner violence such as poverty, alcohol consumption, and the social status of women, a key risk factor is the partner's jealousy (Jewkes, 2002; Kingham and Gordon, 2004). Expressions of male sexual jealousy historically may have been functional in deterring rivals from mate poaching (Schmitt and Buss, 2001) and in deterring a mate from committing a sexual infidelity or defecting permanently from the relationship (Buss, Larsen, Westen, and Semmelroth, 1992; Daly, Wilson, and Weghorst, 1982; Symons, 1979). Therefore, violence in romantic relationships might be associated with mate retention behaviors (Buss, 1988; Shackelford, Goetz, Buss, Euler, and Hoier, 2005).

Foundations in Evolutionary Cognitive Neuroscience, ed. Steven M. Platek and Todd K. Shackelford.
Published by Cambridge University Press. © Cambridge University Press 2009.

Morbid jealousy

Morbid jealousy is a condition of inappropriate or excessive jealousy specific to the sexual partner together with unacceptable or extreme behavior based on a preoccupation with the partner's unfaithfulness (Easton, Schipper, and Shackelford, 2007; Kingham and Gordon, 2004). It is more common in men than in women (Kingham and Gordon, 2004). Nonpsychotic obsessional morbid jealousy has been described as a variant of obsessive-compulsive disorder (OCD; Parker and Barrett, 1997). In fact, several groups have reported successful treatment of morbid jealousy with selective serotonin reuptake inhibitors (SSRIs) widely used in the treatment of OCD (Stein, Hollander, and Josephson, 1994; Wright, 1994). When it becomes delusional and is associated with a false belief in the sexual infidelity of the partner, it is described as delusional jealousy. Delusional jealousy has been identified as a symptom of different psychiatric disorders such as dementia (Tsai, Hwang, Yang, and Liu, 1997), alcoholism (Michael, Mirza, Mirza, Babu, and Vithayathil, 1995), and schizophrenia (Soyka, Naber, and Volcker, 1991). Delusional jealousy can also occur without the presence of another psychiatric disorder, and it is defined as Delusional Disorder – Jealous Type (American Psychiatric Association, 1994). Morbid jealousy is also known as the Othello syndrome (Todd and Dewhurst, 1955). As in Shakespeare's *Othello*, in which Othello's jealousy drives him to kill his beloved wife and himself, this syndrome sometimes includes violence, especially as directed toward the partner, and it can result in disruption of the relationship, and in extraordinary cases homicide and suicide. Stalking behavior is also associated with morbid jealousy (Mullen, Pathe, Purcell, and Stuart, 1999; Roberts, 2002; Silva, Derecho, Leong, and Ferrari, 2000). Therefore, jealousy is an important subject for forensic psychology and psychiatry (Lamberg, 2001; Silva, Ferrari, Leong, and Penny, 1998).

Sex differences in jealousy in response to a partner's infidelity

Evolutionary psychologists have proposed that men and women have evolved different psychological mechanisms to process the cues that trigger jealousy (Symons, 1979; Daly, Weghorst, and Wilson, 1982). Because fertilization occurs internally within women, men cannot be certain of their paternity or genetic relatedness to children produced by their partner. If a woman conceives by someone other than her regular partner, she places him at risk of unwittingly expending scarce resources on another man's offspring. Therefore, men have evolved a special sensitivity to cues of sexual infidelity. In contrast, women are certain that they are the mothers of their offspring. Instead, ancestral women confronted the threat of their regular partner diverting resources, time, parenting, attention, protection, and commitments to another woman and her children. Diversion of emotional commitment is an indicator of diversion of these resources. Therefore, women are predicted to be more sensitive to a partner's emotional infidelity (Buss, 2002; Buss *et al.*, 1992; Daly *et al.*, 1982; Symons, 1979).

There is accumulating evidence consistent with evolved sex differences in jealousy. Previous psychological studies have reported sex differences in the nature of jealousy in different cultures, including in Western and Asian countries. Men tend to be more distressed or upset over partner's *sexual* infidelity than women, and women tend to be more distressed or upset over partner's *emotional* infidelity than men (Buss *et al.*, 1999; Buunk, Angleitner, Oubaid, and Buss, 1996; DeSteno, Bartlett, Braverman, and Salovey, 2002; DeSteno and Salovey, 1996; Harris, 2002, 2003; Pietrzak, Laird, Stevens, and Thompson, 2002; Wiederman and Allgeier, 1993; Wiederman and Kendall, 1999). The majority of studies supporting the evolutionary hypothesis used hypothetical infidelity scenarios, and participants had to choose which type of infidelity (sexual or emotional) is more distressing or upsetting. Studies using continuous measures of jealousy also have found that men were more distressed over *sexual* infidelity than women, and women were more distressed over *emotional* infidelity than men, although a few studies using continuous measures did not find sex differences in response to infidelity (see Sagarin, 2005, for review).

In addition to these survey methods, the evolutionary hypothesis has been supported by studies using physiological and cognitive methods. Buss *et al.* (1992) assessed participants' physiological arousal in response to situations of imagined infidelity by measuring their electroderrnal activity (EDA), pulse rate (PR), and electromyographic activity (EMG). They found that men showed greater EDA for sexual than for emotional infidelity, whereas women showed greater EDA for emotional than for sexual infidelity. Men also showed a higher PR for sexual than emotional infidelity, but women displayed no difference in PR as a function of the infidelity type, and EMG data showed no significant effects in men or women (Buss *et al.*, 1992). A study in which participants listened to a story indicating both types of infidelity and one week later were unexpectedly asked to recall the contents of the story showed that men preferentially recalled cues to sexual infidelity, whereas women preferentially recalled cues to emotional infidelity (Schützwohl and Koch, 2004). More recently, a cognitive study measuring reaction times showed that men and women systematically differ in sensitivity and speed of the processing cues to sexual and emotional infidelity, corroborating hypotheses generated by an evolutionary perspective (Schützwohl, 2005).

Sex differences in brain activations in response to sexual and emotional infidelity

The emerging field of affective cognitive neuroscience and neuroimaging techniques is providing new insights into the neural basis of complex social emotions such as guilt, embarrassment, and pride (Berthoz, Armony, Blair, and Dolan, 2002; Shin *et al.*, 2000; Takahashi *et al.*, 2007; Takahashi *et al.*, 2004). Study of the neural correlates of jealousy and their sex differences might contribute to a better understanding of the neural basis of the jealousy-related behaviors predominantly observed in men.

A study using positron emission tomography (PET) has investigated the neural correlates of sexual jealousy in male rhesus monkeys. In the study, dominant male monkeys were injected with the PET tracer [18F]-fluorodeoxyglucose and scanned when being visually confronted with an interaction between their female mate and a subordinate male. Compared to the control condition in which the female consort was present without the rival male, the males showed increased activation in the brain regions that have been implicated in negative emotions and social cognition, such as the amygdala, insula, and superior temporal sulcus (STS) during the jealousy condition (Rilling, Winslow, and Kilts, 2004).

For practical and ethical reasons, it is not feasible to investigate brain activations in response to actual infidelity in humans. Using functional magnetic resonance imaging (fMRI), we investigated brain activation in response to hypothetical sexual infidelity scenarios (e.g., "My girlfriend had her underwear taken off by another man." "My girlfriend spent a night in her ex-boyfriend's room.") and emotional infidelity scenarios (e.g., "My girlfriend wrote a love letter to another man." "My girlfriend telephones her ex-boyfriend everyday.") (Takahashi *et al.*, 2006). Sexual infidelity might be accompanied by emotional infidelity and vice versa (Buss *et al.*, 1999). For this reason, we carefully chose the situations, although we knew that it was difficult to entirely dissociate sexual and emotional infidelity in our fMRI study. We defined sexual infidelity as a condition explicitly or implicitly indicating a sexual relationship or intimate physical contact, and emotional infidelity as a condition indicating diversion of the partner's emotional commitment to another boyfriend/girlfriend.

We scanned 11 male and 11 female university students. Each participant was heterosexual, had not been married, and was currently in an intimate relationship. The average length of the intimate relationship was 14.8 months (*SD* = 10.6) for the men and 18.5 months (*SD* = 10.9) for the women.

The participants read sexual and emotional infidelity scenarios during fMRI scans and then rated the intensity of jealousy and other basic emotions (anger, sadness, disgust, fear, etc.) using the 6-point Likert scale (1 = *none*, 6 = *extremely intense*). For men, the mean ratings of jealousy for sexual infidelity and emotional infidelity were 5.7 ($SD = 0.4$) and 5.1 ($SD = 0.5$), respectively. For women, the mean ratings of jealousy for sexual infidelity and emotional infidelity were 5.5 ($SD = 0.8$) and 4.9 ($SD = 0.8$), respectively. We did not find sex differences in jealousy in response to sexual and emotional infidelity (Takahashi *et al.*, 2006). The lack of sex differences in Likert scale data might be attributable to several factors. First, the majority of participants rated jealousy as "very" or "extremely," indicating that ceiling effects of the Likert scale existed. Second, the Likert scales for sexual and emotional infidelities were correlated with each other using our method, suggesting that sexual and emotional infidelities might have co-occurred.

As for the fMRI results, men and women showed distinct brain activations in response to sexual and emotional infidelity. For men, the amygdala, hippocampal regions, and hypothalamus were activated in response to sexual infidelity. Emotional infidelity activated several brain regions including the insula, hippocampal regions, and hypothalamus. There was a positive linear correlation between self-rating of jealousy for emotional infidelity and the degree of activation in the insula (Montreal Neurological Institute brain coordinates: $x = -38$, $y = 6$, $z = 8$, $r = 0.88$, $p < 0.001$). Men showed greater activation than women in the amygdala in response to sexual infidelity (Figure 8.1)

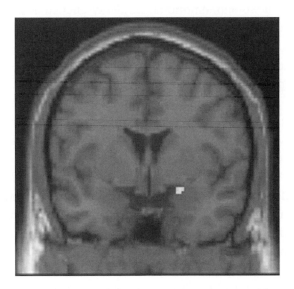

Figure 8.1 Compared to women, men demonstrated greater activation in response to sexual infidelity in the amygdala (peak coordinates: $x = 22$, $y = 2$, $z = -14$). Sex differences were recognized at a height threshold of $P < 0.0005$, uncorrected ($t > 4.59$) and extent threshold of three contiguous voxels.

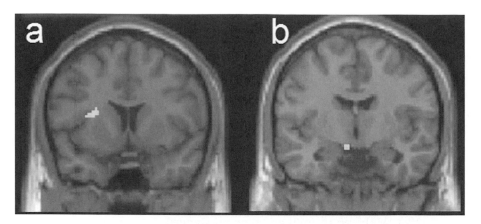

Figure 8.2 Compared to women, men showed greater activations in response to emotional infidelity in the (a) insula (peak coordinates: $x=-32$, $y=14$, $z=12$) and (b) hypothalamus (peak coordinates: $x=-4$, $y=-12$, $z=-12$). Sex differences were recognized at a height threshold of $P<0.0005$, uncorrected ($t>4.59$) and extent threshold of three contiguous voxels.

(Takahashi *et al.*, 2006). Men also showed greater activation than women in the insula and hypothalamus in response to emotional infidelity (Figure 8.2) (Takahashi *et al.*, 2006). For women, emotional infidelity elicited activation in the posterior superior temporal sulcus, which was correlated with self-rating of jealousy for emotional infidelity ($x=-46$, $y=-66$, $z=34$, $r=0.88$, $p<0.001$). Women showed greater activation than men in the posterior superior temporal sulcus in response to emotional infidelity (Figure 8.3) (Takahashi *et al.*, 2006).

Greater activations in the amygdala, insula, and hypothalamus in men were similar to the results obtained in the PET study with monkeys. The amygdala and insula are the central nodes of processing negative emotions (Calder, Lawrence, and Young, 2001; Phan, Wager, Taylor, and Liberzon, 2002; Wicker *et al.*, 2003). In the study with monkeys, males showed increases in plasma testosterone during a situation provoking sexual jealousy (Rilling *et al.*, 2004). Testosterone receptors in the brain exist mainly in the amygdala, hippocampus, and hypothalamic regions that are involved in sexual and aggressive behaviors (Fernandez-Guasti, Kruijver, Fodor, and Swaab, 2000; Giammanco, Tabacchi, Giammanco, Di Majo, and La Guardia, 2005; Lathe, 2001). This means that hormonal transmissions might be responsible for the increased activation in the amygdala, hippocampus, and hypothalamus. Elevation in the testosterone level in the brain and activations in the amygdala and hypothalamus might be a precursor

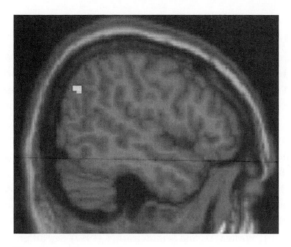

Figure 8.3 Compared to men, women showed greater activation in response to emotional infidelity in the posterior superior temporal sulcus (peak coordinates: $x=52$, $y=-62$, $z=34$). Sex differences were recognized at a height threshold of $P<0.0005$, uncorrected ($t>4.59$) and extent threshold of three contiguous voxels.

of extreme jealousy-related behaviors such as intimate partner violence and morbid jealousy.

The posterior superior temporal sulcus has been implicated in social cognition such as detection of intension, deception, and trustworthiness of others (Gallagher and Frith, 2003; Winston, Strange, O'Doherty, and Dolan, 2002). Considering this function of the posterior superior temporal sulcus, greater activation elicited by emotional infidelity in women suggests that women may be more sensitive than men to a partner's potential deception or trustworthiness.

Conclusion

We used continuous measures and did not find a sex difference in the rating of jealousy for the two types of infidelity. However, using functional neuroimaging techniques, we observed sex differences in brain activations in response to sexual and emotional infidelities, supporting the view that men and women have different neurocognitive systems to process a partner's sexual and emotional infidelity. Because jealousy-related behaviors such as intimate partner violence are more common in men, we expect that our findings will contribute to a broadening of the knowledge pertaining to these behaviors and their possible treatments.

References

American Psychiatric Association (1994). *Diagnostic and Statistical Manual of Mental Disorders*. 4th revised edn. Washington, DC: American Psychiatric Association.

Berman, M. I. and Frazier, P. A. (2005). Relationship power and betrayal experience as predictors of reactions to infidelity. *Personality and Social Psychology Bulletin*, **31**(12), 1617–1627.

Berthoz, S., Armony, J. L., Blair, R. J., and Dolan, R. J. (2002). An fMRI study of intentional and unintentional (embarrassing) violations of social norms. *Brain*, **125**(Pt 8), 1696–1708.

Buss, D. M. (1988). From vigilance to violence: Tactics of mate retention in American undergraduates. *Ethology and Sociobiology*, **9**, 291–317.

Buss, D. M. (2002). Human mate guarding. *Neuroendocrinology Letters*, **23** Suppl 4, 23–29.

Buss, D. M., Larsen, R. J., Westen, D., and Semmelroth, J. (1992). Sex differences in jealousy: Evolution, physiology, and psychology. *Psychological Science*, **3**(2), 251–255.

Buss, D. M., Shackelford, T. K., Kirkpatrick, L. A., Chloe, J., Hasegawa, M., Hasegawa, T., and Bennett, K. (1999). Jealousy and beliefs about infidelity: Tests of competing hypotheses in the United States, Korea, and Japan. *Personal Relationships*, **6**, 125–150.

Buunk, B. P., Angleitner, A., Oubaid, V., and Buss, D. M. (1996). Sex differences in jealousy in evolutionary and cultural perspective: Tests from the Netherlands, Germany, and the United States. *Psychological Science*, **7**(6), 359–363.

Calder, A. J., Lawrence, A. D., and Young, A. W. (2001). Neuropsychology of fear and loathing. *Nature Review Neuroscience*, **2**(5), 352–363.

Daly, M., Wilson, M., and Weghorst, S. J. (1982). Male sexual jealousy. *Ethology and Sociobiology*, **3**, 11–17.

DeSteno, D. M., Bartlett, M. Y., Braverman, J., and Salovey, P. (2002). Sex differences in jealousy: Evolutionary mechanism or artifact of measurement? *Journal of Personality and Social Psychology*, **83**(5), 1103–1116.

DeSteno, D. A. and Salovey, P. (1996). Evolutionary origins of sex differences in jealousy? Questioning the "fitness" of the model. *Psychological Science*, **7**(6), 367–372.

Dijkstra, P. and Buunk, B. P. (2002). Sex differences in the jealousy-evoking effect of rival charactictics. *European Journal of Social Psychology*, **32**(2), 829–852.

Easton, J. A., Schipper, L. D., and Shackelford, T. K. (2007). Morbid jealousy from an evolutionary psychological perspective. *Evolution and Human Behavior*, **28**(6), 399–402.

Fernandez-Guasti, A., Kruijver, F. P., Fodor, M., and Swaab, D. F. (2000). Sex differences in the distribution of androgen receptors in the human hypothalamus. *The Journal of Comparative Neurology*, **425**(3), 422–435.

Gallagher, H. L. and Frith, C. D. (2003). Functional imaging of "theory of mind." *Trends in Cognitive Science*, **7**(2), 77–83.

Giammanco, M., Tabacchi, G., Giammanco, S., Di Majo, D., and La Guardia, M. (2005). Testosterone and aggressiveness. *Medical Science Monitor*, **11**(4), RA136–145.

Harris, C. R. (2002). Sexual and romantic jealousy in heterosexual and homosexual adults. *Psychological Science*, **13**(1), 7–12.

Harris, C. R. (2003). A review of sex differences in sexual jealousy, including self-report data, psychophysiological responses, interpersonal violence, and morbid jealousy. *Personality and Social Psychology Review*, **7**(2), 102–128.

Jewkes, R. (2002). Intimate partner violence: Causes and prevention. *Lancet*, **359** (9315), 1423–1429.

Kingham M. and Gordon H. (2004). Aspects of morbid jealousy. *Advances in Psychiatric Treatment*, **10**(6), 207–215.

Lamberg, L. (2001). Stalking disrupts lives, leaves emotional scars: Perpetrators are often mentally ill. *Journal of the American Medical Association*, **286**(5), 519, 513–522.

Lathe, R. (2001). Hormones and the hippocampus. *Journal of Endocrinology*, **169**(2), 205–231.

Michael, A., Mirza, S., Mirza, K. A., Babu, V. S., and Vithayathil, E. (1995). Morbid jealousy in alcoholism. *British Journal of Psychiatry*, **167**(5), 668–672.

Mullen, P. E., Pathe, M., Purcell, R., and Stuart, G. W. (1999). Study of stalkers. *American Journal of Psychiatry*, **156**(8), 1244–1249.

Parker, G. and Barrett, E. (1997). Morbid jealousy as a variant of obsessive-compulsive disorder. *Australian and New Zealand Journal of Psychiatry*, **31**(1), 133–138.

Phan, K. L., Wager, T., Taylor, S. F., and Liberzon, I. (2002). Functional neuroanatomy of emotion: A meta-analysis of emotion activation studies in PET and fMRI. *Neuroimage*, **16**(2), 331–348.

Pietrzak, R. H., Laird, J. D., Stevens, D. A., and Thompson, N. S. (2002). Sex differences in human jealousy: A coordinated study of forced-choice, continuous rating-scale, and physiological responses on the same subjects. *Evolution and Human Behavior*, **23**(2), 83–94.

Rilling, J. K., Winslow, J. T., and Kilts, C. D. (2004). The neural correlates of mate competition in dominant male rhesus macaques. *Biological Psychiatry*, **56**(5), 364–375.

Roberts, K. A. (2002). Stalking following the breakup of romantic relationships: Characteristics of stalking former partners. *Journal of Forensic Science*, **47**(5), 1070–1077.

Sagarin B. J. (2005). Reconsidering evolved sex differences in jealousy: Comment on Harris (2003). *Personality and Social Psychology Review*, **9**(1), 62–75

Sagarin, B., Vaughn Becker, D., Guadagno, R., Nicastle, L., and Millevoi, A. (2003). Sex differences (and similarities) in jealousy: The moderating influence of infidelity experience and sexual orientation of the infidelity. *Evolution and Human Behavior*, **24**(1), 17–23.

Schmitt, D. P. and Buss, D. M. (2001). Human mate poaching: Tactics and temptations for infiltrating existing mateships. *Journal of Personality and Social Psychology*, **80**(6), 894–917.

Schützwohl, A. (2005). Sex differences in jealousy: The processing of cues to infidelity. *Evolution and Human Behavior*, **26**(3), 288–299.

Schützwohl, A. and Koch, S. (2004). Sex differences in jealousy: The recall of cues to sexual and emotional infidelity in personally more and less threatening context conditions. *Evolution and Human Behavior*, **25**(4), 249–257.

Shackelford, T. K., Goetz, A. T., Buss, D. M., Euler, H. A., and Hoier, S. (2005). When we hurt the ones we love: Predicting violence against women from men's mate retention. *Personal Relationships*, **12**(4), 447–463.

Shin, L. M., Dougherty, D. D., Orr, S. P., Pitman, R. K., Lasko, M., Macklin, M. L., *et al.* (2000). Activation of anterior paralimbic structures during guilt-related script-driven imagery. *Biological Psychiatry*, **48**(1), 43–50.

Silva, A. J., Ferrari, M. M., Leong, G. B., and Penny, G. (1998). The dangerousness of persons with delusional jealousy. *Journal of the American Academy of Psychiatry and the Law*, **26**(4), 607–623.

Silva, J. A., Derecho, D. V., Leong, G. B., and Ferrari, M. M. (2000). Stalking behavior in delusional jealousy. *Journal of Forensic Science*, **45**(1), 77–82.

Soyka, M., Naber, G., and Volcker, A. (1991). Prevalence of delusional jealousy in different psychiatric disorders. An analysis of 93 cases. *British Journal of Psychiatry*, **158**, 549–553.

Stein, D. J., Hollander, E., and Josephson, S. C. (1994). Serotonin reuptake blockers for the treatment of obsessional jealousy. *Journal of Clinical Psychiatry*, **55**(1), 30–33.

Symons, D. (1979). *The Evolution of Human Sexuality*. New York: Oxford University Press.

Takahashi, H., Matsuura, M., Koeda, M., Yahata, N., Suhara, T., Kato, M., *et al.* (2008). Brain activations during judgments of positive self-conscious emotion and positive basic emotion: Pride and joy. *Cerebral Cortex*. **18**(4), 898–903.

Takahashi H., Matsuura M., Yahata N., Koeda M., Suhara T., Okubo Y. (2006). Men and women show distinct brain activations during imagery of sexual and emotional infidelity. *Neuroimage*, **32**(3), 1299–1307.

Takahashi, H., Yahata, N., Koeda, M., Matsuda, T., Asai, K., and Okubo, Y. (2004). Brain activation associated with evaluative processes of guilt and embarrassment: An fMRI study. *Neuroimage*, **23**(3), 967–974.

Todd, J. and Dewhurst, K. (1955). The Othello syndrome; a study in the psychopathology of sexual jealousy. *The Journal of Nervous and Mental Disease*, **122**(4), 367–374.

Tsai, S. J., Hwang, J. P., Yang, C. H., and Liu, K. M. (1997). Delusional jealousy in dementia. *Journal of Clinical Psychiatry*, **58**(11), 492–494.

Wathen, C. N. and MacMillan, H. L. (2003). Interventions for violence against women: Scientific review. *Journal of the American Medical Association*, **289**(5), 589–600.

Watts, C. and Zimmerman, C. (2002). Violence against women: Global scope and magnitude. *Lancet*, **359**(9313), 1232–1237.

Wicker, B., Keysers, C., Plailly, J., Royet, J. P., Gallese, V., and Rizzolatti, G. (2003). Both of us disgusted in My insula: the common neural basis of seeing and feeling disgust. *Neuron*, **40**(3), 655–664.

Wiederman, M. W. and Kendall, E. (1999). Evolution, sex, and jealousy: Investigation of a sample from Sweden. *Evolution and Human Behavior*, **20**(22), 121–128.

Winston, J. S., Strange, B. A., O'Doherty, J., and Dolan, R. J. (2002). Automatic and intentional brain responses during evaluation of trustworthiness of faces. *Nature Neuroscience*, **5**(3), 277–283.

World Health Organization. (2002). *World Report on Violence and Health*. Geneva: World Health Organization.

Wright, S. (1994). Familial obsessive-compulsive disorder presenting as pathological jealousy successfully treated with fluoxetine. *Archives of General Psychiatry*, **51**(5), 430–431.

Index

Locators for headings which have subheadings refer to general aspects of that topic.
Locators in **bold** type refer to figures/tables.